Utopia and Other Places

Richard Eyre has been Director of the Royal National Theatre since 1988. He has directed many premières including plays by David Hare, Charles Wood, Alan Bennett, Christopher Hampton, Trevor Griffiths, Ken Campbell and Howard Brenton, and numerous classics. He has produced and directed many films for television, including *Tumbledown*, *The Insurance Man* and *The Ploughman's Lunch*.

Richard Eyre

UTOPIA AND OTHER PLACES

VINTAGE

A VINTAGE BOOK

Published by Vintage 1994

2 4 6 8 10 9 7 5 3 1

Copyright © Richard Eyre 1993, 1994

First published in Great Britain by
Bloomsbury Publishing Ltd, 1993

This revised edition first published by
Vintage, 1994

Vintage
Random House, 20 Vauxhall Bridge Road, London
SW1V 2SA

Random House Australia (Pty) Limited
20 Alfred Street, Milsons Point, Sydney,
New South Wales 2061, Australia

Random House New Zealand Limited
18 Poland Road, Glenfield,
Auckland 10, New Zealand

Random House South Africa (Pty) Limited
PO Box 337, Bergvlei, South Africa

Random House UK Limited Reg. No. 954009

A CIP catalogue record for this book
is available from the British Library

ISBN 0 0994 2541 6

Phototypeset by Intype, London
Printed and bound in Great Britain by
Cox & Wyman, Reading, Berkshire

TO SUZE AND LU

CONTENTS

PREFACE

When I was younger I wrote bad poetry, a play that was put on at Hampstead Theatre Club and shown by Granada TV, a film that was never made, a successful version of *A Christmas Carol*, and an unsuccessful version of *High Society*, but for many years I wrote nothing at all.

In becoming Director of the National Theatre I found myself a sort of muted celebrity – at least in the sense of being invited (and refusing) to go on *Wogan*, asked for my opinion on whales and rain-forests, courted by charities, and begged to contribute pieces to newspapers. It's an irony that after years of idleness, at least on the writing front, I should have started writing when I had little enough time left from my day (and night) job. However, I am an insomniac and much of this book was written during hours that might more profitably have been spent sleeping, and if there is a consistent colour to the writing, perhaps it is drawn from the cold light of dawn.

Georges Simenon said that he never sat down to write without feeling physically sick. I can understand how he felt. I have never been able to write except at someone else's suggestion, and even then I have to be goaded into it; but few of the important things in my life have happened on my own initiative. If I admire writers above all creative people, perhaps its self-interest – I can't do my work until they've done theirs. Of course I admire the talent of the writers I like, but I admire as much the courage of those who earn a living from it – the solitary ordeal of facing a blank sheet of paper that stares implacably back at you requires the fortitude of the true professional.

As a writer, I'm a dilettante. I'm normally impatient of dilettantes; I don't like to hear actors talking of 'turning their hand to a bit of directing', and, until recently, refused offers of directing operas for the same reason. I have seen the faces of writers when I have told them I am doing a book – a mixture of scepticism and weariness. Not another one, they think.

I had never imagined that I would write a book, certainly not *The National Theatre – My Struggle*. I was approached by Liz Calder, who I can now call my publisher, but up to then called a friend. She said she'd read a piece that I had written and had I thought of writing a book. About what? I said. Oh I don't know, she said, about how you got into the theatre, perhaps. And that's how I came to write about my parents, who had little, if anything, to do with the theatre either before or after I got into it.

My mother's illness had prevented me for many years from communicating with her, and when Liz approached me, my father had just died. I felt an overwhelming sense of unfinished business; there was a lot I wanted to say to them, and there was a lot I wished they could say back. I didn't want to write about them with the triumphant irony of the survivor; on the contrary, writing about them seemed a way of trying to get in touch with them. At first I felt curiously constrained, but when my mother died I found that I could speak to them as I had never done in their lifetimes. It's sad that it happened posthumously, but in writing about them I learned a little more about them, and a lot more about myself. You write to discover what you think.

In my work I've always depended on the kindness of patrons – Clive Perry at Leicester and Edinburgh, Stuart Burge at Nottingham, Margaret Matheson at the BBC, and Peter Hall at the National Theatre. Without their generous encouragement my life would have taken a much less interesting course. As a writer I have had suitors rather than patrons: as well as Liz Calder, there have been David Hare, without whose prompting I wouldn't have written about acting, and Frances Coady, who persuaded me to re-write the last third of the book for the paperback edition. The section entitled 'Misdirection' absorbs much of the material that appeared as essays in the hardback into a first-person narrative larded with personal anecdote. It is therefore no longer possible to pretend, if it ever were, that the book is not an autobiography: the word 'I' occurs much too frequently. This is an imposition on the reader, a demand to spend several hours in the company of a person who will attempt, however diffidently, to grab your collar and talk remorselessly, in a voice marked by the accent of self-doubt, about himself.

When the hardback was published I had several letters from friends of my parents, some saying that they thought I had given a fair and affectionate picture of them, one, 'more in sorrow than anger', saying that he had seen my father in a very different light, and I had traduced his memory. He went on to say this, 'The real question is whether an autobiography written so early in your life is not really a gross self-indulgence.' I plead mitigating circumstances: I was talked into it. Finally, though, I have only myself to blame and I accept that I am guilty as charged.

Autobiography or not, the book is by no means a reevaluation of my private life, nor is it an itemised record of my professional life in the theatre and in television. It does reflect, however, a growing interest in the form of the medium in which I mostly work; becoming Director of the National Theatre has concentrated my mind wonderfully.

Robert Frost has said that poetry is what gets lost in translation. I have become increasingly interested in the 'untranslatable' element in the theatre, the part that isn't a surrogate for television, that isn't prose to be read standing up, the part that can't be translated from stage to screen; the part that is, in a word, theatrical. This word is generally used in a pejorative sense to imply something camp, frivolous and superficial. For me it's come to describe a kind of theatre that exploits the unique properties of the medium – its use of space, of light, of speech, of story-telling: its *theatreness*. This can take many forms: it can be experienced in the spectacle of an anguished vicar standing on an illuminated cross-shaped stage in *Racing Demon*, or in the shock of a man with a brain disorder discovering the unshaven half of his face in *The Man Who*, as much as in the sumptuously eloquent image of an angel ascending over the head of a man dying of AIDS in *Angels in America*, and the surrealistic poetry of all Robert Lepage's work.

I've called this book *Utopia and Other Places*. 'Utopia' means, in Greek, 'not a place', that is, 'nowhere'. It's an imaginary island, and it serves as a powerful metaphor in life and art and politics. However sceptical we are of it in public, all of us privately believe in a utopia, in a form of perfectability, however temporary; it may be in love, in marriage, in work, in society, or in religion. Even when the available evidence is so strongly against its existence, we continue to seek this tantalising territory.

Oscar Wilde is celebrated for having said, 'A map of the world which does not include utopia is not even worth glancing at.' I don't believe that we can avoid carrying this map within us, but I've nevertheless always been cautious about using it – in religion and politics, it's been such a costly and wasteful expedition in terms of human life. In the theatre, however, the search for utopia is a familiar, even necessary, part of the process: to rehearse a play in the company of good actors, sharing a sense of common purpose, mutual respect, and pleasure in each other's company, is to come as close as you can to finding the elusive spot on the map marked 'utopia'. I've never quite found it, but I've had a lot of fun looking.

Richard Eyre
June 1994

LONG SHADOWS

'Everything the Power of the World does is done in a circle.'
– American Indian saying

I

OUR PARENTS CAST long shadows over our lives. When we grow up we imagine that we can walk into the sun, free of them. We don't realise until it's too late that we have no choice in the matter; they're always ahead of us, forever old.

We carry them within us all our lives, in the shape of our face, the way we walk, the sound of our voice, our skin, our hair, our hands, our heart. We try all our lives to separate ourselves from them and only when they are dead do we find we are indivisible.

We grow to expect that our parents, like the weather, will always be with us. Then they go, leaving a mark like a handprint on glass or a wet kiss on a rainy day, and with their death we are no longer children.

When my parents' death came I was in my late forties, and I was unprepared, even with the years of rehearsal, for adulthood. 'You're the one in the red jacket now,' said a friend of mine. 'You're in the Thin Red Line.' And another said, 'Now you're an orphan.' I hadn't known what to expect. Novelists and anthropologists talk of 'rites of passage', but we lack the casual ceremonies, the rituals, and the social habits that give death and grief the familiarity of shared experience and the comfort that we are enduring a 'rite of passage'. Perhaps that's what adulthood means: dealing with desolation alone. Grief and romantic love share

1

some of the same metaphors – heartache and heartbreak, for instance. They seem fanciful from a distance but turn out to be precisely observed descriptions of physiological phenomena. When we're young we rehearse these feelings by falling in and out of love and with odd, teasing glimpses of our parents' mortality.

I had just sat down on a plane, and was beginning to buckle my safety belt, when my name was called out and I was asked to leave the plane. I walked down the aisle, off the aircraft, along a corridor to an office, where I was confronted by an official whose face was moulded into a formal expression of compassion. 'Your mother has had an accident.' I had known this from the instant my name was called. I loved her at that moment with a ferocious intensity, which persisted when I saw her in the hospital, and when she recovered we never quite slipped back into our mutual wariness. My love for her had been dormant, waiting to be goaded into expression by illness or death. The threat of loss made me feel my affections were being tested like an electric current, measured and quantified by both of us.

In the years after, although I didn't see a lot of my mother, I never forgot the vivid, searing moment of pain when I thought I had lost her. It defined with exactness, and guilt, the shape of the feelings that should have existed before. It persisted like the feeling in a phantom limb, shadowing me whenever I saw her subsequently.

I once visited a leper colony in Kuala Lumpur. It was a Sunday morning and patients in varying degrees of decay, from all over the encampment, were going to church. There was a hut set aside for Gurkha patients, ex-soldiers, who paraded, eight of them, in a line outside their hut. Leprosy eats away the body, eventually causing joints and limbs to wither, atrophy and vanish. The soldiers were in tropical uniform – knife-edge creases on their shorts and shirts, sharp caps perkily set on the side of their heads. They stood at ease. Their sergeant brought them to attention, they saluted, and, as eleven o'clock struck, a bugler played the Last Post. Their drill was faultless. Only three of the eight men had two legs, none of them had the full complement of fingers, and all of them lacked part of an arm. Those without a hand raised their upper arm and elbow in a salute, the phantom hand perfectly placed one inch above the right eyebrow. The gesture was no less real for being imagined.

I had little hint of my father's mortality until shortly before his death. When I was eight I saw him on his knees, late at night after a party, talking to the dogs, groaning that he was about to die. I wasn't fooled – even at that age I knew the difference between death and drink, and he was always as indestructible as he was inaccessible. When he did become ill and vulnerable, he wanted to get to know me, and I wanted to get to know him, and we both knew that we had left it too late.

The loss of my parents gets dimmer day by day, and the pain, or the displaced love, translates into curiosity. I find that, far from wanting to distance them from me, I want to draw them closer. I want to know more about them: I am trying to learn what is an accident of nature and what is their indelible legacy. I want to know who I am.

When we lose our memories, we are less than ourselves; in that sense, we are what we remember. What we don't remember we try to reclaim through photographs and anecdotes, the verbal and visual chronicles of a family. We collect photographs as evidence, as if we were preparing for a day when we would examine, explain and judge our past. The day never comes, but we still preserve the photographs, as if their existence provided us with a sort of immortality.

A teacher in a school in Brazil gave his illiterate pupils photographs of themselves and they started to learn to read. Perhaps the photographs of ourselves can be used as a teaching aid – to reveal ourselves to ourselves. I have a photograph of myself in a pram, chubby, round, happy face, torrents of blond curls. I'm none the wiser. I seem to have discarded that person, and his successors, through the years. Childhood, school, university, work: shuffled off like the skin we lose almost as it grows upon us.

Memory is the key to our inheritance. It's said we remember everything; our problem is retrieving it. We talk about the 'dim recesses' of our memory as if the mind were a house that we could wander through at will. Our childhood occupies part of that house – a dense succession of rooms shot through with shafts of milky golden sunlight connected by long bleak corridors pitted with pools of dead water. We can shine a light on to these dark pools but we'll see only dead insects; unhappy childhood memories drift to the surface unasked and unsought for. We want to see childhood as a paradise, free from fear, but childhood's not a paradise, lost or otherwise. It's like one long Sunday afternoon – boredom punctuated by apprehension.

I was born during the War. To talk of 'the War' nowadays is to define oneself as a child of the forties as surely as printing one's birth certificate, but at least until recently you could be confident of sharing a common language; the Falklands and the Gulf have forced us not to take so much for granted. It was 'the War' that provided the basic grammar for my parents' lives.

There are three acts to my family's drama: 'Before the War', 'After the War' and a prolonged and still unresolved coda called 'Growing Up and Growing Apart'. 'Before the War' was for my mother a gilded era of intense social activity and friendships: holidays in France, Italy, Switzerland, New York; riding, golf, skiing, dancing and parties. She had an air of easy laughter that can be seen in countless photographs ('enjoying a joke') – but her laughter looks natural and unforced. She was described by a social correspondent as the 'soul of merriment', and I don't believe it was a flattering exaggeration. For my father: social privation, parental tyranny and naval discipline from the age of thirteen.

'During the War': vivid, intense, passionate, a difficult act to follow. It is one of the consequences of war that life will never be the same for those who are involved and that the casualties are not always the participants. When my parents were together they lived as if it might have been their last time together, and when they were apart my father faced the possibility of U-boat attack in the Atlantic, and my mother the certainty of the casual cruelty of her father-in-law with whom she was obliged to live. And she gave birth to two children – my sister and then me.

Our parents' lives are always seen in the past tense; their children's in the future. The period of the War was invoked with mathematical regularity through our childhood and their memories wound up and regulated our emotional clock. It was unquestionably the time of their lives.

I remember little of the War. A gas mask: a perforated snout with huge round eyes and a flat flappy nose; a 'Donald Duck' mask issued to small children. I remember even the smell and the feel of the rubber, flabby like an inner tube. I realise now that I would have been too young to have worn it, too young even to have been issued with one. So it must have been long after the War and this is a kind of guileless alchemy, turning fiction into fact. I'm not sure I'm a reliable witness to my past.

My first memory. I am standing by our gate, a solid, high, wooden gate which clanged with a hollow thud, never quite shut, every time echoing in a flag-stoned yard by a large cherry tree, which in my memory is always, of course, in flower, handfuls of rich pink blossoms. Perhaps in the beginning it wasn't there. Perhaps it was planted by my mother.

I am playing, perhaps I'm pushing a furry golden horse on wheels. It has a long, soft, bushy tail and it belongs to my sister. I am two years old. The gate opens and there stands the darkest man I've ever seen: skin like bark, thick black stubble, large black eyes. When he speaks I can't understand him, and I run to my mother. She speaks to him, words that I don't understand. She gives him something. Money, perhaps. He goes. I am crying.

The man I remember was an Italian ex-prisoner of war who was looking for work, odd jobs, labouring or gardening. It was years before I could explain his presence, years before I knew that he had been freed from a prisoner-of-war camp a few miles from our village, and it's not until now, trying to parse this infant memory, that I can acknowledge that the thing I really remember is my mother's fear. And her Italian. She spoke Italian to him and I never heard her speak a word of the language again.

There was no compulsion on my mother to conceal her knowledge of a foreign language, but it might as well have been so. Living in a small village in Dorset, Italian was an encumbrance, which dropped away with the passing years; not wanted on voyage.

The Russian poet Joseph Brodsky tells the story of his mother, during Stalin's purges, concealing her knowledge of French for fear of betraying her class origins: 'One day I found her with a French edition of my works. We looked at each other; then she silently put the book back on the shelf . . .' In our country the offence of being the wrong class is never mortal, but it's not possible to grow up in England without learning that you have to negotiate the codes of class with the ingenuity of a spy on foreign territory. You learn the role: when to conceal your origins, when to display them. It's as essential a part of an English child's social anatomy as learning that you can get some food by saying 'please', and more by saying 'thank-you'. Most of us are damaged by this process and even though the wounds can be cauterised they are never superficial.

I used to play in the gutted fuselage of a large military glider with the children who lived down the lane. My friends were known to my parents as the 'village' boys. They found me out pretty quickly. I said 'lunch' when I should have said 'dinner', 'dinner' when I should have said 'tea', and 'tea' when I should have kept quiet. I tried to pass for one of them and was teased by my father for talking with their accent. He called them 'the electors'. They were different from us, he said. This confused me. Far from being my inferiors my friends seemed my superiors in every way: more agile, more confident, more knowledgeable. They knew about 'vartin'. 'No,' said my father, 'farting.' And he illustrated his point loudly. He could be a rough teacher, but I was a keen pupil and I quickly learned the skills of recognition and camouflage.

Life is all loose ends; fiction has shape and coherence, and unravels meanings through epigrammatic anecdotes. There is one incident in my childhood that has the force of a fictional parable. As a rare experiment in performing the role of the conventional parent, my father decided to teach me to play cricket. He bowled and he batted left-handed, but was otherwise exclusively right-handed. He had been taught by his left-handed father, who saw no reason to accommodate nature's error in giving him a right-handed son. When my father taught me to play cricket he passed on his inheritance, and I learnt left-handed too. At the time it seemed natural enough that he made me follow his shadow, even if nature itself was in rebellion against it. Only with the advantage of hindsight does it seem such an uncomfortably resonant cautionary tale. I've often wondered what I would have taught my son if I'd had one.

Like my father, I am exclusively right-handed, but thanks to him I am as unable to bowl with my right hand as I am to meet another English person without consciously attuning my ear to their accent and their vocabulary. The ex-Prime Minister recently revealed that 'class is a communist concept'. She'd obviously not been in West Dorset in the fifties, but maybe she'd have regarded what I saw as a sort of secular Calvinism, the world divided into those who had entered an earthly heaven, and those who would never gain admittance.

In the myth Cadmus sows the dragon's teeth and reaps a harvest of armed men, who fight among themselves and destroy each other. My father's harvest was a lifelong discord with his son. Beyond that his legacy is that I am quick to anger which vanishes like a summer shower, I am stubborn, and I am reluctant to make moral judgements – at least on private matters.

He was a small but strongly built man, with almost

Nordic, snow-blond hair (he was known as Snowy), but his face was indelibly English, all nose and chin. I have his chin but not his nose. He was vain, and with his longish, slightly feathered hair, his colourful ties, his double-breasted, pin-striped suits, he was dapper as a bird, a chaffinch, perhaps.

My mother was handsome, bright-eyed and bright-skinned, confident and assertive, but it was a confidence that was like a skin laid over the bones of a nature that was hesitant, shy and over-eager for approval. She was always generous, even if she often seemed uncertain how to express it. Neither parent had tranquillity in their make-up. Later in his life my father hated travelling, but it did not quell a restless, febrile character. As for my mother – she loved travelling but, as in so many other things, she deferred to him.

Most children dream at some time that they are adopted. I used to dream that I was a changeling, and sometimes I think that my father wished that I could have been. My mother played the peacemaker. She used to say, 'I just want everyone to be happy,' and, as if to teach by example, was always cheerful, in public at least. Like the shape of my face, I've inherited my professional optimism from her. In the rehearsal room I am almost invariably accompanied by constant good spirits. It doesn't always come easily to me, and I'm not sure that it did to my mother, but it's a role to be played, a necessary one for a director, who can never professionally be too far removed from Dr Johnson's dictum on second marriage: the triumph of hope over experience. I don't think it was too far removed from my mother's feelings about her first and only marriage.

II

MY MOTHER WAS born in 1921 in London, in what was then Chelsea and is now called the Fulham Road. Her parents were in their thirties when they married, and she was an only child. Her mother had been an actress before she married, my only genetic link with the theatre. She acted under a name that sounds as implausible now as it probably did then, Malise Sheridan. According to my father, whose testimony was sometimes blinded by wishful thinking, she had eloped with a racing driver whose initials were H.S. For years I imagined this to be the raffish figure of Henry Segrave who stood in front of a gleaming Sunbeam in my *Wonder Book of Daring Deeds*, having broken the world speed record. I now realise that he would have been about four at the time that my grandmother married, so I must reconcile myself to the truth, as always less alluring than fiction. The truth is that she eloped with an amateur racing driver whose initials were G.S. – Guy Sebright, and she decided to become an actress, which presumably caused as much grief to her parents as her elopement.

I don't think she was a particularly good actress. Her first, and greatest, success was in a play called *Diplomacy*, a long-running West End 'society drama' adapted from Sardou's four-act play *Dora*. It starred Gerald Du Maurier, Owen Nares, and my grandmother's friend, Gladys Cooper. The run of this play is well documented in her scrapbook. Du Maurier stares insolently at the camera, a cigarette holder dangling from one languid hand, the other reaching out for a drink being offered by the maid, who is crouching in an awkward curtsey. The maid was my grandmother and I think the photo is a fair metaphor for her professional career.

The part of the maid in *Diplomacy* was, however, no conventional 'Will-that-be-all-sir?' maid. On the contrary, according to the *Sketch*:

> Miss Sheridan is playing one of the comparatively few servants' parts which give the player a real chance, and she is making the most of her opportunities. Her performance is all the more interesting in that it marks her first appearance on the professional stage. She has to use four tongues – English, French, German and Italian – and is equally at home in each.

The play ran in London for eighteen months and then transferred to Broadway, where the production had the same success.

She was always a flamboyant dresser. A friend of my mother's described her to me: on a walk to pick blackberries she was dressed in a purple cloak with a buttonhole of artificial violets. I don't think she picked many blackberries.

She had something of a personal success, or at least her costume did, in *Under Cover*:

> Whatever the merits or otherwise of *Under Cover* – personally I enjoyed it immensely – the frocks are 'bully'. Most striking of all is Miss Malise Sheridan's sleeveless evening gown of red-gold tissue with its whole-skin, sable shoulder straps and swathed, sheath-like bodice, the material forming is caught into a loop just below the right hip and then develops into the square, sable-edged train.

I can't help thinking that something has been lost from theatre criticism over the last seventy-five years, not to mention costume design.

Like millions who were not at the Somme or at Passchendaele or in the Dardanelles, her life was indelibly blighted by the Great War. Her three brothers were all killed in action, and her marriage failed to survive the War. My mother told me that my grandmother remembered nothing of her first husband – or at least she never spoke of him, but she had never forgotten her three brothers. She had few relatives and her death, shortly after my mother's marriage, made my mother's status as an only child seem more than usually desolate.

She continued to act, another maid in *The Girl from Upstairs*, 'She spared no effort to keep things briskly moving'; a small part in a minor Maugham, *Love in a Cottage*, but at the end of the War she relinquished her career and her stage name to marry a naval officer called Charles Royds. I have a beautiful photograph of him: it is mostly occupied by a huge ice cliff, which towers above a minutely small figure of a man standing alongside his sledge, his figure no higher than an inch on the photograph. It is like looking down the wrong end of the telescope, time and distance making him like an insect on another planet.

III

BEFORE HE MARRIED, my maternal grandfather was a Polar explorer on Scott's first Antarctic expedition, responsible for the work of the men on shore and the internal workings of the ship, *HMS Discovery*. A few years ago it used to be possible to see his ship, moored alongside the Embankment just down-river from Waterloo Bridge, when you looked out of the office of the Director of the National Theatre: a rangy, elegant, black, three-masted, one-funnelled, wooden steam yacht. I have a leather-bound calendar on my desk; the day, the date and the month can be changed by turning little milled wheels. There is an inscription on the back:

DISCOVERY
THIS WAS THE CHARTER OF HER LAND
RULE BRITANNIA

The ostensible purpose of the Discovery Expedition to the Antarctic was scientific: meteorological, zoological, ornithological, botanical, biological, geological, geographical. Their real purpose was declared in the traditional pantomime ceremony of 'Crossing the Line' held as they passed over the Equator:

NEPTUNE:	Have I the honour of addressing the Captain?
CAPTAIN:	You have.
NEPTUNE:	And what may be the Captain's name?
CAPTAIN:	Captain Robert F. Scott.

NEPTUNE:	Where are you bound?
CAPTAIN:	To the South Pole.
NEPTUNE:	Oh aye.

Their purpose, whether for science or glory, was to reach the South Pole before any other explorers. They never did reach the Pole, and by the time of the second expedition in 1910 my grandfather was too weary, or too unambitious, or perhaps too disenchanted with Scott, to make the second, fatal, attempt. Even before they landed in the Antarctic they charted undiscovered territory, the *Discovery* making a discovery in good earnest:

> For the first time in its long life, the great ice barrier had been looked on by human eyes ... thousands of penguins crowded to see us: poor beasts, I wonder what they think we are?

They did reach further towards the Pole than anyone had been before, pulling their own sledges by hand after the death of their dogs, and nearly dying themselves in the effort.

They were extraordinarily young. When they set out they were described by the *Daily Mail*, in a style that is all too recognisable, as 'The Babes in the Wood'. They were young, you see, and their ship was wooden ... Scott, then a Lieutenant Commander, was thirty-three. They were mostly, like my grandfather, naval officers and ratings, but they included among the crew of forty-seven a few civilian scientists, including my grandfather's friend the doctor, zoologist, scientist and artist Edward Wilson, who died later on Scott's second expedition. As well as looking after the ship, my grandfather was responsible for meteorological observations, for assisting the botanist Koettlitz, and for playing the piano, the pianola, and the harmonium. He was twenty-five years old when they left Portsmouth in August 1901.

I have my grandfather's journals written, mostly meticulously, in conditions which sometimes beggar belief. The ship is rolling in a gale, the ink is spilled, the cabin is leaking; a blizzard howls outside the hut, the temperature outside freezes the breath, the fingers have frostbite; the writing becomes perhaps a little spidery but still strong, and still legible. The leather-bound books are now quite fragile; each time I open them they shred more shards of their bindings like dry cigars.

Like him, I write a journal. I can't be absolutely confident that I'll never publish any or all of it, but I try to write it as if there was no one looking over my shoulder. It is as hard to keep an honest record of one's feelings as it is to take one's own photograph, and it involves a similar contrivance: it's difficult to avoid the pose of forced naturalness. It is not a matter of 'being yourself', but of being as truthful to the self-deceiving you as well as the artlessly innocent you. As John Updike says in his autobiography, 'What I have written strains to be true but nevertheless is not true *enough*.'

In my grandfather's journals you are always conscious of his intended audience, his family, and now I'm no less a part of that audience than his brothers and the clusters of cousins that he refers to as the 'girls'. I remember one of them from my childhood, his sister Jess. She was less tall than he was, but still monumental at six foot or so, and red-haired as he was and my own sister is. She remained unmarried and by the time I knew her was formidably eccentric. When she came to stay the house would shake as if possessed by a large poltergeist; countless times during the night, she noisily rearranged the furniture in her room, huge chests-of-drawers and tallboys, all subject to her mysterious whims. She was never in the wrong, and took this stance to such an extreme that I once discovered her burying the remnants of a china cup and saucer in the garden to avoid admitting that she had broken it.

Her brother wrote his journal as a testament; he knew that he might not return from his journey. He doesn't present himself as a man without fear, or without a sense of the danger that he was facing. If he has a purpose, a consistent vein, it is to demonstrate that the explorers were far from being extraordinary creatures coping with extreme circumstances. The wonder, if there was wonder, was in their ordinariness. Only once in the two years that he records does intemperance break through the self-control. In June, during the long winter of 1902, he is reading *Through the First Antarctic Night* by an earlier explorer, Dr Cook (even if he did winter in the Antarctic and reached the North Pole, Cook was known as 'a liar and a gentleman', an American Munchausen) and is 'thoroughly disgusted with it'. He spits indignantly at the descriptions of brooding over loneliness, weeping over sweethearts, and growing hair long out of sheer laziness. Seething with disapproval, he quotes great swatches of Cook's elegiac, mournful, and sometimes despairing account. I am bound to say that Cook's account does not strike me as exaggerated, in fact much of it seems remarkably vivid and all too plausible. But then I have never had to confront, and never could, what he describes as 'the everlasting white silence', to which my grandfather adds an almost audibly derisive shriek of exclamation marks – '!!!!!'. 'What we shall continue to do,' he writes, 'is to behave like ordinary human beings . . . The winter cannot be all joy and comfort, and no one could expect it, but with the help of a little tact, a little self-denial, and a cheery face, most of the monotony and discomfort can be overcome.' Is this courage? Is this stoicism? Or is it wilful lack of imagination?

The tone of the start ('At Sea') is characteristic, but its jauntiness didn't last much below the Equator:

> The correct way to start this journal, which is for the benefit of my family, relations and friends, would be, at least some would imagine, 'Well, girls!!' but that would hardly do, so I say, gentlemen and ladies, the following pages are going to be written for you to read and see how we fared and what we did since leaving you, it was only yesterday and it seems years . . . Partings are always more or less painful, and I am thankful to think that the work and continuous bustle has kept one from thinking.

There was, mostly, enough work, and enough bustle.

Blizzard winds, temperatures of minus 60°F, back-breaking sledge-loads dragged across ice floes, glaciers, crevasses and vast white desert wastelands of snow. The pain, the loneliness, the tiredness, and above all the cold, are reported with an uninflected simplicity which is all the more powerful for being understated and unself-pitying.

> FRIDAY. −33°. Taking observations was absolute agony, as the wind cut through all our clothes. Time after time I thought my nose was gone and although it never went quite, it was all but and hurt like blazes, and feels as raw as beefsteak now.

> MONDAY. Have taken to wearing my nose guard. I can't afford to be careless of that prominent feature on my face.
> The daylight is coming on a pace (sic), and at noon observations can be taken without a lamp. It was −57° at noon, and it had been as low as −62° or 95° of frost. What I call pretty chilly!!! One can't help laughing when one thinks of a sore throat and cold in England and thinking how one doesn't dare show one's nose out of doors.

The journey down was comparatively uneventful, if you are undisturbed by dealing with gales in a sailing ship and constant leaks due to poor construction: 'May the man who threw this ship together have bad dreams.' For my grandfather there was the constant routine of standing his watch, monitoring changes in the weather and in the crew (fortnightly measurements of the officers' weights, the dimensions of their chests, waists, biceps, forearms) and trawling daily for plankton to be examined by himself and Koettlitz under the microscope. A crustacean was named after him: *Roydsis formosa*.

There was little leisure time, but what there was was filled by writing letters, playing cricket on the deck, debates, or perhaps mere arguments, about insanity and suicide ('no result as usual'), the rights of women ('I have no opinion'), whether flying fish have wings, and the relative merits of seal, penguin and sea leopard. When they entered Antarctic waters the hunting instinct was allowed full play, the male ego hungry for expression, and an orgy of killing left the ship like a 'regular butcher's shop'.

The piano and the pianola ('The Flying Dutchman' a constant favourite: 'A ripping piece with plenty of go') were played most days and somewhere after the Equator the first sing-song was held in the Ward Room, with melancholy results: 'Talent is wanting in the singing line . . .' and later: 'When we get away for good I must really take the men in hand and have some good sing-songs.' There might have been some relief when the piano broke away from its moorings in a storm round the Cape of Good Hope, but it was repaired when they put in at Cape Town.

The human conditions were no more predictable than the weather. The cook went crazy and had to be put in irons which he escaped from and threw overboard; a sailor fell from the rigging to the deck and was killed ('Sadness and gloom descended'); there were two fires; and Scott proved a trying commander:

I am supposed to be ready whenever the Captain has a mind to get up anchor . . .

Had a row about last night's fire (some Dundee jute had spontaneously combusted) . . . I expected to be blamed for it and was not disappointed . . .

Through the laconic narratives one can detect friendships forming, irritations growing (when voices were raised the warning 'Girls! Girls!' was often enough to break the tension), and, sometimes, a despondency not even the stiffest upper lip can disguise.

Their last contact with civilisation was in New Zealand where they took on dogs, sheep, provisions and coal, and the ship was invaded by visitors eager to examine the Twentieth-century Argonauts:

All come to gaze at the heroes to be! I say Rats to them all. Heard an amazing story of a young lady being asked why she was coming aboard the ship. She replied that in case of any disaster think how interesting it would be to know that she had actually spoken to one of the officers!! Nice way of looking at things, and not very bright for us.

Within hours of landing in February 1902 they had started to build a hut on shore, and my grandfather had a narrow escape from death by freezing or drowning, or both, when he fell into the sea. They started a routine that would last for two years: sledging in the winter months when the temperatures were higher and the days were long and light, and hibernating during the summer, celebrating Christmas on Midsummer's Day when the night and the day were seamless. 'Absence of sun,' wrote my grandfather, 'has a depressing effect on the best of men.'

The sledge journeys resemble each other more than they differ. The men set out cocky and energetic, dragging an 11 ft sledge with a 7 ft one in tow, six men and (initially) four dogs: Nigger, Bismarck, Paddy and Titch – a music-hall quartet. Their feet sink at the ankles at every step. They steer for Mount Erebus, a still-active volcano, or Mount Terror, undoubtedly appropriately named. Little black silhouettes against the plain white canvas. The dogs fight each other, savagely, picking on the weakest, and their feet start to bleed. 'One or two start to bite their traces, and a good flogging is the only way to teach them not to.' They bay at the moon in chorus, a sound, as Scott said, 'that touches the lowest depths of sadness in this vast desolation'.

The men succumb to exhaustion, frostbite, cramp, and snow blindness. When the weather is calm, the sun stabs the eyes like needles or hot grit, even when wearing wooden goggles with narrow, cross-like slits, and the eyes swell and stream with frozen tears. But then the sledging is easy and the landscape is enchanted: ice cliffs like giants' teeth, glaciers like huge slabs of precious stone, blue and green and glassy and infinitely deep, ice-crystals like a gem-strewn carpet, wonderful optical marvels – double haloes, fog bows, prismatic rings, mock suns, iridescent clouds. And silent, stupendously quiet, but for the 'hush' of the snowcrust settling. Just as quickly the spell dissolves, the wind starts howling, the avalanches growl in the distance, the ice crust cracks with a sound like a volley of pistol shots, and the blizzards blanket their vision with an impenetrable dull white. It is like travelling on the moon, but more desolate and more lonely.

Pitching camp in a blizzard, fumbling for the tent poles and the ground sheet. The slow-motion tedium of taking your clothes off to change into dry ones, ice sticking to your beard, your breath icing, your pipe frozen, your matches damp, your tobacco sodden with snow, your flask of water frozen even though you keep it under your shirt next to your skin; your fingers freeze as you take off your mitts to undo your leggings, and you have to put your mitts on again, and then your leggings are too frozen to undo, the knees hard as bricks, but you have to undo them nonetheless; you take the hay from inside your ski boots and put it next to your body, warm for the morning; you get cramp as you are taking off one pair of your several pairs of long socks, your human-hair night-socks are just pliable enough to put on from being kept close to your body, you wrap yourself in fur, you climb into your sleeping bag, you long for some proper food, something to bite on beside biscuit, you are desperate with tiredness and you are too cold to sleep.

They lived in a time that was hungry for heroes. It was the twilight of the Empire, most of the map of the globe had been coloured pink, and penguins and seals had no territorial rights in the Antarctic. The explorers' scientific purpose was serious and the results impressive, even if this served to mask the less noble motives of the expedition: vanity, self-advertisement, patriotism. Only the last had gone out of fashion. I am moved by the heroic folly of it all, by the physical courage and endurance, by their resolve never to submit to despair, by their determination, as Tennessee Williams would say, to endure by enduring. It's a practical creed, and my grandfather and his colleagues were practical men whose adventures in the Antarctic I admire no less than Tennessee Williams' exploration of the extremities of the human spirit. You admire what you cannot do yourself.

I grew up surrounded by my grandfather's Polar memorabilia: photos, letters, maps, drawings, water-colours, his goggles, his sealskin gloves, a walrus tooth, some model wooden penguins that he carved himself, and the piano, specially made by Broadwood and still surviving in my basement. I have a beautiful water-colour of Mount Erebus on grey cartridge paper painted by Edward Wilson. Art, he said, is 'reality touched with emotion'. After the expedition a sailor was asked what he specially remembered of the Antarctic – 'Why, the colours,' he said. 'You wouldn't believe them.'

My grandfather stayed in the Navy, rose in rank fast and retired early becoming, with no apparent qualifications, Deputy Commissioner of the Metropolitan Police. He had a short but very happy marriage and he died, in the arms of his wife, of a heart-attack in the ballroom of the Savoy, rehearsing the first waltz for the Police Ball.

My mother was eleven when he died and I don't think she ever recovered from the loss of him. With time my father resented the mute presence of her father and felt indicted by his example. My grandfather's possessions came to seem like threatening totems, relics that she revered and he scorned. He was an only child too, and his father's phantom presence was every bit as strong, every bit as intrusive but far, far more damaging.

IV

MY FATHER'S FAMILY had some faint fibre of a connection with the Victorian passion for exploration. The blood runs rather thinner these days, not only in my family, and if the appetite for adventure hasn't dwindled, the opportunities are finite. Our horizons have contracted and the only unexplored territory now is the territory of the human soul. Instead of gazing out at an unknown continent, we peer inwards to a landscape that is often as mysterious and inaccessible.

I was once asked by a friend, in front of my father, if Lake Eyre in Australia had been named after a relation of mine. 'Oh yes,' I said blithely, 'my great-grandfather's brother.' 'He wasn't,' said my father. 'I think he was,' I said. My father stood up and shouted, with a violence that astonished my friend, but not me, 'Don't tell me about the history of my family!' And I was wrong, of course.

Edward John Eyre, a distant cousin of my paternal great-grandfather, set out from Yorkshire, the son of a parson, to discover the legendary inland sea in Australia. He had arrived at the age of seventeen in New South Wales, where he spent a short time on a sheep farm and as a cowboy, an 'overlander', driving stock from Sydney to Adelaide. He was then twenty-three. As he reflected in his forties, 'I was impelled by an innate feeling of ambition and a desire to distinguish myself in a more honourable and disinterested way than by mere acquisition of wealth. I was wrong, no

21

doubt – though I think it is a noble fault to fall into.' Between 1839 and 1841 he opened up huge swathes of uncharted territory.

Fuelled by camp-fire tales of the unrevealed paradise in the centre of the continent, a giant oasis fed by a vast lake, he set off from Adelaide in 1840 with a party of six white men, two aborigines, thirteen horses and forty sheep to 'lift the veil from the still-unknown and mysterious interior of this vast continent'. At his departure he was presented with a Union Jack which he was to plant in the centre of the continent 'as a sign to the savage that the footstep of civilised man has penetrated so far'.

It was not long before 'civilised' man was humbled by nature; there was no inland water, no solace, no triumph, only barren tableland and mirages which bewitched them: 'A vast sheet of water appeared to intervene between us and the shore ... the whole scene partook more of enchantment than reality, and as the eye wandered over the smooth and unbroken crust of pure white salt that glazed the basin of the lake ... the effect was glittering, and brilliant beyond conception.' It was a monument to ambition and vain hope.

He was a religious man, a man who interpreted impossible conditions not as real obstacles, but as the workings of destiny, who stubbornly refused to recognise the furnace-heat of the desert, the lack of water, the intractable hostility of the terrain as anything more than challenges to be met and be overcome. He could not accept nature's mockery of man's insignificance. He was certainly stubborn, but he was not stupid and therefore not without courage; a determined romantic, you could say. He was always seeking the beauty, glorying in the grandiose terror and majesty of exploration. He did it. I dream about it, and in dreaming know my own limitations. 'All was uncertainty and conjecture in this region of magic,' he said after his discovery of the salt lake.

Shortly after I was sent away to boarding school I would read nothing but POW stories and mountaineering books. The model escape story was *The Wooden Horse*; prisoners in Stalag Luft-Something-or-Other dig a tunnel under their gym horse during recreation, and the bags of sand or earth are carried away inside the wooden horse. It was embroidered with the usual seductive detail of forged passports and work permits, cameras made from tins, official stamps and soap, suits made from sacks, uniforms from blankets, and a cast of characters whose weaknesses weren't hard for me to identify with. It fulfilled most of my basic needs: it was frightening, ingenious, difficult, painful, and, above all, true. The penalties for failure were fatal, but the prisoners succeeded in burrowing out of their prison, while I failed to burrow out of mine, even if it was only the tedium and petty oppression of school that I sought to escape from.

Like many bookish schoolboys I read epics of mountain-climbing with an almost pornographic fascination. I loved the vicarious danger and I loved the jargon: bivouacs, abseils, arêtes, crampons, belays, pitons, karabiners, ridges, couloirs, chimneys, slabs and seracs. My favourites were *The White Spider* by Heinrich Harrer, about the climbing of the North face of the Eiger, and *Annapurna* by Maurice Herzog. Both these tales involved terrible physical privations and mental torment. The physical trials included spending the night in a sleeping bag suspended from a vertical cliff by a clip attached to a piton, and losing toes from frostbite on the descent. It wasn't that I was attracted to physical pain – masochism has never held a lure for me – it was the conquest of fear that I found so fascinating. The triumph of the will, I suppose you could say.

My tenuously related ancestor found as bad conditions, or worse, in a journey along the massive natural fortress of the cliffs of the Great Australian Bight that rim the waste-land of the Nullabor Plain. Australia ends suddenly with a sheer drop of hundreds of feet, as if a giant or a god had casually broken off the land and flung it in the sea like a piece of old cheese. After the death of his companion and the defection of his servants, he walked for weeks in the company of a young aborigine boy. They walked nearly a thousand miles. Death was a pleasure kept at bay by the force of an imperative that would have been recognised by my maternal grandfather but not, I think, by me: duty. 'Nothing but a strong sense of duty prevented me from giving way to this pleasing but fatal indulgence. I felt that I could have sat quietly and contentedly, and let the glass of life slide away to its last sand . . .'

I wish I understood this sense of duty; I think that it has vanished along with the other certainties of the last century. I understand duty to friends and to family as a form of love, but not as an abstract, mystical virtue. Perhaps he meant nothing more, or nothing less, than his duty to protect the life of Wylie, the aborigine who had saved his.

There is a terrible paradox in this story. Eyre was one of the few early Australians who thought, and said publicly, that the Europeans should bear in mind that the aborigines regarded them not as legitimate settlers but as invaders and expropriators. After his epic days of exploration he became the Protector and Administrator of the Aborigines in South Australia. He even, for better or worse, educated two aborigine boys in England at his own expense.

He entered the colonial service and in 1865 became Governor of Jamaica. To suppose that you can hold absolute power and not behave like a despot is like supposing you can drink all day and remain sober, and he succumbed to power's fatal lure. The Governor of Jamaica presided as absolute ruler of an island of 16,000 whites and 300,000 blacks. Slavery had ended only in 1833.

Terrible poverty and systematic cruelty provoked a riot led by an inspired revolutionary demagogue. 'It is time for us to help ourselves, skin for skin . . . Every black man must turn out at once, for the oppression is too great.' The riot provoked Eyre into panic: martial law, mass executions, floggings and punitive destruction of property. He was regarded as the saviour of Jamaica by the white settlers, but he was dismissed from office and recalled to London, where his hearing in front of a parliamentary commission provoked riots in the streets. It was a test case for the British Empire: liberal conscience protested against the thuggish brutality, economic pragmatism defended the necessity of harsh measures to protect British interests. Dickens, Carlyle, John Stuart Mill, Ruskin, Huxley were embroiled in the debate.

There were street riots against Eyre – the London working class identifying with the oppression of the Jamaican blacks; there were street riots in Manchester – the Lancashire working class celebrating the use of force in defence of the cotton and the sugar industry. In the middle dwindled the discoverer of the great Australian salt lake; sour, sad, and bitterly confused. He had, after all, done what he thought was his duty.

There is a River Frome in Southern Australia, which was explored by Edward Eyre. It may have been named after the river that ran through the village in which I grew up. The novelist Sylvia Townsend Warner lived in a Victorian house with a corrugated iron roof at the edge of the River Frome on the way to Frome Vauchurch. I spent countless hours with my sister on the river bank opposite catching minnows and sticklebacks with a net, or tadpoles in a jar, or, later, trying vainly to catch trout with a rod made with a bamboo pole taken from the garden shed. I longed for a world outside our small village where people dealt with the great matters of the world – love and politics and art, I'd say now – but then anything that would have lifted me out of my social corral. A few feet away was this remarkable apostate revolutionary who lived there all through my childhood. I knew only that she was a 'Communist and a Lesbian', and therefore socially consigned to an oubliette as dark as the one that contained the 'village' boys.

V

MY GRANDFATHER AND my father were proud of what they described as their 'Irish' ancestry, but I've never spoken my surname with much confidence whenever I've been in the West of Ireland. There's an Eyre Square in Galway City, a village of Eyrecourt, and, near by, the picturesque carcase of a large country house. It's roofless, but most of the walls survive, brick here and there peering through the weather-stained white stucco. It was built by John Eyre in the late-seventeenth century when Galway was a remote colonial outpost whose population were mostly Royalist and almost entirely Catholic. John Eyre, an Englishman from Wiltshire, was a Protestant settler, rewarded by Cromwell for services rendered in the Civil War. He had been persuaded of the strength of the Roundhead cause by the King's treatment of his father, who had been punished savagely, even by today's standards, for objecting to an ill-conceived and hastily constructed tax – he was castrated for refusing to pay Ship Money. It was to be drawn from those who lived on the coast to fund the Navy, and was applied with Thatcherite rigour to Giles, who objected, not unreasonably, that Wiltshire was a long way from the sea. His house was plundered by the King's soldiers, he was robbed of £400 and, as a nineteenth-century biography has it, he was 'XXXXed'. Fortunately for the survival of the family he was already the father of eleven children.

The decay of the house, Eyrecourt Castle, looks as though

it might be a legacy of the Troubles. The truth of the fate of the estate is less interesting, but its ruin no less deserved. It was a house built for entertainment: a ballroom for dancing, large stables for hunting. It encouraged excess. The pride of the house was the staircase – a double one, carved by Dutch craftsmen and transported from Holland. It is the only part of the interior that remains in existence. It was removed, piece by piece, in the twenties and transported to a museum in Detroit. It was flamboyant and eye-catching, but what really caught the eye of the guest was the inscription over the entrance: WELCOME TO THE HOUSE OF LIBERTY, which was taken so literally in matters of hospitality by successive generations that by the beginning of the eighteenth century the family had exhausted its capital.

A distaste for learning is a family tradition more honoured in the observance than the breach. My father didn't want me to go to university. He wanted me, he said, 'to fuck my way round the world, and learn in the university of life'. I felt wholly unqualified by nature for this, and, as much to defy him as for any other reason, I insisted on breaking the family tradition; I tried, and succeeded, in getting to university. It was the first of many disappointments for him. The son of the founder of the Irish dynasty (another John) had entered Trinity College, Dublin, at the age of sixteen. The following year he was back home, married, with sufficient education to satisfy himself and his father.

In 1760 John Wesley was preaching in the West of Ireland. He brought an unpopular message: no drinking or spirituous liquors, no fighting, or quarrelling or 'doing what we know is not for the glory of God, as putting on of gold or costly apparel'. He observed that the 'ill-breeding' as it showed itself in behaviour was to be found among the 'well-dressed people', and that 'we rode on to Eyrecourt where threatened great things' but, he observed with a Pooterish pun, 'all vanished into air'.

Someone in the family, uncharacteristically, must have concentrated their minds on more substantial matters than spirituous liquors because by the late-eighteenth century the family had acquired 85,000 acres and a peerage. But they reverted to form and a style of living consistent with the family's strengths: 'We hunted all day, danced all night, and strolled about with our lovers.' At least they shared their largesse; they were not absentee landlords, and they lived with an obedience to the household motto which verged on fanaticism. In his old age the noble lord became well known for his hearty appetite and his enthusiasm for cock-fighting. He lived a life described by a contemporary observer that my father read to me with undisguised envy:

> His Lordship's day was so apportioned as to give the afternoon by much the largest share of it, during which, from an early dinner to the hour of rest, he never left his chair, nor did the claret ever quit the table. This did not produce inebriety, for it was sipping rather than drinking that filled up the time, and this mechanical process of gradually moistening the human clay was carried on with very little aid from conversation, for his lordship's companions were not very communicative, and fortunately he was not very curious. He lived in an enviable independence as to reading, and, of course, he had no books. Not one of the windows of his castle was made to open, but luckily he had no liking for fresh air, and the consequence may be better conceived than described.

It was not in the nature of the family, as a biographer commented, to push and strive. The first Lord Eyre died without an heir, the title disappeared and the estate passed to his nephew, Giles, who dedicated himself with wholesale enthusiasm to a life of pleasure:

> To keep game cocks to hunt the Fox
> To drink in punch the Solway
> With debts galore, but fun far more
> Oh! that's 'the man for Galway'.

The 'man for Galway' kept thirty or forty horses for hunting, took no more than two bottles of claret after his dinner to 'drive the gout to his head', and is alleged to have spent £80,000 in bribes during an election – and failed to get elected to parliament. He was approached once by an opponent with a piece of paper in his hand, an offer to retire from the contest if the Squire would sign the declaration. He was confident of his opponent's enviable independence of the skills of reading and writing.

Giles Eyre's lasting claim to fame was his Mastership of the Galway Blazers Hunt. It might be thought that this referred to the pack of hounds, blazing a spirited trail across the countryside in pursuit of the uneatable. Not so. The name was earned by the habit of the Master and his followers putting up at hotels after a hard day's sport and, like a Heavy Metal band high on speed and spirits, setting fire to the hotel. It was perhaps as well for the hoteliers of Galway that overindulgence of all sorts brought the family into debt. Always barely one step ahead of bankruptcy, his son appears to have spent several years in the debtors' prison in Dublin, which does not seem to have hindered his fathering a number of children.

The nephew of one of these children was my great-grandfather, Philip. He was intended by his father for the Church, but bored by the prospect of a life of rural penury, and no doubt tormented by the family's tradition of noisy licentiousness, he ran away from home, enlisted as a private in the South Staffordshire Regiment and left for the Crimea. Here he distinguished himself in battle at the Siege of Sebastopol, was decorated and offered a commission. He was killed thirty years later at the Battle of Kirbekan, leading his regiment as its Colonel. His death was reported in the same week as that of General Gordon, the 'Pacificator' of the Sudan. The *Illustrated London News* reported that he died with these words on his lips: 'I am a dead man. Lord have mercy upon me. God help my poor wife.' It's in the same vein of fiction as the caption that I once saw under a photograph of Indian troops sitting in a trench shortly before Passchendaele: 'They took the fortune of war with the utmost cheerfulness and found considerable solace in the cigarette.'

VI

MY GREAT-GRANDFATHER'S military career cast its shadow over the lives of all his descendants, even my sister and myself. He was clearly a forceful man and I was aware, even as a small child, that his son was cowed by his reputation and diminished by his presence even in death. His portrait hung at the end of the dining-room in my grandfather's house, a stern, patriarchal man, with a large walrus moustache, in full military regalia. The dining-room had dark, dirty, plum-coloured wallpaper, a heavy oak sideboard, a high window that reached from ceiling to floor, and a thick, uneven oak table. My grandfather always sat beneath the portrait of his father and stared malevolently at his son, sitting at the opposite end of the table. He invariably cast a sepulchral silence over meals, punctuated occasionally by a timid dribble of conversation from my sister or from me. During one of these joyless meals she told me that she'd met someone on a train and talked to him. My grandfather slammed his fist on the table, shaking the glasses and the cutlery: 'No one's ever spoken to me in a train, thank *Christ*!'

My parents were never great readers, a novel 'on the go' for my mother from the World Book Club, a military biography for my father, Wellington or Nelson for preference. Beyond that the only required reading was Damon Runyon, P. G. Wodehouse, or *Cold Comfort Farm*. With these exceptions they both preferred the harshness of facts. We were subscribers to the *Reader's Digest*, which ran then, and maybe still does, a regular feature: 'The Most Unforgettable Character I've Ever Met'. My father always said there should be a feature about his father: 'The Most Unpleasant Character I've Ever Met'. When he said that, I never felt he was exaggerating.

Neither Kafka's name, nor his books, were known in our house, but you could get to know Kafka's father through my grandfather. They were brothers in spirit (and in looks) and my father felt about his father as Kafka did of his: 'Often I picture a map of the world and you lying across it. And then it seems as if the only areas open to my life are those that are not covered by you or are out of your reach.' Throughout his life my father struggled to clear a space left unoccupied by his father, and I've made no less an effort in my life. It's a costly operation.

I imagine that my grandfather saw very little of his father, who died when he was eight. He followed his father into the Army but he had a desultory career, and retired early as a major. I asked my father once what his father had done during *his* war, The Great War. 'Sat twenty miles behind the lines at HQ warming his arse on a stove,' he said.

He married my grandmother Joan when they were both in their early twenties, but they were childless for eleven years after their marriage. My father, born in 1916, was their only child. He was very close to his mother and whenever he spoke of her to me his natural reticence about his feelings almost disappeared and a rare tenderness softened his face.

It was always my father's claim that his mother had been killed by his father. I don't think he meant it literally, but I was never quite sure. She died of a stroke when she was fifty-eight, worn out by bullying, long periods of silent disdain followed by eruptions of volcanic severity.

He was even-handed in his brutality and dealt with his son in the same currency. His concept of discipline, at least in practice, was derived from Prussia, or even Sparta. My father was taught to ride before he could walk, tied to a saddle before his legs reached the stirrups. I've seen photographs of him on the back of a plump pony, looking like a pea or a finger puppet. Whatever fear he felt he disguised and it was a lesson he never forgot. Like a wolf child, he was always more at ease with animals than people, and throughout his life could only accept those people who could embrace his love of horses. Try as he might, he found it hard to find fellow feeling with those who had less rigorous childhoods than his own. He was beaten with a riding crop for minor misdemeanours, and when he became a naval cadet at the age of thirteen the consistency and anonymity of the rigid military discipline must have seemed like a benediction. His hair was cut shaved close, within a hair's breadth of his scalp, until he was eighteen; in photographs you can see his skull gleaming through his thin hair. Throughout his adult life he tried to show his independence from his father by growing his hair long, or at least just long enough to make his point but, characteristically, not too long to be unacceptable to convention.

My grandfather lived in a late-eighteenth-century house in North Devon in a small village near Bideford, 'Mau Mau country' my father called it, unfriendly and impenetrable. The house was detached and stood in a few acres of parkland dominated by a huge horse-chestnut tree. On the front of the house two of its large windows were blocked up, legacies of the refusal of a previous owner to pay the Window Tax. It gave the face of the house the look of blindness, as if its eyelids had been sewn together. My grandfather was not rich. He lived on his major's pension and the evidence for this was all too obvious in what he would never have called his lifestyle. If the past is another country, it's one that he had become a native of. He had stopped his personal clock somewhere before the First World War and he dressed always as an Edwardian: narrow-trousered, pale-brown tweed suits, or breeches with puttees and a Norfolk jacket, and always a high-necked, round-edged stiff collar. He was not amused to be told, shortly before he died in the late-fifties, that he was a real Teddy Boy. His hair, though, hardly fitted the bill, shaved Prussian-style close to his scalp like emery paper. If he had a role model it must have been Bismarck, although the suggestion that he resembled a German would have earned the retort: 'I hate the bloody Germans. And the bloody French. And the bloody Italians, for that matter.'

His house was warmed, and I use the word advisedly, by a fire in the dining-room and in his bedroom. There was a firm and unbreakable rule about fires: they were never to be lit before the 1st of October or after the 1st of April. If it snowed on the 2nd of April, so be it; you complained at your peril. He never had electricity installed in the house. All the lighting was done with candles and oil-lamps, all cooking was on a large, black, open, coal-burning range in a kitchen with a flag-stoned floor and a smoke-stained ceiling. The water was pumped in the yard from a well, inhabited by dead cats, rats and frogs. I wish I exaggerated.

The house seemed, to a child's eye, a continent of fearful possibilities: dark, labyrinthine panelled corridors, cellars, creaking floorboards, cupboards that were never opened, rooms that were never entered. The drawing-room was forbidden territory. It was the only room in the house that was light in colour and in feeling, airy and cheerful. We never used it; the grand piano that had been played by my grandmother remained locked, and her collection of musical boxes lay untouched. Her spirit was a palpable presence in the room, and to creep into the room unobserved was to find a calm sanctuary from the potential terrors that lay in the rest of the house. One of these was to be caught by my grandfather using the lavatory at a time when he wanted to use it. This was a common fate of mine, as I could never resist the lure of the only reading matter that was kept there – copies of Old Moore's Almanac from years back. The lavatory, an early work by Armitage Ware, was set at the end of a stone-floored tack room, unheated and supplied only with old shredded copies of The Times for use as lavatory paper. You'd sit there shivering from fear as much as cold as the door, unadorned by a lock, clattered open and my grandfather stared malignantly: 'How much more bloody time are you going to spend in here?'

In fact there were two lavatories, but the more accessible and, I imagine more comfortable one was reserved for the use of women. They were not however allowed to enter his smoking-room. He may have smoked a pipe but beyond that the purpose of the room was uncertain, or perhaps its purpose was defined simply by its inaccessibility to women. The walls were spread with haphazardly hung rows of sporting and military prints, sepia photographs of Army officers, and brown-paper-covered, dog-eared copies of the Army List dating from before his father's death. Even from the hall the room smelt musty and on the rare occasions that I was allowed in it seemed as welcoming as a monk's cell. It was a melancholy shrine to his past.

His bedroom was furnished with a miserly asceticism: it contained only an iron single bed of the sort found in boys' preparatory schools or prisons of the better sort, and a rough-looking kind of sack or skin, which acted as a carpet, by the bed. This had a rare sentimental value which he revealed once to my father's cousin who was staring at the floor-covering with some curiosity about its origins: 'Viceroy,' said my grandfather. 'Best damn pony I ever had!'

There were always household tasks to be set for a child: pumping the water in the yard, cleaning the funnels of the oil-lamps, rubbing the rust off the old iron cutlery, and sometimes, as a treat offered by my grandfather to provoke my father, fetching rough cider from the barrel in the cellar in a heavy, thick glass jug. At the age of six or seven, my sister and I would be encouraged to drink this potent local brew and it never failed to provoke a heady vagueness in us and a full-scale row between them.

I think it was the rows that first attracted my attention to the possibilities of drama, which, unlike fiction, is all about the spaces between the lines. I was fascinated not so much by the obvious entertainment of the inventive streams of violent invective as much as the silences that followed: epic, giant, immense, terrible, and terrifying. Maybe they're magnified by the eyes of childhood, but to me each look had the weight of a hammer blow, each blink a fist. Only the scraping of the cutlery on the plates distracted from the dense absence of words, and broke the almost palpable thickness of the space between them. It was as if the atoms in the air were charged with the anger that they generated and when my mother offered more fish pie (was it always fish pie?) the storm would break again, thunderous threats culminating in my mother leaving the room in tears, my sister and I silent as sea anemones, and the two men standing with their fists extended at each other while the shadows made by the flickering oil-lamps danced on the dark ceiling.

Outside his family my grandfather's displays of violence were rare but celebrated. He was bound over to keep the peace several times for assaulting motorists with a horsewhip. He saw himself as a private avenger, keeping the roads free of the alien motor car. When he heard, or more likely scented, an approaching car, he would position his horse across a narrow lane, forcing the driver to stop, and plead to be allowed to pass. Iron-hearted, confirmed in his role as the Scourge of Progress, he resisted all pleas for mercy. The driver would be wound to a pitch of anger and exasperation and get out of his car to move the stubborn object. Then he would be lashed for his insolence, and my grandfather would ride on. 'That'll teach you, you bastard!'

Psychopathic or just plain mad, he was alleged to have many friends, at least as a young man. Like many psychopaths he was fond of practical jokes. He had a cousin who was on the Board of Governors of Bristol Zoo. He rang the zoo pretending to be his cousin and said he was giving a tea-party. He'd be most grateful for the loan of two elephants to be displayed in his garden and was particularly keen that their manure be put to use on his roses. The elephants were delivered on a Saturday afternoon when his cousin was indeed giving a tea-party. He wasn't amused, and I think my grandfather exhausted that friendship as he exhausted the others.

My grandfather had another friend who was a zoologist.

He wrote a letter to *The Times* in his friend's name saying that he'd sighted the Loch Ness Monster, a long-necked, long-tailed, pinniped, or fin-footed mammal, some thirty feet in length, which blew like a whale. There was a great deal of excitement, the zoologist was besieged by the press, and his life, at least temporarily, was made hell. This would have given great satisfaction to my grandfather who was an expert in that department.

My mother had a shrewd idea that her life could become hell if she stayed in his house as he'd taken against her on sight and could only be persuaded to speak to her if he wanted some service performed or in order to defame his son. In later years whenever we stayed with him she was banished to the kitchen, or forced to shave his head with fearsome-looking trimmers like crab's claws, but during the War my mother wisely chose to rent a house in a village near him on the estuary of the River Torridge rather than share his house. He was the closest available family: her mother had died soon after the birth of my sister, her uncles had been killed in the previous war, my father was at sea, and London was still being heavily bombed. Her only companion was her nanny, a gaunt, lonely, distant, but kind woman who had been with her since her birth and consequently never quite regarded her as being capable of looking after a child, let alone two. On my mother's honeymoon, spent in the Great Northern Hotel at King's Cross The Day That France Fell, her nanny accompanied her, in a separate room, and my mother was obliged to spend part of the night with her chaperone. Unsurprisingly, my mother always seemed faintly daunted by her, and asserted her rights of access to us as if she lacked the natural conviction in them. My sister and I grew up between the two of them, never quite certain whose authority to defer to.

I was born on a Sunday in March 1943. I was once persuaded to visit a foot-reader, or 'reflexologist' as he called himself. He told me I had been born late and that my mother had been unhappy during my pregnancy. The rest of your life, he said, you will be trying to make up for your late entry into the world; your mother didn't want to let you go. As it happened, it was true what he said. I was late, she was unhappy, and I don't think she did ever want to let me go. She missed my father, and it was six months before he saw me. For a few months she kept a diary of my growth, interspersed with her visits, announced at very short notice, to Derry, or Dover, or Plymouth. On these short visits she had 'a marvellous time', 'a heavenly week-end', 'a thrilling time'. When my father had his first sighting of his son it was said by my mother to be favourable.

My grandfather wrote that he was pleased to hear of the safe arrival of 'the gift from God' (I assume that was heavy irony). 'Some day soon I will give you my considered opinion of your effort.' I have no idea what his considered opinion was but it may well have been reflected in his instruction that I was to be christened 'Richard Fitzrichard', or, as I understand it, bastard son of Richard. Fortunately, the vicar was deaf and christened me 'Richard . . . er, just Richard'. A small act of mercy.

We lived in North Devon until the end of the War, and returned there annually on a pilgrimage that was penitential, at least for my father. It wasn't so for me. I liked the strangeness of it all; it was like time-travelling. I was fascinated by my grandfather and his house, and during the long hot summer days we'd often go back to Instow where we'd lie on the beach looking across the Torridge to Appledore waiting until low tide to walk across the estuary to go shrimping in the pools.

It was on one of these shrimping expeditions that I had my first sexual experience. We'd had a picnic on the beach, a lot of drink for the grown-ups, a lot of noise. I remember my mother telling everyone not to go swimming, they'd had too much to drink. As a child, she said, she'd been in Deauville and seen the town band go swimming after a huge, drunken lunch; they'd staggered across the flat sand into the sea, and several failed to return, drowned. But the tide was too low to swim and we all trooped off to the shrimping pools. I'd watched slyly earlier as a friend of my mother's changed out of her wet bathing suit into her dress. Now she slipped on the wet sand and fell back into a pool with a shriek of laughter. She wrung out her dress, and, as she did so, once again observed by me, revealed what I already knew – she wore no knickers. She caught my eye and smiled, a smile of sweet complicity.

Throughout those summers I lived with a lightness of spirit, shoeless, with a minimum of clothes. Occasionally I would be sunburnt, but even that had its compensations. Going up to my room with the green-painted cupboard up the narrow back staircase, carrying a Wee Willie Winkie candle, to lie on my bed while my mother rubbed Calomine lotion on my back and then read *Struwwelpeter* to me, the only children's book in the house. But not even the tales of chopping off fingers and eating babies destroyed the pleasure of hearing my mother's voice as the soothing pink lotion on my back dried like cracked clay.

My grandfather had a mistress. She was a widow, who lived in the village, and was occasionally glimpsed by me on one of my reconnoitres of forbidden territory. I'd be drawn by the sound of hushed voices and doors which mysteriously closed as I approached. I once went into the dining-room as his friend, the exotically named Mrs de Las Casas, was being ushered out rather indecorously over the low sill of the window. It was a compulsory fiction that the affair was not taking place, but her presence made itself felt at second hand: 'My friend, Mrs de Las Casas, says . . .' while my father muttered, 'I don't give a bugger what your friend Mrs de Las Casas says.'

She was revealed in her true colours at my grandfather's funeral, an occasion which my father said was no less welcome for having been so long awaited. 'It just goes to show that there's a God,' he said. He sat at the front of the church during the funeral and at one point, being aware of someone getting up behind him, he looked round and saw Mrs de Las Casas leaving the church carrying a large shopping bag. His curiosity got the better of his filial affection without much difficulty and he followed her. She crossed the road and went into my grandfather's house, through the back door, down the dark corridor from the kitchen to the hall, and into the dining-room. For a few moments my father waited, listening to a shuffling, chinking sound. When he went into the room, she turned, frozen, her hands full of silver cutlery. 'He always wanted me to have this,' she said defiantly.

My grandfather's sole concession to the twentieth century was a large radio, or rather, 'wireless', which was powered by a large accumulator. Its use was permitted only twice a day: *The Nine o'Clock News* in the morning, and *The Nine o'Clock News* at night. Parsimonious as this was, I always loved sitting round the wireless, focusing on the art deco panel in front of the loudspeaker, and the portentous, dinner-jacketed voice of the news-reader. I liked the ritual and the forced family gathering.

I was away at school when my grandfather died. I'd persuaded my father that he should give me a radio to replace my crystal set and when they came to see me they were going to bring it. But their visit was cancelled: 'Your grandfather has died and your parents won't be able to bring your wireless. I expect you're sorry about that.' I was, but I was sorrier still that Grandpa had died. I wasn't sure why. Something had gone from my life, I wasn't sure what.

VII

We all grow up in the same way, more or less;
Life is not known to give away her presents;
She only swaps.
                    – W. H. Auden, 'Letter to Lord Byron'

THE ABSENT FATHER is a literary commonplace drawn from the commonplace of life. My father's generation had yet too become self-conscious about the role of the father, or willing to articulate the frustration of the mother, and I'm none too certain that he would have stayed at home if he'd had the choice. Like many of his generation, he was emancipated by his life in the Navy, and although it was undeniably dangerous to be at Dunkirk and hell to be on a convoy in the Baltic, there was a licence for him to see the world during and after the War, and an implicit licence for the sort of behaviour dictated by the thrill of beating death: a licence for licence.

Until I was eight I have only intermittent memories of my father but I do remember trying to get him to teach me to swim. There was a picnic, friends and their children, and food and drink spread out on the grass of a water-meadow beside a large weir pool, sheltered on the other side by white willows and osiers. There was the smell of an English summer, fresh river water, grass and the faint scent of cowshit on the breeze. The weir itself had several floodgates which could be wound up and down according to the level

40

of the water, and a flat area beneath the gates where the water collected before spilling into the river below. I longed to be able to swim from the weir to the shore, a distance of perhaps fifty feet.

I tried to distract my father. He was engaged on an apparently endless anecdote about how he had to put his hand down a woman's dress to extricate a hearing-aid that had fallen down the front, and then shown a couple to the coal-hole who 'couldn't wait to do it'. I waited until the end of the story and asked him to teach me to swim. 'If you swim from the weir to the bank,' he said, 'I'll give you ten shillings,' and he brandished a note. Greed overcame fear and I ran to the weir. I confidently assumed that he wouldn't be watching, secured a large piece of timber which supported my weight, and paddled like a sodden dog to the shore. As I lay in the water panting, preparing to collect my reward, a condom floated towards me. I held up my find. 'What's this? What's this?' I yelled in the face of a blast of laughter. 'It's a trap for catching eels,' said my father without pause and that was the extent of his swimming tuition, and, for that matter, sexual education. I was expected to acquire knowledge by osmosis.

Years later I was on the beach at Southsea with my mother. She fell asleep, and while she slept I was convinced that I could learn to swim by the power of positive thought. I strode out into the sea towards my sister, who was an able swimmer. I was soon out of my depth and unaccountably my flailing arm movements failed to keep my head above water, and I clung to my sister's neck, dragging the two of us downwards. The role I'd inadvertently given my sister was typical: she was supporting me. When I asked her years later if she remembered this episode I remembered only my part. I'd forgotten, typically again, that I'd almost dragged her down with me. We were saved from drowning by a prompt spectator and I was carried, before the fascinated gaze of the entire beach, back to my sleeping mother. She woke to see a bluish child deposited at her feet. In gratitude she gave my saviour £5; even in my bleary, sodden, tear-clouded state I can remember the look of grateful surprise as he took the large white note, and I thought: Oh, that's what I'm worth. I learnt to swim for free a few years later.

As a young girl my mother had been a keen swimmer, a golfer, a skier, even a rider, but with time and marriage these enthusiasms dropped away. My parents' real passion was for parties, and I was conscripted reluctantly into these as a truculent waiter, ferrying drinks to guests who would have preferred a direct connection with the bottle. They seemed to have discovered the secret of circular breathing, talking seamlessly, without the need to pause to take in drink or air. From the child's-eye view I saw their huge chests as mere containers for liquid and their braying voices as mere devices for making noise. If they spoke to me I was paralysed by shyness, and if I spoke to them it would be to experiment with the code of address in which my father had instructed me: all male adults (of a certain class) were to be called 'sir'. My levelling instincts rebelled and I took a malicious delight in public refusal in spite of the inevitable punishment, often being chased round the garden to evade the hard slap of my father's hand and the incarceration in my room, where I steamed for hours with righteous indignation.

My father never lost the habit of treating parties as if the War had cast the mould for 'a good thrash', and anything less would be a betrayal of the past. He had a rapacious attitude to pleasure, underpinned by a kind of urgency. His creed, borrowed perhaps from the 'House of Liberty' of his profligate ancestor, was this: 'Enough is too little, too much is enough.' If the Suez Canal was said to flow through the drawing-room of Anthony Eden during the Suez crisis, rivers of gin seemed to flow through ours. It may have been a legacy of the War years, or it may have been a rebellion against an abstemious childhood, but it persisted almost until his death. He had a contagious energy, and, when his insistent enjoyment joined with my mother's exuberance, they were a hard couple to resist. They never seemed more themselves and more together than when they were on the opposite sides of a room hosting a party, radiating a mutual warmth and defying the guests not to enjoy themselves. Their charm was not so much infectious as guileless, but for me at least, it was a sort of tyranny of fun – there seemed no room for dissent.

There's a cartoon that people often send to me on first nights, when I put my head on the professional block: 'How to Behave at a Preview'. A couple stand at an art exhibition, the man's elbow is poised on an imagined mantelpiece, a glass in his hand, the woman is seated below him. HE: 'This is my masterpiece – hand and glass locked in a tension of opposites.' SHE: 'Don't be a wally, Nigel – people will hear you!' The context clouds the picture. My parents would have been as likely to be seen at a Nubian fertility dance as at an art exhibition, but their masterpiece was indisputably hand and glass locked for a lifetime in a tension of opposites.

If they enjoyed themselves with a passionate intensity, when they fought it was no less intense. I had a miniature bricklaying set, a sort of crude precursor of Lego, tiny terracotta bricks, stuck together with a sort of soluble mortar. I had spent a day building a bungalow, pitched roof and bow windows, which I carried before me down the stairs like a burning Christmas pudding to display to my parents and bask in their admiration. As I opened the door our white Bakelite radio, propelled by my father, flew across the room towards my mother and seemed to stick to the wall: valves, wires, condensers, resistors, transformers, all slipping slowly down the wall like entrails or jelly. Violence freezes the senses. It's often shown on film in slow motion and it seems meretricious. Yet there really are two simultaneous time-scales, the real and the perceived, the objective and the subjective. I was once beaten up, in Singapore. I can remember every moment of the impact as if it had been minutely catalogued, yet it was over, with startling force, in a matter

43

of seconds. The radio seemed to take the rest of my childhood to drift down the wall.

Like most children of my class I was sent to boarding school
when I was eight, and progressed, according to the custom
of the tribe, from prep school to public school. Evelyn
Waugh's much celebrated view of the public school now has
the status of a revealed truth: 'Anyone who has been to an
English public school will always feel comparatively at home
in prison. It is the people brought up in the gay intimacy
of the slums . . . who find prison so soul-destroying.' It's
an observation that's often quoted in a self-congratulatory
fashion by those who'd have you believe that their education
has done them no harm and, as if to prove the proposition,
they intend to send their sons to endure the same treatment.
Leaving aside Waugh's fantasies about the 'gay intimacy of
the slums', there is much truth in the comparison between
public school and prison. Both institutions harbour people
who would rather not be there, both apply a senseless discipline in the name of self-improvement, both insist on class
solidarity, both pay lip-service to remedial education, both
encourage the suppression of natural feelings, and both
encourage an orthodoxy of homosexuality.

At least prisons have a rational justification for their existence; the justification for the seminaries of the English
middle class is harder to find, but its consequences are all
too visible. The custom of sending children to boarding
schools at the age of eight has an air of calculated cruelty
that does not have the excuse of ignorance or helplessness.
It is no exaggeration to say that the moment I was left
alone in late September on a playing field in Hampshire as
my parents drove away inspired a pain and resentment that
the wisdom or forgiveness of hindsight hasn't diminished.
Perhaps I was more than usually thin-skinned, but I knew
then as I listened to the cawing of the rooks and gazed at
the bleak faces of my fellow new boys, all struggling to
conceal their misery, that it was a high price to pay. To be
taught to survive is one thing, to be taught that it is unwise,

unmanly and unsafe to share your feelings is quite another. This is the fate of English Middle-Class Man.

No one has written with more eloquence of the English middle-class educational system than Orwell, and yet, as if unable to eradicate his tribal loyalties, he obliged his own (adopted) son to endure the same rites of passage that he so despised. Perhaps he wanted his son to learn the same lesson he had to learn, as a child poorer than the other children: 'A child conscious of poverty will suffer snobbish agonies such as a grown-up person can scarcely even imagine.' Through suffering he would learn; a political education, but at what cost? More often, fathers who have suffered themselves will, like homeopathy, apply a little of the same treatment to their children as if to assuage their own memories, or simply to convince themselves it was all for their good. It made men of them. More pathetic still is the spectacle of those who didn't have the dubious benefits of this education, craving it for their own children as the essential qualification for membership of the club that they've been taught, by the existing members, is essential for their social advancement. Easy enough for me to say, of course, as a member of the club.

We are a deeply conservative, and a deeply religious people. The only possible explanation that I can see for the survival of, and deference to, the Monarchy, the House of Lords, the Honours system, the British Constitution (or lack of it), is that we have a kind of mystical faith in our systems and institutions that is not susceptible to reasoned analysis and debate. They are regarded, in a real sense, as sacred. Our feelings are passionately religious – no less so than Islam – and are all the more powerful for not being acknowledged as such; it is, after all, an *English* religion. The clock was stopped when the mortality of the Empire was perceived and progress was frozen somewhere around the Jubilee in 1897. It's not a coincidence that the form of many of our 'time-honoured' pageants and rituals was conceived by committees in Queen Victoria's reign in the wake of Disraeli's coinage of the title 'Empress of India'. They are as synthetic as the annual gathering of the Druids on Primrose Hill to celebrate the Summer Solstice. We call congenitally retarded children, the sufferers from Down's Syndrome, 'mongols'. In Japan they call them 'Britons'.

To judge by the standards of the voluminous literature of the English middle-class education, my prep school was typical, and I was happy enough there. There were some excellent teachers: an American student who loved to talk about the French Revolution – I can still remember his rhapsodic description of the importance of the Gabelle, the tax on salt, as a trigger to the Revolution; a Latin teacher with one eye, tall as a poplar tree, severe but kindly; an ex-Commando major who had lost his leg in Normandy and used his tin leg to gain our attention, banging it with his stick, or, in extremity, hurling the same stick like a lance to hit a recalcitrant pupil with the rubber end right between the eyes. He loved reading aloud and had a wonderfully alluring voice, like an English Spencer Tracy, and he gave us, over four or five lessons, the whole of Matthew Arnold's epic narrative poem about the Norse Gods, *Balder Dead*. It was dense, vivid, and unflaggingly exciting. I looked at it again the other day and realised what an alchemist my teacher had been. But the reading that converted me to the power of descriptive writing was Hemingway's *The Old Man and the Sea*. In the classroom we unhesitatingly identified the Old Man with the teacher, our old man, and when he finished the story there was a silence that could have been carved into a monument. The Major took an interest in me, thought that I had a talent for acting, and wrote a play for me – *The Man Who Won the Pools*, and I was that man. We performed it after the school prize-giving, to applause that intoxicated me and corrupted me irrevocably.

His interest in me was of a different sort to Uncle Willie who taught French, and kneaded one's legs just above the knee, and to the Headmaster who weighed us twice a term in our underpants and then confirmed his measurements by sitting us on his knee and bouncing us up and down in a fairly unscientific fashion. We were cynically aware of the

Headmaster's follies, but not cynical enough to encourage them. Sex seemed innocent enough and we discovered the delights of masturbation, lying in small huts we constructed in the woods out of branches and warm hay after smoking pipes turned on the lathe in the woodwork shop and stuffed with the tobacco from discarded cigarette ends.

It was a school mostly for the sons of naval officers, and its maritime bias was expressed in a large flagpole, like a mast, which stood in the forecourt. Every morning the Union Jack and the flags for four admirals who had given their names to the 'houses' at the school were raised by the boys. It was a much envied privilege, and I count among the more useful things I learnt at school the knowledge of how to roll a flag, run it up a pole, and unfurl it on cue.

Weekends always had a particular flavour, part desolation and part exhilaration. It was a mixed blessing to have a visit from one's parents – the strain of having to spend time with comparative strangers and one's anxious awareness of their efforts to be entertaining were at war with the pleasures of remaining at school. A melancholy walk on the esplanade at Southsea followed by a meal spent with half an eye on the clock could hardly be preferable to being left to enjoy the film on Saturday night – a short, often a *Ma and Pa Kettle*, followed by a feature, perhaps *King Solomon's Mines*, an Ealing comedy, a George Formby, or, exceptionally, a bona fide American movie.

And on Sunday nights anarchy ruled. There never seemed any evidence of staff after the church service and the meal on Sunday evenings, and this invisibility enabled a wild, atavistic display of violence to occur. The whisper went round the school: 'Chain He in the gym,' and by seven o'clock about a hundred boys had collected. One was chosen 'He' and formed a chain which grew and swung and swept the length of the large echoing gymnasium gathering its victims in its jaws. To be one of the last to be caught was to know real excitement and real fear: the sight and sound of nearly a hundred small boys drunk with infectious savagery, screaming with demonic glee, thundering towards me with plimsolls thudding like hooves on the springy floor lives with me still. I loved the feeling of fear as much as the feeling of power.

My public school was exceptional only in that it had a more stubborn hold on the nineteenth century than others at the time, and that I was finally expelled from it – for a mixture of boredom, rebelliousness, exasperation on their part and sheer bloody-mindedness on mine. In my last year I'd engineered a kind of no man's land between science subjects and English. I convinced the science teachers that I was occupied with English, and the English teacher vice versa, and I filled the ensuing vacuum by breeding a contagious discontent and editing the school magazine. Its satirical tone was ahead of its time, but that was all that there was to recommend it under my editorial hand. A stray copy of the proofs reached the Headmaster's eyes; the issue was plucked from the presses and an apparatchik was installed as a substitute editor. The incident coincided with a trip that I made to a sixth-form conference at Watford Grammar School. Suitably dressed in black shirt, white tie, drainpipe trousers and winklepicker shoes, I made my way to the station. 'Where are you going?' said the school chaplain. He spoke mildly, in fact somewhat in the tone of a man musing on his text for next Sunday's sermon, but my fuse blew. I told him it was no business of his where I was going, caught the train, and by the time I returned I was the only person in the school who didn't realise that my half-life was over. Shortly afterwards, when I was eighteen, I became a barman. I revealed to a customer that I'd been expelled from school. 'For rogering behind the pavilion,' he said, and I couldn't satisfy him with the truth.

When I was expelled I was confronted by the Headmaster. He told me that I would regret leaving under these circumstances all my life, and cited the change of heart of Alec Waugh, Evelyn's brother, who had been expelled some forty-five years earlier for writing a novel about the school that indicated that homosexuality and bullying were the most conspicuous educational disciplines on offer. It didn't seem like fiction to me. The Headmaster was still pretty steamed up about it, but the point he made was this: 'Alec Waugh lives abroad now and he returns to this country twice a year. The first occasion is the Lord's Test, and the second occasion is the Old Shirburnian's Dinner. I think there's a lesson to be learned there, don't you agree?'

I didn't.

I don't think the parting of the ways with my father was entirely my fault – but then I don't think it was entirely his. When I was nine he was sent to South-East Asia, or, as he called it, and it seemed accurate enough to me, 'The Far East'. He was away for over two years and he became a series of X's on a postcard: his cabin on a P and O liner, the bridge of his ship – the destroyer *HMS Consort*, the Peak in Hong Kong, the old palace of the Rajah Brooke's in Sarawak. The postcards got less frequent, the X's disappeared, and I was left with the Esplanade in Macao, the City of Tokyo, the Island of Formosa, and a remoteness as wide as three continents.

We waited for several hours on a cold night at Stansted Airport to meet him on his return. Somehow I expected to see him in uniform, the sharply pressed white-uniform shorts that he wore in the bleached black-and-white photographs he had sent us. I was disappointed by the man I met, undoubtedly my father, but less big, less romantic, and, above all, less welcoming than I had hoped. Perhaps I didn't make it easy for him, but instead of kissing me as he had when he left, he patted me on the shoulder, perhaps with awe: I was no longer the child he had left behind.

The next night we went out to dinner at Quaglino's – a supper club whose great days belonged to a past when nightingales sang in Berkeley Square. I sat next to my father feeling somehow as if I'd won the evening as a prize in a competition. Stirring the conversational pot my father asked me how my riding was going. To him it was an accomplishment as casual, and as necessary, as tying your shoelaces.

'I don't . . . er . . . much like riding,' I said, staring at my plate. He snapped back without hesitation. 'That's because you're no bloody good at it.'

The truth, which amounted to the same thing in his eyes, was that I was frightened of it. I was naturally physically quite timid, and as far as horses were concerned my timidity had been reinforced by breaking my arm while trying to mount a pony bareback like Tonto, and by seeing my sister dragged by a bolting horse along a gravel path. But my fear drove him away as surely as if I'd declared that I had cholera.

I sat in silence for the rest of the meal and when we returned to the Cadogan Hotel, I was a little older and a lot sadder. Many people think of Oscar Wilde's arrest when they pass the Cadogan Hotel. I think of the night my father gave up on me. What we have to admit is that the failures are not only those of other people; they are our own. If he was punishing me for failing to live up to his expectations, I was doing the same to him. And I should not assume that it cost him less than it cost me.

'There are only two classes of good society in England: the equestrian classes and the neurotic classes. It isn't mere convention: everyone can see that the people who hunt are the right people and the people who don't are the wrong ones,' says Shaw in *Heartbreak House*. I'd declared myself a member of the neurotic classes, but for several years I failed to concede the divide and made strenuous attempts to redeem myself in my father's eyes, before conceding the impossibility and resigning myself to years of armed truce. When I was appointed Director of the National Theatre there was a characteristically inaccurate item in the *Evening Standard* about how I was seeking to 'ascend into the squirearchy' by joining the hunting fraternity, 'turning from red to pink'. They weren't to know the painful irony of their fiction. They printed a correction from my father: 'Someone's been pulling your whizzer,' he said. 'My son is grown up and I don't dictate to him whether he should go hunting, or drink a bottle a day, or have three women a week.' That at least had the unmistakable tone of his voice and what he said of himself was true, but not through want of trying.

My mother too belonged to the neurotic classes, and she compensated for her alienation with an engaging and restless energy which defied nature in a form of perpetual motion. She was an organiser with an idiosyncratic but systematic method of reducing chaos to order: list followed list as she marshalled her resources with the flair of a natural general. It wasn't unusual to be asked at supper what you wanted for breakfast, lunch *and* dinner the next day, or to find her planning her Christmas shopping in June. Her cooking was self-taught and by any standards touched with genius; the secret of the perfect meringue has died with her. She was a dedicated, knowledgeable and enthusiastic gardener who spoke of plants by their Latin names with the confident certainty of an expert.

My father retired from the Navy in his early-forties when I was twelve. He became a farmer. In spite of the fact that for years he was anything but a dilettante, he liked to be referred to as a 'gentleman farmer'. For a while my mother ran a catering business, cooking for large, sometimes huge gatherings, and my father must have thought that they were coming perilously near to being 'trade'. She was happy in her work, he was happy in his, and even, for a while, so was I.

His farm was a mile and a half from our house by foot – over the railway line, up the steep hill scarred by lynchets from the Bronze Age, and into the next valley. The farm was hilly chalkland, covered with bracken and rabbit holes. I loved helping him clear thorn bushes, fields of thistles, build fences, and mend barns. He transformed this unpromising land into something that was, for a while, almost profitable: there were beef cattle, corn, even turkey for two seasons. It's a Nature Conservancy Reserve now, and has reverted back to its natural wildness; it's home to species of wild orchids and a rare butterfly.

I once saved his life. He pierced an artery in his arm on barbed wire and I made a tourniquet from his shirt. I wasn't generally as useful but I was tolerated, and at harvest-time made to feel that I was doing real work. I drove the tractor pulling the baler, even sometimes the combine-harvester. For a few years I was too small to lift straw bales on to the trailer, but I was never happier than when I was allowed to stack them and sit on top as we drove back to the barn with the sun setting and the stacked piles of straw rolling like a galleon in a heavy sea.

At heart my mother was a town girl, but she made spirited attempts to counter this impression. She was never too much worried by the Muscovy ducks wandering into the kitchen from the garden, or Rex the Ram following them and drinking out of the dogs' water bowl. But her most conspicuous identification with the farm was her adoption of our bull. He was a hornless Hereford, brown-and-white, who she bottle-fed as a calf, and watched over in our orchard as he grew into a creature of awesome size. She was very fond of him and she had very mixed feelings as we walked him one day up the hill to present him to his wives.

My father started to race horses, or, to be more accurate, he raced his one horse 'over the jumps' and I tried to share his sport vicariously. I visited most of the National Hunt courses in the South of England, trailing after him, trying to convince him that, although of the neurotic classes, I was still acceptable in a man's world. He was never fooled, and neither was I, but I enjoyed the life on the courses and I still do. Out in front over the fences, he was a hero: black-and-yellow quartered jersey, quartered cap, thundering, thumping, crashing through the fences. Falling sometimes, his shoulder dislocated, he would bellow at the St John's Ambulancemen, 'Leave me, don't touch me,' crawl on to a stretcher, and I'd follow him to the doctor who pushed his shoulder into its socket as if he was forcing a leg into the seat of a chair.

There's something comforting about race-tracks. They're

always the same: the camelhair coats, the British warms, the anoraks and the Barbors; the thick, rubberised Burberry raincoats of the trainers, bookies in sheepskins and Max Miller trilbies; large, check Viyella shirts, hairy ties, flat-brimmed, grey-brown felt hats over piggy, Gainsborough-pink round faces; ageless aristocrats with light-brown, velvet-collared overcoats; dark-brown, furled-brim trilbies perched like apostrophes on chinless heads of under-employed Army officers, the sharper, more jaunty trilbies of the touts or the trainers, the bowlers of the race-course officials, the plaids, the checks, the tweeds, the whisky, the gin, the beer, the beer, and the beer, and the piss splashing back on your feet from the wall of a galvanised-iron urinal; the faces marinated in alcohol and broiled in rain and strong winds; the gorblimey caps of the stable boys, the pony-tails of the girls; the shield-shaped tags that admit you to the paddock, the display ring, the holy of holies, where you stand self-consciously brushing shoulders with the riders, trainers, owners, officials; and the horses sleek, and tense, and beautiful, gaped at by the knowing, cynical and unim-pressed crowd pressing at the rails; bulky binoculars, wads of notes, torn betting slips, tote tickets, thick ham sand-wiches. And the talk, the crack, literally over my head, of the form, the going, the SP, the tips: 'from the horse's mouth', 'he's a goer', 'he won't run'; 'he's a donkey', 'know what I mean?'; the villains, the bent jockeys, the real gents – Fred Winter, made in heaven; and the courses that still ring like a catechism for me: Wincanton, Newton Abbot, Plumpton, Chepstow, Cheltenham, Exeter, Taunton, and Fontwell. There's a kind of day in February or early March that always makes me think of the races: scudding clouds, strong winds, fugitive glimpses of pale sun, a downpour, then a bright, glistening sunlight that seems to put a polish on everything, followed by a sunset the colour of a dying bruise.

Apart from riding, my father's main enthusiasms were drink and sex; often, if we were to believe the stories, all three were combined on the hunting field. He had an astonishing constitution for drink. Maybe it was the war-time training, or maybe it was the pint of water that he drank every night before sleep, but he rarely showed signs of damage the next day. He found it hard to understand a teetotaller, and regarded a reluctance to get drunk as a weakness of character. He had an equally forceful attitude to sex. He was attractive to women and was acquisitive. His approach was frank and, I hope, more sensitive than his public performance as the wenching squire – all slap, pinch and tickle. His conquests, real or imagined, and those of my mother, were the seed-corn of his banter, and, if my mother was embarrassed by this, that suited his comic turn. He made much mileage out of an incident at our village railway station: he was stepping out of the London train as my mother's lover was returning to London on the opposite platform. I never tested this tale against the railway time-table; it was the status of folklore, and I preferred it that way. Only later did I learn the true extent of their mutual infidelities. My father may have encouraged my mother to imitate him, but there was no disguising his shock when he discovered a list of my mother's lovers, real or imagined, that she had kept in her dressing-table. I'm sure then that he wished that he had known nothing, and I, of course, wished the same for myself.

He encouraged me to think that conquest was all, invok-ing a sort of competitive promiscuity, which, far from eman-cipating me, made me feel anxious and inadequate for failing to fulfil his implicit quota. I was never sure where the banter ended and reality began. We did not speak of love, or happiness, or even of pain.

It was difficult to bring my girlfriends near him without passing through a drizzle of teasing or worse. He would either attempt to seduce them (once, to my everlasting bitter-ness, successfully), or he would frighten them off with his robust wit. He could be counted on to greet a new girlfriend with the refrain: 'Time is short and we must seize/ Those pleasures found above the knees,' and then he'd laugh with a goatish snort at my pained embarrassment.

In matters of sex he was impatient with euphemism. He despised Hardy's novels for that reason. I tried to get him to read *Tess of the d'Urbervilles*, not least because much of it is set within miles of where we lived. 'Why doesn't he say they do it, when they do it?' He was a man who would call a spade a spade. Or to be more accurate, a bloody spade. Or to be more truthful, a fucking spade. Only now can I see the small boy in the grown man, bullied and beaten by his father into a resolve to show no softness in public, least of all to his son.

Am I being fair to him? He had great energy, a sharp wit, Rabelaisian inventiveness, great charm when he chose to apply it, and a rare tenderness, even if it was often reserved for animals, or for my sister, whose view of him was almost the polar opposite of mine. He caricatured his father to me, and perhaps I'm doing the same to him. Perhaps all of us do that of our parents; the reality is too complex. I paint my mother too white, my father too black. The real picture is too shaded with guilt, love, hatred, resentment, and wish for approval to be rendered accurately. I am standing too close to the canvas.

As we grew apart my mother became an uneasy negotiator, her loyalties confused. At school I distilled my resentment of my father into a kind of ideology that lay somewhere between anarchy and communism. My cardinal principle was to oppose whatever my father stood for. 'The Tories are it; the others are just politicians,' he said, and I found no difficulty turning that adage on its head. I clamoured for attention, and found it in acting. The fact that it interested my father as much as the economy of Albania made it all the more attractive. When my father said that he didn't want me to go to university, that it was a waste of time, it was an act of defiance to try. I wanted to colonise a world that he hadn't invaded.

I never spoke to my mother much about all this. She was modest about her intellect and often hesitant about stepping on uncertain ground, she represented herself as less clever than she was. She always felt intellectually inferior to my father, and he endorsed her inadequacy. At first it was playful teasing; then it hardened by use into a sort of systematic bullying.

My father never came to see my work in the theatre, but, on one or two occasions, my mother did. She came to see *Comedians* in London and we went to dinner afterwards. She didn't often come to London and she was quite different when we were alone. No longer parroting my father's opinions or his tone of voice, she was something like herself, soft, tentative, and instinctive. She was trying to understand who I was, and I was doing the same with her. She told me that she wasn't happy, she hinted at trouble with my father, but she was not disloyal. She asked gently about my own life, and we spoke about the play, and about the central character: a violent, almost psychopathic, romantic, dispossessed working-class boy, consumed by a raging despair. 'I'd never realised how much you hated your school. I'm sorry, I should have asked,' she said.

In one sense we never grow up. To our parents we are always children and we view their marriage through the eyes of a child. It is hard enough to penetrate the façade of any marriage; we never have the necessary evidence to condemn or acquit, to allocate blame or innocence. Some marriages sustain for years an inscrutable face to the world, then collapse with a terrible suddenness which unnerves friends who had counted them as the fixed point in their moral and social constellation. Other marriages, fuelled by constant public attritional warfare, miraculously survive – the more secure perhaps for never having been perceived as exemplary. The evidence for our parents' marriage is always hopelessly tainted by our own prejudice and wishful thinking. We long to believe that the happiness we saw was not superficial, assumed for our benefit, and that the pain was a temporary accident of circumstance. In later years it was apparent to anyone, even to their children, that my parents' marriage had reached a bitter stalemate.

But when my parents married they were very much in love. I don't say this as a sentimental attempt to salvage a sunny beginning from a story that became increasingly dark. I know it to be true. I was going through their papers after my father died, trying to sift what should be saved, what should be discarded. It was like an archaeological dig: layer after layer of dust, photographs, chequebooks, bank statements, Christmas cards, solicitors' letters, mortgages, press cuttings, magazines, the whole detritus of their lives impacted like peat in layer after discarded layer. Like the burn-marks on stones, the papers gave evidence to the fact that they had *lived* but, with the exception of some photographs, not *how* they had lived. And the photographs told little to the archaeologist: it was always summer, these people were always smiling, *ergo* they were always happy. But among the hundreds, perhaps thousands of photographs, there was not a single picture of a family group: mother, father, son and daughter. It's unscientific of me, but I'm reluctant to draw conclusions.

The Rosetta Stone was a small, heavy brown-leather suitcase, full of letters, elastic-banded bundles of them, hundreds, perhaps thousands, mostly on blue air mail paper: 'AIR MAIL LETTER CARD USE OF HM FORCES ONLY.' I stared at the letters, certain that I was never meant to see them. I recognised my father's handwriting and tentatively withdrew a letter. I read only enough to blush at the invasion of their privacy. For a long time the suitcase was there as a *memento mori*, a relic that could only be revered.

The day after my mother died I realised I was on my own, free at last of the influence of both my parents. It was what I thought I'd always wanted, and yet I felt utterly bereft. I felt a hopeless desire to get in touch with my mother, talk to her, touch her. I was free of all restraint and I opened the suitcase full of my father's letters.

It's always a mistake to read things that are not intended for one's eyes – a school report, an assessment, a reference, a letter. These were no exception. They were lustful, bawdy, playful, loving, blunt, larded with a profusion of inventive endearments, and a cascading litany of sexual address that made me smile, and blush, and smart, and drop large tears on to the sheaves of pale-blue envelopes. I was glad they'd been happy once.

VIII

WHEN SHE WAS fifty-two my mother fell downstairs on her head carrying my sister's daughter. The baby, who was two at the time, was unharmed, but my mother fractured her skull. The fracture healed and at first it seemed as if the only further damage was to my mother's nervous system. She lost her sense of smell and her sense of taste and, naturally enough, her skill and enthusiasm for cooking. But then, little by little, other things dropped away. She easily recognised her pre-war dancing partners on the TV, although I suppose in the case of Ronald Reagan she had opportunity enough ('Dull man, but frightfully good dancer'), but she started to forget her previous sentence halfway through the new one, and she would stare speculatively at her knife and fork as if unsure of their use. She started to cry in frustration when she forgot how to write the M in her Christian name, Minna, and when she took my daughter, aged four, to the village shop, a journey of a few hundred yards, my wife thought it safer to follow them as the two set off hand in hand, chatting simultaneously, uncertain who was leading whom.

For a while it seemed as if her behaviour was a painful plea for attention, and with the arrogance of self-interest I constructed a rational cause for her illness. I wanted it to be a psychological disorder rather than a corrosive physical decay of the brain. I wanted to believe that there was a reason for it: that she had been ignored and rejected by my father. I wanted her illness to serve my cause, but when I opened a door for her and she stared at the door, then at the doorway, and asked me with undisguised terror, 'Which side do I go?' I knew she was losing her mind, and that there was no one to blame except God.

Alzheimer's Disease is a terrible illness. If there is a physical disease it resembles it is leprosy, which eats away the body as Alzheimer's does the brain. The first signs are a loss of short-term memory, but forgetfulness, *non sequiturs*, and vagueness give way to loss of bodily control, as if the brain can no longer remember what to tell the body. The personality starts to disappear, and with it the humanity, and the soul, leaving, as if in mockery, only the body to breathe and be fed. The disease is spun out with a malicious cruelty, in my mother's case for ten years after it was diagnosed. Before that she was said to be suffering from 'Presenile Dementia'; it was the same thing by any name – she was old before her time.

For years she was losing her mind, and for years death seemed ashamed to approach her. Little by little she was slipping away, and we never knew when to say goodbye.

For a while she was living at home but it became impossible to look after her properly. She had bouts of terrifying rage, followed by incoherence, followed by blankness, followed by clear breaks of sanity that were more frightening to her than anything that had preceded them.

In most ways she had loved Dorset, and I have indelible memories of her, tanned and shoeless, dressed in a halter-necked cotton dress picking raspberries or tending the bull in the orchard on hot, carefree summer days, but her heartland was London, the world of her childhood, and when her mind became disordered she longed for that heartland as if her life, or her sanity, depended on it: 'Please, please, please, please, please, please ... take me home ... take me back to my mother ... my friends ... take me to London ... let me go in a train ... please, please, please, please ...'

There was a silence, an absence of words and a despair

so deep that it almost seemed as if her breath were speech, then a sigh: 'I think I am dying.'

But for years she lived on in the hospital, lying on the floor in a foetal position on a beanbag. No sight, no hearing, no sense at all. She breathed and ate and wasted away. She became an emblem for the nursing staff, and they treated her with great kindness and something like love. When the ward was turned into a surgical ward, and the patients decanted to private nursing homes in the name of 'cost-efficiency', they wept at her departure.

I would sit with her, with my hand on her forehead, year after year. She seemed inexpressibly lonely, but she'd seemed like that even before she lost her mind. Grief became muted over the years, but I never lost the distress of things unsaid. There are those who leave us without our detaining them; we have said all there is to say. It wasn't so with her; there was a continent of regret and guilt.

Her face and her body wasted away. Her mouth was set in the shape it became in the later years of her marriage when she was steeled in bitterness. I asked my father once when we were driving to the hospital, united for once in mutual despair, if things had been strained between the two of them for the last few years. Oh yes, he said, for about the last thirty.

I can still hear her voice even though it's hard to remember her face as it was before she lost her mind. I can still see her hand, bony like a claw, plucking at her face, as if she was surprised that it was still there. When I was a small boy I'd sit by her dressing-table to watch her as she did her make-up. 'I'm putting on my face,' she'd say.

When she died her body was like a child's.

It was a cruel paradox that my father knew he was going to die before my mother. He always seemed indestructible; when he became seventy he had lost nothing of his energy. He had acquired a girlfriend, and when my mother moved into hospital, his girlfriend moved in with him. For some time we regarded each other with mutual suspicion. Later I felt churlish in the face of their obvious happiness, but I found it difficult to forget my mother's distress in the early days of her illness when she suspected their affair, and suspected her sanity when it was denied.

My father's friend was a woman of about my age – large, loud, loving and tolerant (at least of him), and more often than not, like him, hiding her intelligence and sensitivity behind a wall of noisy banter. They lived like students, in an accumulated glacial deposit of old food, magazines, newspapers, photographs, sewing machines, clothes and crockery. They'd bicker and banter in his private argot which she had willingly learned even if it had become increasingly wearisome to those for whom it had been staled by overuse. They were content. 'Happy as pigs in shit,' my father would have said, and he must have been as surprised as anyone when he had a stroke. He'd gone up for a sleep in the afternoon, and at seven he hadn't come down. He was lying on the floor. 'I didn't know if he was drunk or something more serious,' said his girlfriend.

I went to see him and he could barely speak. Neither could I. Confronted by him – weak, vulnerable, mortal – I felt very shaken. He seemed terribly diminished, in terrible pain and worse depression, deprived of his energy and his mordancy.

A few days later he could speak. He told me that his mother had died of a stroke, his father had died of a stroke, and that these things are meant to shake you up; they are meant to change you.

He was moved to a new hospital and for a few weeks he occupied the same space in the same ward as my mother had seven years before. It was a deeply unsettling echo. I talked to my sister once on the phone after she'd seen him, and wrote as she spoke:

> can't read
> can't walk
> won't try

He came home and his girlfriend looked after him with

astonishing patience, enduring his rage and despair with unexpected equanimity. When he was seventy-four we gave a birthday party for him. He seemed barely to acknowledge me but at the end of dinner he made a speech, thanking everyone for their kindness, my sister and her children, myself and my family, his friends and his girlfriend. He staggered to his feet, and for a while – an eternity – he was unable to speak. When he spoke at last it was in short, uncompleted, bursts, choked with feeling like an over-charged light bulb, shining for a moment with great intensity, then breaking down in shuddering flickers. After a lifetime of guarding his feelings like Masonic secrets, emotion was breaking through in wild disorder.

A month or so later I had a letter from a vicar. He said he'd spoken to my father while he was in hospital, and that my father had begun to make his peace with his Creator. My first reaction was pure incredulity. On the rare occasions that I had been in church with him, when he was in the Navy and, as Commander of a naval base, had to read the lesson, he had muttered throughout, noisily proclaiming his resistance to liturgy and his ignorance of the difference between a psalm and a hymn. Priests he referred to as 'God-botherers' or worse, and he'd always seemed to me defiantly resistant to the idea of life after death. Perhaps he was moved by the idea of retribution, or even forgiveness. Perhaps he was simply afraid of death. I don't think he'd bought the Christian line on suffering, but he did recognise one of the great moral equations, perhaps the only one: all our actions have their consequences.

The vicar was young and utterly guileless, and I think my father was touched by his honesty and lack of evangelical certainty. He asked me to help to put my father's 'house in order' before he 'faced the Evening Light'. The vicar recognised, he said, that he had not been an ideal father.

I went to make my peace with him. He was pleased to see me, coherent and shy of me. He knew, I think, what he wanted me to say and he knew that I was probably going to say it. We circled around each other for a bit, while the

racing commentary babbled on the television; the Cheltenham Week. He asked me repeatedly when the Gold Cup
was on. In two days' time, Dad, in two days' time. He said
he hadn't fallen into dissolution yet, although some people
thought he'd gone already, and, as if to prove that his
memory was intact, he recited the name of all the destroyers
in the Navy in 1938, eight different classes, followed by the
names of his year at naval college – the Hawke Term at
Dartmouth in 1929, thirty of them. He only stumbled on
the last three.

His mind started to stray, and he said he had a terrible
hangover. No, Dad, I said, you've had a terrible stroke. He
said he'd been dancing all night; his ankles were swollen
and he'd had to take to his bed. He'd woken up with three
women and he'd had to prod them to make sure he wasn't
dreaming.

'I'd like to be an oar,' he said.

'?'

'Yes, an oar.'

'What, like in a brothel?'

'No, idiot, *oar*.'

'Why?'

'It would be restful.'

He talked about the Fall of France; the day he got married. 'Send Ma some flowers,' he said. 'I'm bleeding, bleeding in my brain.'

I asked him about seeing the vicar. He was silent for a
while before he said he'd got a great deal of comfort from
him. 'One of the straightest men I've ever met. You'll find
it a rich joke coming from me but I've been taking Holy
Communion.' But I didn't see a joke, even though it was
hard for him to speak to me without irony, or punning,
putting his feelings in inverted commas, the habits of a
lifetime. He struggled with the words, tears threatening.
Until his stroke I'd never seen him cry.

'Was I as bad a father to you as my father was to me?'

'No, of course not. I wish we'd got on better, that's all.'

'He was a tyrant.'

'You weren't a tyrant, just a bit neglectful, perhaps. But I don't feel any anger against you. I love you.'

He gripped my hand, almost spasmodically.

'I don't know if I was neglectful, I just didn't appreciate you. I'm sorry if I made you unhappy. When is the Gold Cup on?'

'In two days' time, Dad. In two days' time.'

Then he paused. A long time. Minutes, perhaps, and, when my tears dropped on his hand, he gripped me tighter, and smiled, gently.

'Is Lucy a happy person? I hope so.'

She is happy, my daughter; it's a gift, like dancing.

He died in his sleep a few weeks later. Apparently everyone who dies in their sleep dies peacefully; I hope that's true. My sister rang me to tell me. 'Dad's gone,' she said. Just that. She sounded like him. And I said, 'Oh, he's gone.' Terse as ever with our feelings; we'd learned it from him. I was in a bar when Samuel Beckett died; it was on the TV. 'Ah well,' said an Irish voice. 'That's another one gone.'

I drove down to Dorset to see him before the undertakers took him away. The French writer Saint-Exupéry talks of 'seeing through the heart', and I've never seen the country-side around my home looking more intensely beautiful than on that day. Little churches, sandstone villages, valleys, hills, downland, slabs of incandescent colour – dark-green woods and hedges, fields of butter-yellow oilseed rape, blue of linseed, red of poppies, opiate-rich, and the barrows, lynch-ets, burial mounds, earthworks, ditches and standing stones of Celtic Britain. I drove up to Eggardon Hill, a few miles from our house. It's a Bronze Age hillfort that commands the surrounding countryside like an Aztec temple, an oval plateau dipping down hundreds of feet to woods and farm-houses and fields that stretch out to Golden Cap on one side, the sea beyond, and the Blackdown Hills of Somerset on the other side, and, with the exception of a spider's web of electricity pylons tracing across the valley, the landscape can't have changed for hundreds of years. Sunlight hung over the hill like a benediction. I've always loved this place: it's vast and mysterious and awesome. When I was a teenager, rich in time and suffocating from boredom, I used to come up here and it felt like a foreign country. Now it seemed uniquely English.

I was brought up in a part of England that seems centuries away from the England I belong to now: the England of the city and the suburbs, of power and money, of art and politics, of poverty and people less lucky and privileged than I am, and I was. But this is where I started and something of who I am must be here, in this landscape, as much as in the body of my father.

He lay naked beneath a blanket, his arms crossed over his chest. He looked calm, at peace. He had shrugged off the tense, childlike, febrile look that he'd had for the past year. He looked very dignified and for once he seemed to me utterly authoritative and mature. My father. He had grown a beard, his last twitch of mild self-display, and he looked now like a patriarch, like Gielgud – all nose, and all English.

His skin was waxy and pale. I kissed his forehead and sat beside the bed. We end as we start. With the death of our parents we enter a second childhood, and once again confront the question: Am I loved? – but this time it's in the past tense. Only then, sitting by the dead body of my father, I realised what all my efforts had been for, why I'd been striving, what I was trying to prove. I'd been signalling, waving in a frantic semaphore: Look at me, look at me, look at me. Too late now. Whatever seam was available to me when I was very young, ways of making myself impressive to my father, I had exhausted long ago. When I failed I chose a life as remote from him as Antarctica. It was a means of advertising my independence from him, but I realised now it was another form of dependence – I'd been indentured for life. I had my freedom now; all I wanted was his love.

Mary Soames, who is Churchill's daughter, told me that she was sitting with her father in his old age late one evening. Long silence followed long silence. Then she asked him if there was anything in his life that he had wanted to do but hadn't, any honour that he'd wanted but hadn't received, anything that he regretted. And he said, 'I'd like my father to have lived long enough to have seen me do something good.'

IX

AFTER HIS FUNERAL we returned to the house, and I heard his voice. I darted into the room where he had died, convinced that I had heard him calling for me; a household ghost. I once saw a ghost in Cambodia. I went to Angkor, to the temples, when the jungle was a worse predator than Pol Pot. I arrived there from Hong Kong via Phnom Penh in a Royal Air Cambodia plane, one of whose two engines caught fire in flight. 'Excuse me,' I said to the stewardess, 'the wing is on fire.' The passengers, eleven of us, were consoled by a bottle of spirits apiece, and I travelled in more comfort to Angkor by bus, sandwiched on the front bench with the other privileged passengers – a handful of saffron-robed monks – while the remaining passengers, hundreds of them, clung to the inside, outside, and roof of the vehicle with children, chickens, pigs and vegetables carried like a second skin. All the way to Angkor, a day's journey, there was a constant cacophony of chatter, but what I most remember was the laughter. Within a few years all this had gone and the only laughter was the laughter of the grave.

When I arrived in Angkor it was getting dark, and after going to the hotel I walked to the main temple Angkor Wat. There was a full moon and I could see the vast scale of the temple quite clearly and the thick, serpent-shaped handrail over the bridge that crossed the huge moat to the main gateway. There are five, or maybe seven, I can't remember now, rectangular cloisters of diminishing size surrounding a tower like a ziggurat in the centre. The outer rectangle is about a mile by a little less, and is lined by carved friezes, a bas-relief gallery that seemed to me to run for centuries.

As I passed through the outer wall I looked along an infinite colonnaded gallery. The bright white moonlight stabbed through the gaps between the columns and striped the floor like a giant animal skin; these patterns were followed by areas of shadow, whose black seemed so dense that they might have been solid. The wall carvings were in darkness, outside the edge of the slanting moonlight.

I walked for a while along the gallery and stopped in an area of shadow. Everything was still. Only the regular chanting of the crickets disturbed the pure silence of the night. I felt a small hand in mine, a child's. I looked down but I could see nothing. The hand led me towards the wall and placed my palm over some carvings – elephants, dancers, horses, warriors, Buddhas – I was guessing but it all felt like a seamless undulation, as if what it felt like was more important than what it was. When we reached a slab of moonlight I turned into the light, but the hand left mine and seemed to vanish. I could see nothing, and heard no breathing, no feet, no movement. The child, or spirit, had vanished as mysteriously as it had appeared. I've never known what to make of this encounter but I've never felt such tranquillity, such total lack of apprehension, as when my hand was pressed to the wall in that immense temple.

I told this to my father once. He probably wanted to show you his sister, he said.

I loved being in South-East Asia, travelling uncertain of my destination. I have always felt restless, a lack of a sense of place. I'm more at peace now, but too unsure to settle, as if to rest were to become dormant and to become dormant were a slow retreat to the fears of childhood. I have a love and a hatred of small villages; I long to belong, but I hate to be claimed. I have the same feeling about families: I envy what I imagine to be the enveloping security of a large family and the confidence that engenders, but I fear its inescapability at the same time. It's why I like the theatre, a surrogate family that has the advantage over the real thing of being temporary and of being chosen, rather than involuntary and for life and, oddly, if I like running a theatre it must be that something within me makes me want to play the father.

I don't think I had an unhappy childhood, even if I do sometimes still see happiness as the absence of unhappiness, like the relief of a dull ache. The body has a mechanism for forgetting pain; the brain is more stubbornly retentive.

We should never try to describe happiness. Like staring at the sun, you are blinded, you close your eyes, and there is an image left on the retina that is without definition. It fades and you are left with a blackness that is more bleak than before; an absence of light. We don't need to stare at the sun to see where we are going.

Sometimes I think of a time when I was happy; when possibilities hung in the air like motes of dust in the sunlight. I am driving with my mother, early in the morning, to Sherborne to take a scholarship exam at the school. It's a windless June day. We drive through woods, thick colonnades of tree shadows flick the black car as we pass through villages where the houses cast deep shadows on the road dark as reflections in glass. But for the car everything is motionless: cows, leaves, dogs, birds. My mother is wearing a wide-shouldered flower-print dress. I am wearing a school uniform, black blazer with maroon piping, grey shorts, and black shoes. My geometry set is sitting on my bare knees: compass, protractor, set-square, ruler. My mother smiles at me: 'It's going to be all right.'

I dream about this sometimes, and when I wake I want the journey to go on for ever.

ACTING PROPERLY

'Well, now that we *have* seen each other,' said the Unicorn,
'if you'll believe in me, I'll believe in you. Is that a bargain?'
– Lewis Carroll, *Alice Through the Looking Glass*

FOR A LONG time I wanted to be an actor. Like a stammerer
I wanted the gift of fluency, and like an orphan I wanted
the gift of love. The search for approval, for requited love,
is the sustaining force behind all actors; it's what sustains
the bad ones and often spoils the good ones. Insecurity is
their fuel and I wasn't lacking in that respect. What I lacked
was the actor's Philosopher's Stone – the talent that is more
than a facility to observe your elders and imitate them,
more than a readiness to be the comic turn at parties, more
than a knack for dazzling the class when reading aloud, and
more than a dizzying simulation of self-confidence. If you
don't have it no amount of effort or education will compen-
sate for the injustice of having been cast out of paradise.
Actors are born, not made, but it took many years for me
to accept that this truism might also be true.

Like many children, I preferred to pretend to be someone
else; perhaps for no other reason than because it was so
difficult to be myself. I was part Walter Mitty and part
Baron Munchausen, and my tales from school painted me
as the hero of my own exploits, the star of my constellation,
and, probably, the object of my own affections. For much
of the time I think I carried it off, at least if the reactions of
my mother and my sister were anything to go by. But
perhaps they were paying me the highest compliment (but
somehow the least welcome) that an actor can receive: 'You
didn't appear to be acting.'

My father was less sympathetic to my fictions. He had a Churchillian phase during which, inspired more by the bricklaying than the oratory of his idol, he made paths and walls, once crushing his thumb under a concrete block and emitting a scream that was silent, as if he was searching for words to match the pain. He laid paths in thick, glutinous, grey, glistening concrete irresistible to a small boy. I walked barefoot in one of these when it was setting, and my father's rage was formidable even by his own immodest standards. 'It was Chico,' I said. Chico was a dog who looked like a soft-tufted lavatory brush and smelt worse but was, in all other respects, entirely innocent. The evidence of my footprint was indisputable but in my terror I imagined that the strength of my conviction in the lie, the force of my performance, would prevail. It didn't. I was soundly beaten, but not soundly enough to convince me that acting was outside the range of my accomplishments.

My performance as Peaseblossom in an open-air performance of *A Midsummer Night's Dream* at my primary school at the age of six did little to persuade me either way. I remember it only for Puck's habit of bursting into tears whenever she forgot her lines (frequently), and for making me aware of how difficult it is to sustain dramatic illusion against the intrusion of real life. During our scene with Bottom, who was equipped with a very notional ass's head, a horse, which had up till now been quietly and uninterestedly grazing in a field beyond our stage, contrived to open a gate, and strolled towards his fellow quadruped with a sort of speculatively seductive air. There was a great deal of screaming from the cast and the audience and a satisfying (at least to the cast) descent into chaos.

Like many aspiring (and aspired) actors I was shy, I was reserved, and I was more comfortable speaking in any voice but my own. The English get a lot of practice at this. Coded from birth by our accents, it's often more comfortable, or more liberating, to pretend to be what you are not. I acquired a skill as a mimic, partly as my passport, partly as a weapon. I was able to mimic my friends, our teachers, and for many years I was able to copy, like Chinese boxes, all the many voices of Peter Sellers – an actor, if ever there was one, who experienced a mortal difficulty in being himself. My enthusiasm for this vein of mimicry died in a restaurant in my early twenties. I'd just set out on the satirical travelogue: 'We enter Balham through the verdant grassland of Battersea Park . . .' and the words died on my lips as I caught the unamused gaze of Peter Sellers.

The only theatres in Dorset during my childhood were the Pavilion and the Alexandra in Weymouth, the Pier and the Winter Garden in Bournemouth. My mother occasionally took us to a pantomime there but I was as resistant as she was to the tyranny of audience participation, the witless slapstick, the graceless (and sexless) drag acts, the artless comic routines and the pretence that we were all enjoying ourselves. I hated the assumption that we'd all consented to this miserable ritual and, as supplicants, were expected to show our devotion in laughter and applause, but I liked the painted gauzes and the transformation scenes, and my heart always beat faster when the orchestra played the overture, the curtain rose and we were once again on The Village Green Outside the Baron's Castle. Many operas seem to begin in the same way and, as with so many operas, disappointment sets in rapidly.

I've seen one decent pantomime; it starred Stanley Baxter and Ronnie Corbett and was as different from the others as Nijinsky to Morris dancing. I find it sad that many people make their only visit to the theatre an annual penitential pilgrimage to the local pantomime, and it's little wonder that so few care to go inside a theatre again. Can there be anyone, apart from theatre antiquarians, who actually enjoys this pathetic annual parade of self-revealing national bathroom habits, fourth-rate comics, superannuated pop stars, has-been sportsmen, jokes about jokes about jokes about television, all of it marinated in the basest traditions of English 'variety'? Never was a word more inapt.

If variety is the spice of life (and it was in the case of Max Miller and Jimmy Wheeler) we saw precious little of it in Dorset. I did, however, see both Jewel and Warris and Morecambe and Wise in Weymouth, and although I am ashamed to say that at this distance I can't distinguish between them in my memory, I knew even then that I was watching something out of the ordinary.

My father didn't accompany us to the theatre but he would have enjoyed the pantomime that Roy Hudd told me about years later. At the start of his career Roy was apprentice and stooge to Jimmy Wheeler ('Ay ay, that's yer lot') who made no secret of his hatred of pantomime. He left the adult members of the audience mute and open-mouthed with horror, like the first-nighters in *The Producers*, when he invited the little boys to put their hand on their little girls' Polo mints, and the little girls to lick the little boys' lollipops.

Jimmy Wheeler was a comedian of the old school. It was Roy's melancholy task to wait behind for him after the show, standing outside the dressing-room while the comedian entertained a brace or so of chorus girls. After an hour or so of laughter, slaps, squeals, squeaks and the tinkle of bottle tops, the girls would spill out of the door, followed by an empty crate of beer, and the comedian himself: 'A very entertaining evening, Roy.'

This was possibly not far removed from my father's idea of an entertaining evening, but the nearest we got to it in the theatre was an annual visit to the Victoria Palace to see the Crazy Gang. They were the genetic link between music hall and the kind of comedy that started to appear on television in the late-sixties – Benny Hill with a hint of *Monty Python*. The sketches of the Crazy Gang were paragraphed by the routines of the Tiller Girls, 'sixteen long-legged lovelies', who linked arms, tapped and high-kicked like automata, wearing smiles that seemed printed indelibly on their faces. We sat, for reasons that were not then obvious to me, in the front row and I felt oppressed by the sheer bulk of buttock and breast and the acres of fleshy thigh encased in 'fishnet tights. I preferred the caperings of Flanagan and Allen, Nervo and Knox, Naughton and Gold, and 'Monsewer' Eddie Grey, who had energy and anarchy and the kind of seductive vulgarity that was the hallmark of Max Miller and the direct antithesis of the miserably bland TV comedy of the late-fifties – *Bilko* always excepted, of course. I can still see Jimmy Nervo, round, bald, pink and leery, being chased round the stage in a pram by Teddy Knox, chased by the rest of the gang as the audience rose to a pitch of fevered laughter.

I had a Pollock's Toy Theatre painstakingly cut with large, sharp scissors, scored and folded along the dotted lines, and stuck together with fishy-smelling glue. During the war, to while away the hours at sea when he wasn't on watch, my father had two hobbies: knitting and making small model steam locomotives from kits. The knitting produced a pink pig for my sister and a blue one for me, and the kits produced meticulously, and in my eyes miraculously, detailed miniature steam engines out of cardboard sheets the size of postcards. My father passed on the technique of model-making, but showed little interest in my toy theatre and less in the performances I staged with the two-dimensional cardboard cut-outs of characters from *The School for Scandal*. I think my apathy for the drama of that period stems from my frustration with the depressingly finite possibilities of staging a play with two hands and more than one character: I needed no less than three hands to slide the actors onstage while raising the front curtain or changing the backdrops. I should have bought cut-outs of Olivier and Claire Bloom in *Hamlet* – at least the scenery was simpler, and it's possible that I would have become a better actor with their inspiration, but somehow I doubt it.

I became bored with the limitations of my toy theatre and started to make puppets out of papier mâché – layered scraps of newspaper stuck together with flour and water, painted with poster paint and glazed with a thick, clear varnish. I liked the way that a puppet acquires its own personality: your hand becomes a metaphor for the body, the puppet a metaphor for the person. It's pure theatre.

A play with two characters is known as a 'two-hander' and my hands performed duets that, like most improvised drama, were resolved in savage arguments and physical assaults, which cracked the lacquer on the puppets' faces and shredded the papier mâché like a pernicious skin disease. I deserted my puppets for Plasticene and, inspired by a lavishly illustrated location report in *Photoplay* of a Vincente Minnelli movie, made a model of a camera and film lights. The actors were recruited from my model medieval army – half a dozen knights in armour with lances and livery. They sat on horses, bright with their heraldic devices, and around them I deployed the camera, the lights, the flags, and the foot-soldiers from another century, and I still thought I wanted to become an actor.

The arc of my acting career describes a parabola shaped like an eighteenth-century military cap, or a bishop's mitre, bowing out at the side, rising to a peak (my university years?) and plunging, at first gently, and then with undignified haste, to the level at which I began. I didn't travel far, but at least I learned from the journey.

At my public school, initially at least, I was encouraged to act as I had been at prep school. Slightly against my will, and in the face of my instinctive contempt for its ennervating rhythms and wooden-topped melodies, I was cast as one of the Three Little Maids from a Sem-in-ar-y in *The Pirates of Penzance*. I was considered to have made a success of the part, but I was divided between being flattered and embarrassed at being told that I made a very pretty Kate. It was impossible to be unaware of the sexual potency of the situation: with our unbroken voices, our boyish figures, our unselfconscious flirtatiousness and an audience of teenage boys in a boarding school, not even the insistent blandness of Sullivan's music could extinguish the heat of androgynous sexual promise. No doubt the show was crude and maladroit, but there was enough there to alert me to the power of the theatre to excite and enchant – particularly with its sexual allure.

I don't think my experiments in cross-dressing in *The Pirates of Penzance* were enhanced by the large rugby socks that I stuck down my dress for breasts; my characterisation was all too literal, and my sexual identity had all the mystery of Violet-Elizabeth in *Just William*, but maybe, like all bad actors, I was simply trying to get the audience to look at me. If I didn't have the largest part in the play, at least, I thought with the prosaic sexual imagination of a thirteen-year-old, I could have the largest breasts.

Most female impersonation is satirical, underwritten by a palpable misogyny, but when it is done truthfully, observed with psychological and physical accuracy, it begs questions about the sexual roles we have been allocated. In a sense all acting, good or bad, is a criticism of life: human beings are represented and offered to us on a stage to observe and assess. In a wholly successful performance the gap between the actor and the character is seamless, and the judgements we make then are as confused, complex and ambiguous as those we make in life itself. But however well observed, in a performance that involves an impersonation of the opposite sex there will inevitably be a gap between actor and character; there will be an edge of comment, a touch of parody in the voice and the gestures. It will always be an imitation, never a state of being. Kabuki actors believe that women are too close to femininity to capture its essence; they mean its essence to men, of course.

Nevertheless, it's a marvel of the theatre that it is possible for an audience, regardless of sex, to look at a man playing a woman – even if his large feet and chest hair are visible – and believe in his femininity, just as an audience can willingly join the conspiracy to accept that a statue has come to life, or a puppet gained human characteristics. Like religion, the theatre can make us believe in the unbelievable.

There's a peculiar intensity to the way that an audience identifies with the actor and actress in drag: it is acting taken to its apotheosis, not only changing to another character, but another sex as well. Sitting there in the dark staring at an individual who is trying to impress you is a sort of sexual encounter, and if the sexual address is ambiguous, then that encounter is heightened. It's why the characteristic that all great theatre actors and actresses have in common is a touch of the androgynous.

Marlene Dietrich, who was a great star but far from being a great actress, used to say, 'I got into drag because I wanted to attract men and women.' Not me, I'm afraid. Her attraction for me was anaesthetised by her behaviour at the Lyceum Theatre in Edinburgh, where I was working when she did her *Late Night Show* at the Festival. Her conditions were stringent: the dressing-room must be decorated to her specifications, the Ballets Nègres from Senegal must be out of the theatre before she entered the stage door, and rose petals must be flown in from Israel in order to be dropped from the flies in a spontaneous gesture of generosity from the management after she had taken a score or two of curtain calls. When she came offstage after her first show, which I had watched from the wings, she was asked by a stagehand (he who had dropped petals on cue) for an autograph. 'Fuck off, darling,' she said. She changed quickly, went out of the stage door, stood on the bonnet of a car, and signed autographs for thirty minutes. When she died I heard on the radio that she'd visited her former husband after he had lost all his chickens in a landslide following a rainstorm in California. 'You should have stuck to ducks,' she said.

By the age of fifteen I had become a vicarious follower of the 'New Drama' – *Look Back in Anger, Roots, The Caretaker, The Hostage* and *The Long, the Short, and the Tall*. I hadn't seen any of these plays but I had read them and, at least as important, I had read Tynan's reviews of them. The attractions to a schoolboy of *The Long, The Short, and the Tall* were obvious: the story of a group of British soldiers and their Japanese prisoners in the Malayan jungle, it was bawdy (in so far – not very – as the Lord Chamberlain would permit), it was violent, it was funny, and it had an all-male cast. It couldn't have been long after its short run in the West End that we played it in the school hall to the satisfying disapproval of many of the staff and the undiscriminating praise of our contemporaries. I have a photograph of the production – against a serviceable set of a bamboo and corrugated iron hut and a primitive jungle backcloth, stand six or seven fifteen-year-old boys carrying rifles like large toys, their faces daubed with thick tan make-up (Leichner 5 and 9), painted beard stubble and glycerine sweat. We look like children engaged in a grotesque game, but, in spite of the make-up, not implausible. Most wars are fought by boys not much older than we were then. When I made *Tumbledown* I was told by a Falklands veteran that if the average age of the soldiers in the front line was much over twenty you'd never get anyone to fight. I didn't see any reason to doubt it.

I acted in two Shakespeare productions at school – as Benedick in *Much Ado* and Antony in *Julius Caesar*. I struck no sparks off my (male) Beatrice, but my Antony was alleged by a critic in the school magazine to presage a career as an orator. Perhaps if I'd played Macbeth my career prospects would have given more pause for thought. I was sufficiently swollen-headed by my notices for my housemaster, mindful of Antony's fate and my newly inflated ego, to tell me that actors were often taken over by the characters they played. With the exception of the inmates of long-running sitcoms, and the odd actor who, playing a character gifted with great sexual success, assumes that fiction can become reality, I've rarely seen this happen.

My performance as Antony had been crippled by seeing Brando in Joseph Mankiewicz's film of *Julius Caesar*. I idolised Brando and, as president of the Film Society, I was able to programme the film shows, operate the projector, and steal six frames of *On the Waterfront*, which I kept in my wallet along with two unused condoms for many years. I still regard Brando as the best film actor ever; he had – and maybe still has, but how would we know? – an almost mystical authority, great beauty, a persona that was mercurial, feline, melancholy, witty – and androgynous. He had the facility in spades that makes some film actors so alluring: the ability to appear to think slowly, so that the audience feels that it's being admitted to the intimacy of the thought processes, and embraced as conspirator in the emotions. Stage acting demands a radiant energy, a quickness of wit, a lightning ability to change thought and speech, and a virtuosity which, on screen, often makes theatre actors look like vulnerable show-offs. In the movies, they say, you keep everything in, in the theatre you let everything out.

Brando's unwillingness to work as an actor is profoundly sad and revealing. Something, I think, to do with the feeling that acting – 'play' – is not a proper activity for a grown-up, well, for a grown *man*. I have never known a woman to express this feeling. At a technical rehearsal, when the actors wear their costumes for the first time like anxious guests at a themed costume ball and stalk around the set like animals marking out their territory in a new habitat, it is inevitable that, at some point, at least one actor will say, 'Oh God, what a life for a grown-up.' Women don't share this problem. Maybe they are more used to being looked at, examined and assessed, or to having to pretend for the benefit of men, that a larger, paying, audience is a small shift of the imagination. Maybe they're more grown-up than men and consequently less anxious about their adulthood, or maybe they are simply unembarrassed by a process that is, after all, 'creative': giving birth – even if it is only to a character in a play.

After my expulsion from school, I became a barman and wine waiter in a restaurant in Somerset, and I continued to work there intermittently during my university years. I had qualifications enough – my 'work experience' from the age of eight as a waiter at my parents' parties. The restaurant where I worked had been started on the cusp of a social revolution; outside London it was rare then to find a restaurant that wasn't in a hotel, and as surprising as snow in the Sahara to find one that had cabaret and stayed open until one o'clock. They served modestly ambitious food and presented stars of the dying London cabaret circuit – Noel Harrison, who sang about the 'windmills of his mind'; Cy Grant, to whose Othello I was later to play Third Cypriot; Los Valdemosas, a Majorcan singing group to whom I lost my first four weeks' wages in a game of poker; and conjurors, charlatans, crooners, and undergraduate wits. The most memorable of the performers was a man whose name no one who is now under forty-five would recognise: Hutch. He was the authentic voice of post-war supper clubs like Quaglino's, Les Ambassadeurs, The Stork, names tinged with raffish, but faded, elegance. Hutch was black, romantic, effortlessly elegant: he sang with a touching grace and the ease and charm of Dooley Wilson in *Casablanca*. Hutch's song was 'This is a Lovely Way to Spend an Evening' and he sang it with an air of weary melancholy, which may have had something to do with having had to sing the same song for thirty or so years, but may have had as much to do with the way that women fell in love with him when he sang it. My girlfriend, who was French and a waitress in the restaurant, was no exception and he treated her with a practised courtesy and tenderness that I regarded with undisguised envy. 'Don't worry, young man,' he said, 'I won't be around much longer.' He died soon after and I missed him as much as she did.

Working in a restaurant was a rehearsal for working in the theatre, and I was attracted to it for many of the same reasons. As in the theatre you live to please, and of course, please to live. There's a satisfaction in being able to recognise your success as it occurs – the satisfied customer, the gratifying applause. If a restaurant manager is asking if everything is all right with your meal he needs your approval no less than the actor demanding the audience's applause. I found the hours attractive; I liked working during other people's leisure time, and having time off when everyone else was working. Being a night person gives you a sense of living by different rules, you can deride the tyranny of the daily routine. It's an illusion, of course – there's no more

demanding routine than that of the actor in the long run –
but it's a fantasy that sustains many actors, dressers, directors, and, I suspect, waiters and chefs.

I was the only English member of staff in the restaurant.
There was the German manager, his Swedish wife, who
worked as a waitress, a French waitress (my girlfriend),
my fellow barman and wine waiter – a surly, dough-faced
Frenchman, and his irascible compatriot and room-mate,
the chef – a tall man with a large Alsatian dog. The dog
bayed and barked with understandable anxiety whenever the
two Frenchmen made love to the Irish twins who worked in
the nearby hotel, while my girlfriend and I followed the
catechism of teenage romance: listening to Chopin, reading
Verlaine, and murmuring, 'Do you think it's right for us to
sleep together?'

The day started at about eleven o'clock with clearing out
the empty bottles, and restocking from the store. The Irish
twins might wander in and mockingly tease me with
accounts of their sexual exploits that they knew had already
been advertised for me by the baying Alsatian. We'd have
a few customers at lunchtime, see a film or go to sleep in
the afternoon, and assemble again for the staff meal at six
o'clock – usually the chef's best efforts of the night. Then
a long evening during which we worked for five hours or
so without stopping. We bantered like actors in the wings
whenever we passed on the restaurant floor, shouted at each
other backstage in the kitchen, winked, glared, and corpsed
above the heads of the unsuspecting customers who we
regarded with a kind of compassionate superiority, and who
we served with fixed smiles and courtly gestures as if we
were engaged in an exaggerated comedy of manners. When I
was behind the bar, I could listen to confidences exchanged,
seductions made, partners betrayed, friends defamed and
retain an inscrutable deafness.

The last customers left about one o'clock and then we'd
sit around the bar dissecting the customers' characters and
table manners, and telling multilingual jokes while we
played Twenty-one Aces with liar dice – the first person to

throw an ace chooses a drink from the bar, the second pays for that drink, the third chooses another drink, the fourth pays for that, the fifth drinks it. I don't recommend the cocktail of malt whisky and Tia Maria but, as Groucho Marx said, the great thing about whisky is that it makes you drunk.

I went to Cambridge in the early-sixties. It may not have been quite then, as Larkin suggests, that sexual intercourse was invented, but a few other practices were: pot smoking, academic vandalism, and undergraduate professionalism. I tried them all to a greater or lesser extent. I am no stranger to feelings of remorse, not least about my time spent at university. I was as wasteful of my time as a murderer's prayers.

I had taken my entrance exam in physics and chemistry and I knew, even as I sat the entrance exam, that this was not for me. I had learned my limits and for the first time in my life I'd discovered that it was impossible to bluff my way around my inadequacies. There are moments in your life when you confront the limits of your capabilities: you will never play the saxophone, become a polyglot, or ride in the Grand National. There are other things that you admit to never having the will to do: walking the Pennine Way, giving up alcohol for life, seeing the entire *Ring Cycle* or reading the novels of Barbara Pym. Perhaps these small defeats occur every day, but you adapt yourself unthinkingly to the known horizons of your personality. Beyond that there are genuine failures – expectations, or delusions, that have provided you with an identity that draws a thick, containing frame round your character. For me there have been two such sustaining fictions: 'I am an actor,' and 'I am a mathematician.' The latter died when I realised that, beyond the theorems and axioms that I could comfortably embrace, there were hypotheses and a language of speculative thinking that were as inaccessible to me as the mind of God.

I slipped into Cambridge on my science subjects and

confessed my false pretences to the Senior Tutor who suggested that I changed to what he, enchantingly and temptingly, described as 'the humanities'. 'Try English,' he suggested, making a virtue of a necessity as the college had just invited Kingsley Amis to become an English supervisor and needed some students to justify their uncharacteristic act of free-thinking. Apart from nurturing one of the discoverers of the structure of DNA, and many solid but unexceptional right-wing clerics and historians, the college's most celebrated feature was its well-endowed kitchens.

The influence, or at least the reputation, of Leavis was strong in the English faculty, and I always feel a little awed by those of my contemporaries who cite him as a potent influence in the formation of their literary thinking. Leavis is alleged (by Amis) to have sneered at my college for having appointed a 'pornographer', but, make of it what you will, I learned far more from Kingsley Amis than I did from F. R. Leavis.

I tried English, and I had a lot of catching up to do. My fellow students gave the impression of having been reading Pope while I was reading *Boy's Own*, but I made up for my prodigious ignorance by assiduously listening to jazz, reading the *Sporting Life*, researching the interiors of betting shops, going to the movies, and acting in as many student productions as would have me. I have made up for it since by becoming a voracious, even obsessional, reader.

University drama was centred on the ADC Theatre, which was housed in a converted cinema. It had most, if not all, of the technical apparatus of a modest repertory theatre, and in every sense tried to mimic the professional model to the point, I can see with hindsight, of extreme parody. Intrigues, jealousies, stars and careers were conceived on the lines of what were imagined to be the real thing. Actors vied strenuously for parts, and if rejected often started their own groups, shining in their separate constellations.

We were cocky, immodest, self-regarding, ostentatious, vain and self-important. Some of us may even have been talented. We were not especially iconoclastic; after all, the professional theatre of the day had at long last caught up with the cinema, and it seemed, and not only in retrospect, a golden age for the theatre. Barriers were broken in style, in content, in taste and in appetite but at Cambridge there were no eviscerations, no graphic sexual representations, and, apart from three semi-nude but wholly static Girtonians in a scene from *Expresso Bongo*, no nudity.

This was the occasion of my first, indelible, encounter with the press. Fleet Street had got wind of the intoxicating combination of female brain and body and descended *en masse* to seek names and photographs. The director of the show was Stephen Frears and he had his first taste of public controversy. I was its star and I got a no less edifying induction into journalistic blackmail. 'Are you intending to do this sort of thing professionally?' I was asked by a figure who uncannily prefigured the *Spitting Image* hack. I modestly asserted that I hoped so. 'Well, chum,' he said, like a baddie in a Basil Dearden movie, 'we can ruin you before you've even started.' He worked for a newspaper called the *Daily Mail*; I've read it with caution ever since.

A director is usually a cook; he assembles the best ingredients, follows his recipe and serves it up as impressively as he can. Occasionally, and very rarely, a director is an alchemist, transforming dross into theatrical, even real, gold. More often, however, a director is like a dowser or water diviner, trying to detect the potential that lies below the surface of an actor's talent. *Expresso Bongo* was a limp musical satire of the burgeoning pop industry, whose tunes gave ample evidence of why audiences were deserting the musical theatre in preference to the emergent pop culture. During rehearsals of this show Stephen sent me to a hypnotist. He was convinced that within my unpromising shell lay a rich seam of untapped talent, a Promethean vigour that could be unlocked by hypnosis. Alas, it failed; I was too anxious about disappointing the hypnotist, let alone the director, to abandon myself to the swinging watch chain. Even so I enjoyed a brief celebrity with my performance which may not have been entirely due to my proximity to the Girton nudes, but more to the gold lamé suit that I wore to sing several of the glutinously unappealing songs.

There were some of us who were involved in the theatre for the sheer pleasure of it, and there were as many who had their eyes on 'the profession', as it was awesomely described. There was a lot of talk about the preceding generation of directors (Peter Hall, John Barton, Peter Wood), actors (Ian McKellen, Derek Jacobi), and wits (Peter Cook and Jonathan Miller) as well as speculation as to who would be their successors. There was never much doubt about Trevor Nunn. I played Seyton in his first production of *Macbeth*, and learned from Trevor my first piece of theatrical jargon. Thinking that there was some urgency about muttering my first and only line, I raced on to the stage as if I were being chased by a swarm of wasps, fell to my knees and slid to a halt at the feet of the eponymous hero. 'TheQueenmylordisdead,' I gabbled. 'No, Richard, no,' said Trevor. 'Milk it.'

I'm ashamed to say that I remember the production most vividly for an incident of unforgivable irresponsibility in the ranks of the supernumeraries. For reasons not entirely clear to us at the time, eight monks crossed the stage diagonally at the beginning of the English scene. In the ranks of the monks we thought it would be amusing for one of our leading pair to put his monkish habit on back-to-front and we promised him that, given the difficulty of walking backwards in a straight line, he would be guided by a hand on his elbow. We set off across the stage; about halfway across his elbow was released, and, like a robot with a short-circuit, he careered towards an increasingly unnerved audience, who saw a lone, faceless monk with a mask of matted hair bearing down on them. Compassion overcame the remaining monks, and we sped downstage in perfect formation to retrieve our lost brother, who later became president of MENSA – which must say something about something.

At Cambridge there was a contagious condition that I didn't start to recognise until I had stopped being an actor myself and realised that I'd suffered from the same affliction. I've come to know it as 'university acting', although it persists in some actors long after their university years, and occasionally infects actors without a hint of higher education. It's the kind of acting that is all architecture and no heart, assembled by an intelligent mind conscious of meanings, of content, of style, of history, *over*conscious, in short, and saddled with an implicit editorial commentary that runs parallel to the performance, telling the audience what to think about the character and his predicament – and that the actor is more important, or more intelligent, than the character he is playing. It's like music written by computer.

Intellect, like beauty, is no bar to great acting, but beauty, unless it's animated by the breath of real talent, will seem gauche and plain, and intellect alone will make an actor seem doltish, describing a performance rather than giving it. I don't know a good actor who is not intelligent, but this intelligence is like a musician's, to do with timing, rhythm, hearing, sensibility, physical co-ordination rather than with cleverness and the ability to express ideas. Actors have more in common with spiritualist mediums than with dons, and the world of their work occupies a different globe to the articles of intellectual faith that underwrite university life.

I don't know that directors should be that much different. It has taken time in my case to learn to say, 'I don't know,' before rushing to rationalise, and I've learned to defend instinct against the intellect. It's not something I learned at Cambridge, which has been a breeding ground for a number of successful theatre directors. I have often heard it said that a kind of Mafia, or at the very least a Masonic brotherhood, exists in the theatrical profession among Cambridge graduates. While there may be a certain amount of circumstantial evidence for this, I don't believe it to be true. Opportunism has always been a more powerful bond than tribal loyalty. The privilege of Cambridge can't however be denied: there was a rare landscape of opportunity, well-endowed facilities, enough time, and a concentration of gifted actors. It was a sort of *de facto* directors' training course.

With the development of drama courses in several universities, the construction of university theatres, the expansion of the NUS Drama Festival, the elevation of the Edinburgh Fringe, and the voraciousness of TV and radio, student drama everywhere has acquired a much more conspicuous and egalitarian profile. Nevertheless, many of the newer directing talents, male and female, continue to emerge from Cambridge. Perhaps it's the water.

As for myself, I directed nothing at Cambridge but a short film that was plagiarised from Buster Keaton but which I've learned to describe as *hommage*, and I failed to prove to my satisfaction that I was a bad actor. That took a little longer.

I became a professional actor much as I might have become a soldier in the nineteenth century; I didn't seem to be fitted for anything else. Anyone can become an actor, all you have to do is to find someone to conspire in your delusion by offering you work – and obtain an Equity card. In my day you simply applied for one and paid a subscription, nowadays there's a little more to it; you have to serve a mandatory twenty-week apprenticeship. The catch, of course, is that to get the work you need the card, and to get the card you need the work ... I heard the other day of an actress who'd been the stooge in a knife-throwing act to get her card; well, an actor always needs to be equipped to take personal criticism. I had no such training, and I embarked on my life as an actor armed only with my availability, my optimism and my defiant description of myself as a professional.

A friend of mine, a pianist, played the piano once for Bill Gore, a clog dancer who did a club act – dancing in coloured lederhosen. At the climax of the act the lights were switched off, and with the aid of ultra-violet light, the fluorescent clogs would come into their own. 'How do I see the music?' asked my friend. 'Use these,' said Bill, handing

him spectacles with a torch taped to the side. 'Pro gig, lad.'
My professionalism was much the same brand of wilful
assertion: I advertised my services in *Spotlight*, the actors'
catalogue, I went for auditions, I wrote begging letters to
directors, I bought the *Stage*, I learned the jargon, and I
railed about the injustice of 'the profession'. Eventually
someone at Hornchurch Rep invited me to act for money.

My induction into the professional theatre was as inaus-
picious as is imaginable. After the long journey via Dagen-
ham on the District Line, I entered a rehearsal room which
had the air of a parish hall after an air raid. If people had
been huddling under blankets it would have completed the
picture, but in all other respects the image is exact; cups of
tea, dour faces, inert bodies, an air of desolation and one
energetic and voluble man who might have been the ARP
Warden, but in this case was the director. He was attempting
to engender sufficient enthusiasm in the cast to begin a read-
through of the play, which was *Henry V*. The actors, most
of whom had worked for him, looked about as likely to
follow him once more unto the breach as into the doors of
a gas oven.

'Hello,' trilled an actor I'd just met. 'Just joined the
Titanic, then?' It's rare to encounter this degree of pessimism
on the first day of rehearsal. More often the reverse is
true – there's a contagious nervousness and self-doubt, but
everyone is nevertheless determinedly optimistic. So much
so that it often takes a wholesale evisceration of a production by the critics and mass defection of audiences to
dent the optimism of a company of actors. It's usually possible on the first day of rehearsal to gauge whether the production is going to turn out all right, and at Hornchurch,
even with my as yet untrained antennae, I could tell we
were in for a bumpy ride.

Rehearsals proceeded from worse to terrible, and not even
the replacement of the director in the third week (of a three-
week rehearsal) could save us from certain catastrophe. Our
spirits were kept alive by the remorseless camp banter of
the wits in the company. Camp is the ghetto language of the

theatre. It's not exclusively a gay slang, even if it annexes most of the characteristics of that argot; it's a way of looking at the world that seeks to deflect seriousness and asserts, at least on the surface, that nothing really matters. It's a different thing altogether from 'camp' in art, which is a critical term that describes high seriousness dressed up in implausible costume: post-modern architecture, Wagner's operas, Queen's videos, High Church liturgy. Camp speech is a levelling device (I heard it said of one of Hitler's speeches: 'Oh, she's in a right old state') and a lingua franca, like that of any closed society – the Army, rugby clubs, public schools, prisons or gentlemen's clubs. At heart camp is like the slang of nurses and doctors, a carapace against suffering – in the case of actors the suffering caused by failure and public humiliation.

We were a collection of adults, some of whom were trained, experienced, and very gifted, and, like soldiers in the trenches, we were being sent out with no leadership and no protection between us and the audience but a few ill-designed costumes rented, or more likely borrowed, from someone else's conflict – a previous encounter with *Henry V.* I played Mountjoy the French Herald, in a costume that made me look like a rather worn playing-card. On my first entrance I faced a somewhat depleted but impish-looking English army. I spoke my first line: 'You know me by my habit,' only to be greeted by barely concealed gestures of self-abuse under the knitted chain mail. Later in the evening I doubled as a member of both the French and the English armies, who ran intermittently across the stage stopping only to fire arrows which bounced off the wall of the theatre and returned forlornly to the foot of the archer, who picked them up, ran offstage, changed a helmet, and returned in the other direction to repeat the process as the opposing army. I still smart with shame when I think of it and of the audience who endured it without criminally assaulting the actors and the management of the theatre.

Theatre is often embarrassing, inept, awkward, silly, in a word, tatty, and those who dislike the theatre cite its tattiness. One could say that it's as if you were to condemn Tolstoy for using the same medium as Barbara Cartland – but that's not really a serviceable analogy. While there's no danger of Tolstoy mutating to Barbara Cartland, there is *always* the danger of theatre, however fine, however 'grave', however 'serious', becoming absurd. At the moment of Lear's death, it only needs a member of the audience to sneeze loudly, or an actor to slip on stage, for the consent of the audience to be broken. However sophisticated its aims and its effects, it's never more than two boards and a passion, and it's precisely its ability to enchant, its *unreality*, that makes it so potent, but also, of course, so fragile. It's this very fragility of theatre, its potential for tattiness, that makes it so humane, so difficult and often, so absurd, and it's why one feels more comfortable sitting in theatres clad with 'humane ' materials – wood, lath and plaster, faded gilt – than with unforgiving chrome and concrete.

No jobs followed, but at least none were lost, as a consequence of the Hornchurch débâcle. I was given a small speaking part (lost from the final cut) in a feature film, and I learned that the adage 'There's no such thing as a small part' is a pernicious lie. I felt as if I'd been taken out of a box marked *English Middle-class Male, Young*. I had no idea why I'd been chosen over the infinity of alternatives. At least when I went for an interview for a GUARDS cigarette commercial I knew why I was rejected. 'Too short,' they said as I walked into the room.

I had a part in a TV play. Rehearsals were conducted in a dilatory fashion in a church hall in Tooting. Actors were more raffish, or lazier, in those days, less concerned with 'image', 'career', and becoming 'personalities', and had yet to be soaked in the baptismal waters of the opportunism of the eighties and born again as pundits or politicians – which is really to say that there was more drinking at lunchtime and after an hour or so in the pub many of the cast were too tired to rehearse in the afternoons. So I'd walk round Tooting Market with Meier Tzelniker, who had once met

Stanislavski and had worked in the Yiddish Theatre Company in Vilnius.

I was offered the opportunity of settling for a few months – a season at the Phoenix Theatre in Leicester: Play as Cast. The Phoenix is a theatre built cheaply, unpretentiously and wholly successfully in the early-sixties. It was next door to a bus depot, and lay parallel to a factory that made boiled sweets and glacier mints. I've not often recaptured the mixture of smells – acrid diesel fumes mingled with the vapour of sickly-sweet synthetic fruit and mint – but it's always recalled that period of my life with an almost nauseous intensity.

I lived in a bed-sitting room with peeling wallpaper, brown lino, a candlewick bedspread, gas meter, and a landlady who I only saw smile once – when I left. She was like the woman who a friend of mine overheard discussing a play she'd seen. 'How did you like it?' 'All right, if you like laughing.' It was not a glamorous life but, like most young actors, I was sustained in it by the fantasy that my life could be changed at the flick of a coin – stardom was just round the corner. If I'd been honest I would have had to say that my text was drawn from the film *42nd Street*:

> Miss Sawyer, you listen to me ... and you listen hard. Two hundred people, two hundred jobs, two hundred thousand dollars, five weeks of grind and blood and sweat depend on you! ... You've got to go on and you've got to give, and give, and give. They've got to like you, got to. You understand? ... You're going out there a youngster, but you've got to come back a star.

This theatrical eve-of-Agincourt speech is actually as near as most accounts, fictional or documentary, get to describing what it's like to work in a theatre. Perhaps other professions are as ill served; journalists constantly complain of the poverty of fictional accounts of newspaper life – although I've never heard them trying to dispel the enduring and improbable stereotype of the Journalist as Hero. But like actors, journalists know that the reality is too prosaic and too dull

to share with the public. To protect our fantasies we conspire in the fiction that life beyond the stage door is a
combination of the Land of Oz, Dante's Inferno, and one
of the more remorseless orgies of Caligula. I once met a
brigadier who asked what I did for a living. 'I work in the
theatre.' 'Mmmm,' he said, 'must be a lot of fucking.' To
which I should have said, Not as much as either you, or I,
would like, but probably no more than at the House of
Commons, or *The Times* newspaper, or anywhere where
there is a highly charged atmosphere, intense but carefully
prescribed relationships, an air of sexuality, banter and fun,
and hours that leave people of opposite, or even the same,
sex together late at night.

Life on stage at Leicester was less fun than off, but at
least I was learning. I was taught the meaning of 'blimping'
from an actor who was playing Willie Mossop in *Hobson's
Choice*; it meant being able to see up the women's skirts
through the floorboards of his ill-constructed cellar. He later
became a popular presenter on a children's show. I endured
the wrath of an ageing actress in a sub-Chekhovian tragi-
comedy; I was playing her servant – aged fourteen – and
had to spend much of the play kneeling at her feet where
she kicked me whenever she felt my concentration was straying. That wasn't unreasonable. It was more dispiriting to
have to prompt Othello in his dying speech and then be
taken by the neck as if *I* was the 'circumcis'd dog' when he
killed himself, and that was not the worst of my indignities.

The production of *Othello* was a companion piece to
Henry V and was watched by the audience with mute horror
– as if they were watching a surgical operation performed
without anaesthetic. It was acted in a style that I've come
to know as 'dog acting', derived from the habit of actors
in classical plays of seeking out a piece of furniture and
placing a foot on it, uncannily resembling a dog's relationship with a lamppost. It's prevalent at all levels of the acting
profession and is a sort of received idea of how to behave
when encountering a classical text. It embraces sonorous
voices, bombastic verse-speaking, and, because the language

is heightened and archaic, a suspension of the normal criteria of human behaviour. Life stops being the model, and in its place a kind of coded conduct is substituted – pewter tankards clash, whores lift their tattered petticoats, lords laugh demonically, lovers coo and simper, kings bellow their authority, and victims are stabbed with the ease of a spoon entering a blancmange. It's very difficult to animate a text in a language that is alien to us – rhythmic, non-naturalistic, compressed and expressive, and it is rarely that actors are able to achieve it, particularly in the case of Shakespeare, without years of practice.

There are other orthodoxies of bad acting that can be observed in modern plays, and are endemic to most TV drama. How often have you seen an actor on TV finish a phone conversation and stare at the mouthpiece, and how rarely have you seen anyone do this in life? It is possible to see this sort of 'telephone acting' spread, like echolalia, throughout an entire cast, just as in TV sitcoms actors suffer from a collective deafness that necessitates shouting at each other in ritualised exchanges which are resolved only by bursts of synthetic laughter from a phantom audience.

We should be able to judge good and bad acting more easily than any other art – after all, we are all practised observers of human behaviour – but, given that, it's odd how audiences are so easily contented with performances which, as Hamlet says, 'imitate humanity so abominably'. The truly real, or truly natural, performance is rarely seen, and, perhaps, rarely desired. An audience seems to want something more than imitation of nature, something that is somehow different from itself. Often it's fantasy that is required, but more often merely something that is observably real and yet more exotic, more idiosyncratic, than we feel ourselves to be. We want to be reminded of the singularity of each human being, and at the very same time be made to acknowledge that we swim in the common pool of humanity.

The Christmas show at the Phoenix Theatre was *The Boy-*

friend. There must be those in remote corners of the English-speaking world who think that this pastiche of a pastiche of a twenties musical is delightful, but I found its winsome melodies, its saccharine charm, its camp, smug, self-regarding milieu, as alien to me as an Aztec sacrifice, and at least as repulsive. Like an advocate, the actor is supposed to remain detached from the content – he is the servant of the play and not its judge – but I was as impartial as a hawk with a dead mouse.

I wasn't alone; like prisoners of war counting flies, the chorus, or at least the male half, developed their own survival techniques. We sat motionless in our dressing-room before the show, our feet on the table, staring inscrutably at ourselves and our colleagues out of the corners of our eyes. The challenge was to see who could be the last to get changed, made-up (regular Riviera tan, Leichner 5 and 9), and get onstage for the first bar of the opening number. It was often the first note of the (shortish) overture that signalled an explosion of activity, with a degree of manic energy and commitment that disappeared as soon as we arrived onstage in our white shirts, trousers and deck shoes and told the audience that it was 'Nicer, much nicer in Nice'. Given our views on Leicester we could have sung that it was nicer in Anchorage, Alaska, with as much conviction.

My personal nemesis arrived when I came onstage, took my partner, and she whispered to me that she'd forgotten to put her knickers on. Mercifully the choreography was too demure to involve high kicks until the end of the number, at which point the girls dipped down on one leg, kicked high the other and leant backwards supported by their partner. A kind of laughter, like bubbles in a pan of thick soup, was building up inside me, and it burst as I dropped my partner on the stage in my efforts to defend her modesty. I stood still, shaking hopelessly, until I was dragged offstage. Perhaps it was forgivable in the circumstances, but it was becoming clear, even to me, that it was unfair to release my contempt for my own inadequacies on a paying audience. I was beginning to think of acting as the Captain does of

Joxer's singing in *Juno and the Paycock*: 'I hate to see fellas thryin' to do what they're not able to do.'

I decided to give up acting one Saturday afternoon just before the matinée. I can put a date to it: it was the 30th of January, 1965, the day of Churchill's funeral. I'd listened to the commentary in the morning, and on my way to the theatre I stood in a silent crowd outside a TV shop to watch the coffin conveyed from Tower Bridge to Waterloo Station along the river in a launch. Harold Wilson said at the time, 'There is a stillness and in that stillness each has his memories.' What my memories were I wasn't certain, and, although I felt profoundly moved by the funeral, I wasn't sure why. It seemed, and I don't think this is hindsight, as if a world had died with him. It was my parents' world, and in spite of my desire to see their world reformed, in my heart I felt only regret. Whether it was real or imagined, they were grieving for a lost utopia, an English Eden.

That afternoon I stared at my face in the mirror and felt like Magritte's portrait of a man looking at himself in the mirror; like him, I saw only the back of my head. I wasn't sure who I was, but at least I knew I wasn't an actor. I no longer had the will to continue. It was more than a lack of talent; I felt as if I'd been cushioned by a combination of exhibitionism and vanity, fuelled by sufficient confidence for the audience to supply the missing part and put it down to inexperience, and there had been enough co-conspirators in my fiction to encourage me to think I could earn a living out of acting. Confidence is nine-tenths of the business of acting, and when my cushion of confidence deflated I was left with nothing but despair.

Acting is a mystery: in the medieval sense it's a handicraft, and yet it's also something that is obscure, enigmatic, and beyond comprehension. All of us, consciously or not, are actors – we simulate feelings we don't feel, we lie, we pretend to be what we aren't. It is this latent, though well-rehearsed, skill that lures so many people to believe that they can become actors; if everyone does the actor's job in life, then anyone can do it on a stage. Couple this to a desire to assert an alter ego, and you go some of the way to explaining why the acting profession is so overcrowded with hopeful aspirants. It's a tantalising paradox that what seems so familiar and attainable to us should be so exasperatingly difficult to do; without talent, will, and character, it's impossible.

Good acting embraces a number of paradoxes: actors must be conscious of themselves, but not be self-conscious; they must know themselves, but they must also, on stage, forget themselves; they must be self-less, but will undeniably be selfish; and they must find the balance, while acting, between the heart and the head, reason and instinct, that Diderot describes as 'the true point':

> An actor who has only sense and judgement is cold; one who has only verve and sensibility is crazy. It is a peculiar combination of good sense and warmth which creates the sublime person; and on the stage as in life he who shows more than he feels makes one laugh instead of affecting one. Therefore never try to go beyond the feeling that you have; try to find the true point.

It's difficult to achieve this in life, which is probably why we give such extravagant praise to those who achieve it in art. To act properly, in life as in art, implies a moral dimension that makes us want actors to be exemplary beings. It's an impossible prescription – to seek attention for oneself but not to be narcissistic, to perform but not to show off, to communicate, but in someone else's voice – is it any wonder that actors often seem as ill-at-ease offstage as politicians outside the House of Commons.

The best actors have much in common. They know how to use a space and invariably make the space they occupy onstage or in the frame of a film seem expressive. The bad ones just stand there. Nureyev said, 'A great dancer is not one who makes a difficult step look easy, but one who makes an easy step look difficult.' It's the same with actors, the ability to transform the commonplace; to make gods of men, and men of gods. The best actors need to communicate with each other and with an audience; the bad ones never make contact, or make themselves heard. Courage is essential to the good actor; in the bad it is mere folly.

To express anything an actor must have a physical technique. It may be latent, but it must be trained. The training will always be empirical, learning by doing, and adding to that by watching other actors, listening to them, copying them, stealing their tricks, and reinventing them for yourself. Stanislavski was trying to give shape to an inchoate process; his 'Method' is a vast concordance of common sense. The fact that few, if any, good actors invoke his work is not to say that they don't recognise and follow most of his pragmatic precepts.

I'm never surprised that the question that actors are most often asked is not, 'Who are you sleeping with?' but, 'How do you learn your lines?' The question is not naive; what should be inferred from it is the desire to know how another human being transforms themselves into another. It is a form of magic, as mysterious as the ability to conjure sweet sounds out of a piece of varnished wood with catgut stretched over it.

There are as many 'methods' of working as there are actors, and, unless they are subject to the collective discipline of an expressionistic production or of a musical, most actors will work like scavengers, picking up ideas, images, 'business', and occasionally, like panhandlers, pure gold. A structure is imposed on an actor's work by the rehearsal process; the lines acquire meaning, the moves evolve, ideas become animated, against a rigid and remorseless storyline – rehearsals begin at a known point, they end some weeks later when the play is decanted (sometimes disastrously) from the rehearsal room to the stage. There is always a result: a triumph, or a catastrophe – or, more often, something in between. During the rehearsal period some gifted actors seem exasperatingly slow, some bewilderingly stubborn, some alarmingly quick, leaping from conclusion to conclusion like scaffolders on rooftops.

For all the disparate ways of working, and the apparent self-absorption and navel-watching, there is one inviolable rule: you have to play with your fellow actors – the solipsist will always be left marooned on an island of his own making. Strong actors can appear, often unfairly, to dominate a rehearsal and a stage at the expense of other actors. They radiate an energy that has an almost physical heat, and, like poultices, they draw the heat from the actors who surround them. Being combative, impatient, irascible, and frustrating is often an implicit demand to be challenged and stimulated, to be given competition by their fellow actors. Even accounting for this, some actors seem to need to make it difficult for themselves, even painful. It's as if they are fighting to achieve a mystical dimension by suffering, when that dimension, which unquestionably exists, is achieved only by practical means.

Take any actors, and you will find their working methods are as distinct as their personalities and backgrounds. To take three actors, not entirely at random: Judi Dench, Ian McKellen, and Michael Bryant. None of them would confess to a working 'method', any more than they would own up to a 'lifestyle', but they all have processes that they have, consciously or not, developed over many years; serendipity may play a part in their work, but little that they do is accidental. Judi Dench is an actress who works almost entirely on her instincts. Someone once told me that John Williams, the guitarist, never needed to practise, his technique is effortless. Like him Judi has technique to burn – she can turn a line on a fragment of a syllable, a scene on the twist of a finger. She doesn't *study* a part but works through a process of osmosis, soaking up the details with a sometimes disconcerting randomness. She'll ask questions that seem hardly to bear on the character and, as if she'd disturbed you while reading a book, leave you as soon as you answer as if afraid that more talking would muddy the instinct. When I directed her in *The Cherry Orchard* for TV, she beckoned to me thoughtfully just before we went for a take; it was a long scene in which Ranyevskya talks about her life with her lover in France. 'She's a terrible old tart, isn't she?' she said, with a mixture of charity and envy. When she's rehearsing the elements of her performance seem disparate but gradually, and invisibly, the elements come together: head, heart, voice and body into a marvellous synchronicity. She reminds me of what Peggy Ramsay told me once about recognising whether an actor is in character, 'Look at the feet, dear.'

At first glance Ian McKellen is a scientific actor. His performances form like crystals in a saturated solution; you hang a small crystal from a thread and little by little, facet by facet, the crystal grows until it hangs like a large diamond. As a young actor he wore his talent like a jewel, turning it in the light, holding it up for the audience to marvel at, but over the years, as his public and private life have fused, so have his talent and his character. It's not always true of actors, and of people in general, that they desire to improve themselves; in this sense Ian is exemplary. 'Everyone has talent at twenty-five,' said Degas. 'The difficulty is to have it at fifty.'

Some actors start with trying to establish the details of how the character will look, some with how they will think or feel. It was said of Olivier that he started with the shoes; with Ian it's the face and the voice. I have a postcard he sent me when we started to work on *Richard III* – a wry cartoon of a severe face, recognisable as his own, with sharply receding hair, an arrow pointing to a patch of alopecia; at the throat is a military collar, above the shoulder the tip of a small hump. He is a systematic, fastidious and exacting actor; each word is picked up and examined for its possible meanings, which are weighed, assessed, discarded or incorporated. In rehearsals he is infinitely self-aware, often cripplingly so. His waking, and perhaps sleeping, dreams are of how he will appear on stage – his position, his spatial relationships with the other actors. But in performance that inhibition drops away like a cripple's crutches and he is pure performer. All the detail that has been so exhaustively documented becomes a part of an animate whole. In sport, in a great performance, there must always be an element of danger. The same is true of the theatre. I wouldn't say there is not a good or even effective actor without this characteristic, but there is certainly no celebrated one.

After acting with Ian, Irene Worth said, 'We were jazzing.' Like a musician, he composes his performances; he writes a score for his own orchestral forces and then allows himself to conduct it. Sometimes you can see the conductor at work, but more often the conductor becomes subsumed in the character and what you are watching is an act of possession.

The most mysterious, even mystical, element in acting is the element that has the characteristics of demoniacal possession – the phenomenon in which the devil besets the soul inside the body, when Satan is said to 'inhabit' the victim. Virtuous people were supposed to be immune from it, and perhaps the facility of actors to be possessed not by demons but by the characters they are playing has made some contribution to the fiction that they are in some way less virtuous than the normal run of society.

The phenomenon of possession is often apparent in flashes during rehearsals when an actor suddenly develops a particular rhythm, an inner ear for the character, and the voice and movements of his body no longer seem his own. It is as if, rather than the actor occupying the character, the character has occupied the actor. During an early run-through of a play, the actors are always charged with a febrile nervous energy, and at this point the 'spirit' of the character often seems to drive the actor's imagination and invention, and things that have never happened in rehearsals occur spontaneously and effortlessly. It is almost unnerving to see the actor's own personality, which may be quiet, unforceful, and inarticulate, be wrenched, thrown about, transformed, and, literally, possessed by another persona. At the end of the run-through, when this has occurred, the actor is left exhausted, etiolated, as if the 'spirit' has departed and left him to learn how to summon the demon again, and how to harbour and accommodate it. In effect, the actor's problem is how to repeat the experience without the wasteful energy; an actor cannot live the experience every time, he must learn to simulate it. This is the true test of the professional – he or she must experience possession, endure passion and yet, like a firewalker, remain untouched by the experience.

For all its sensational associations, it's a remarkably unsensational event to witness. To some degree it's an essential part of all rehearsals and, if not entirely taken for granted by actors, is no more celebrated than the rising of a soufflé would be by a chef. Audiences take it for granted and recognise the phenomenon only when it's inescapable – in Edna Everage, for instance, when they're struck over the head with a gladiolus by a rather studious, thoughtful, mild-mannered man.

There are those, and not only from primitive societies, who hate to be photographed; they feel that it steals their soul. Paradoxically, some actors, when they are unprepared, out of character or rehearsing, feel the same, and they conceal themselves behind a prickly wall. Maggie Smith is one of these. Onstage she is luminous, brilliant and wholly accessible to the public, and in private, she is – well, private. I made a film with her of a Tennessee Williams play. For much of the time she was not feeling well, and was enduring conditions that would have tested my namesake along the Great Australian Bight: shooting over eight minutes of dialogue a day in a studio with the temperature rising to 110°F, and the humidity of a tropical rain forest. Maggie said that she felt like Alec Guinness in *The Bridge on the River Kwai*; I felt more like the Camp Commandant. And yet, when I look at her now on the screen, there is an effortlessness in her performance that shows nothing of the pain. It is not merely that she acts with astonishing skill, she seems to render the description of 'acting' inapplicable; alchemy would be more appropriate. Her playing of the half-mad Mrs Venable doesn't seem like imitation; it seems more like theft – she has stolen her soul.

Most actors hate to talk about their work; they are rightly reluctant to intellectualise about processes that are idiosyncratic and instinctive. Alfred Molina, a hugely gifted, droll, mercurial actor, insists that acting is just a matter of mechanics, and yet when you work with him you witness an invention, and intensity of intuition and feeling that is anything but mechanical. Miranda Richardson appears to have a translucently thin skin as an actress; you can almost *see* the feelings. She has an unearthly ability to transform herself, but you will discover no more about how she does it than you will about the plant life on Mars. Robert Stephens said in an interview, 'I have no great views about acting except this. Number one: If you are going to act be serious about it. Number two: For God's sake speak properly.'

Michael Bryant is firmly of this persuasion. To hear him talk you would imagine he is a carpenter or a farmer, and is as reluctant to theorise about acting as about a piece of wood or a cow. He has as much interest in 'experiment' and 'research' as a farmer has in veterinary science or a carpenter in tree surgery. When he was rehearsing *Wind in the Willows* Nicholas Hytner invited the actors to study the behaviour of their respective animals: toads, rats, weasels, ferrets, rabbits and badgers. Michael took a video of a badger-watch away with him and returned a day or two later with this revelation: 'I have made a discovery about the habits of badgers: their movement and their posture has an extraordinary resemblance to Michael Bryant.'

Actually, in his approach to a part he reminds me most of a badger-watcher: silent, strategic, patient, unobtrusive; he stalks a part. He talks little in rehearsal and needs, or wants, only the most basic information – where he is to stand, what the furniture is, louder, softer, quicker, slower. He regards the text as the only hard evidence at his disposal, and matter-of-factly builds his character like a detective assembling a case until one day, sometimes alarmingly late in rehearsal, the character is there – complete. It's as if he'd been marinating the part in secret until it was ready, and if you enquired about the recipe you would be bluntly rebuffed. Yet for all his blimpish, witty, portly, plain-man persona, there is no actor more sensitive, more subtle, or more private than Michael Bryant. If the mystery of acting is the combination of craft and enigma, no one embodies it more fully – to which I can hear him saying, 'Oh bollocks!'

'Scratch an actor,' said Laurence Olivier, 'and you find an actor.' He should have known, but I don't think it's true, or any more true of actors than politicians, or priests, or teachers, or strippers, or anyone else engaged in acts of public self-display. What *is* true, I think, is that if you scratch an actor you will find a child. Not that actors are inherently less mature than politicians, priests, etc, but actors must retain a child's appetite for mimicry, for demanding attention, and above all for playing. They must see with a child's heart, innocent of judgement.

Like all children (and all artists), actors crave approval. With actors the craving is more acute than in other performers, because you cannot make the distinction between approving the performance and approving the actor himself. In applauding the performance, like a grateful parent, you are bestowing love not on a fiction but on the actor who stands before you.

Directors are far from immune from the desire for approval, even if they are more insulated than actors from the raw immediacy of rejection. When I first became a director I visited the Odeon Theatre in Paris; it is still my favourite theatre in the world, inside and out. I saw Jean-Louis Barrault play there, and imagined, as I watched, that a production of mine might one day occupy that stage. In 1990 I took *Richard III* there, and at the end, in the amiable tradition of European theatre, I was pushed onstage to take my bow with the actors. I walked forward like a sleep-walker, gazing at the audience as if surprised that it had intruded on my dream. 'Bow,' hissed Ian McKellen. 'You BOW.' I did, and felt the intense pleasure of what for an actor is all in a night's work; love requited.

MISDIRECTION

'Only a garden can teach gardening.'

Douglas Dunn

I AM SITTING in a theatre, late at night, wishing that it would burn down. Acre after acre of empty seats fan out in the dark auditorium, threatening as the cave of the gods, bleak as an empty aircraft hangar. I stare at a piece of scenery that is moving with glacial torpor across the stage of the Olivier Theatre. A few stagehands stand motionless, staring at the object as if it were an obelisk or a pyramid – there for a millennium and for a thousand years to come. I am wishing the stage were bare, or that the theatre were smaller, or that I were dreaming, and I am longing to be delivered from the bonds of a production that has gone wrong, or is going wrong, or will go wrong. 'Football isn't a matter of life and death, it's much more important than that,' said Bill Shankly, and I know what he meant. It's only a play, but I'm feeling less like a football manager, more like a pregnant mother, terrified of a still-birth.

Truffaut directed a comic fantasy about making a film called *La Nuit Americaine*. There is only one moment in the film, enjoyable as it is, that strikes me as observed from life: the director of the film within a film, played by Truffaut himself, lies awake, tormented by fears for the work. 'Let it live,' he mutters to himself like an anxious surgeon. 'Just let it be alive.' Peter Brook identifies this life, the necessary spark in a piece of theatre, as a fisherman's treasure, a 'golden fish':

In the case of the well-made net, it is the fisherman's luck whether a good or a bad fish is caught. In the theatre, those who tie the knots are also responsible for the quality of the moment that is ultimately caught in their net. It is amazing – the 'fisherman' by his action of tying the knots influences the quality of the fish that land in the net!

More often than not in the theatre you land a dogfish, too fat to slip through the web of your inadequately constructed net, and too ugly to be worth catching.

I caught a carp once, not a metaphor, I really did: a Brobdingnagian goldfish, heavy as a flagstone. I was in Sarawak in Borneo, and I'd fallen in with, or had been snared by, a man who I later discovered was a collector of alligators and young boys. Perhaps the idea was that the latter would be fed to the former. He was a distinguished-looking Chinese, large, not entirely inscrutable, but no more nor less so than Sidney Greenstreet, to whom he had more than a passing resemblance. We had a long Sunday lunch of Malaysian curry and Tiger beer in the 'Club', as it was unironically called: large flaking fans, dark, almost ebony-black polished wood floors, bulky green leather armchairs, humidity sticky as a flypaper, and servants as painfully deferential as they would have been to the imperial sahibs.

I was taken to his farm, which consisted of about thirty large ponds surrounded by iridescent green grass. Many of the ponds held alligators, who stirred malevolently at our approach and looked anything but a joke; *not* floating handbags, I thought. 'Come on,' said my host, 'now you see a bit of action.'

We crossed to a yard by a long low hut, which lay alongside a poultry pen. About fifteen men, mostly middle-aged, sat on benches and packing cases, forming a small square arena. From inside the hut came the sound of squawking, an angry sound, fierce and far removed from the cluck of a domestic chicken; the pre-match banter of fighting cocks. Out of the hut came two men holding huge hooded birds, running like a sledge behind huskies. The men took up positions at opposite corners of the makeshift ring; the cries of the cocks merged with the yelling of the betting. Fanned fists of notes changed hands as the voices rose and exploded when the hoods came off and the cocks rocketed towards each other with huge plumed tail feathers, gold, auburn, blue-black, waving in a rabid frenzy. Beaks pecked at breasts, at necks, at eyes, and spurred feet, little scimitars, flashed like kick-boxers' ankles. Feathers flew, blood scattered like crimson corn. They parted, they feinted, they parried, they clung to each other, a bare-fisted prize-fight – heavyweights, solid as Gibraltar. I don't know how long it lasted, hours, perhaps, but to me it seemed barely a second before one of the birds lay panting on the ground, pulsing out his life's blood, and only then did I feel anything like revulsion or shock or horror.

This was a prelude to the carp fishing, which was offered much as you might offer a sorbet to someone who was already gorged. The ponds were about thirty feet in diameter, and perhaps three or four feet deep. To catch your carp you had to trawl across the pond with another person, water never below your waist or above your chest, holding the net as wide as your arms would stretch, your lower hand scraping as close to the bottom as possible. When they sensed the threat the pond started to boil, and the fish jumped ferociously, several feet out of the water, some of them within inches of our faces, and we closed the net, dragging them, like cats in a sack, to the bank. Catching the golden fish, I thought, nothing easier. After I'd caught a few the owner of the pond told me that the head of the carp is as hard as marble. 'If it hits you between the eyes,' he said, 'you're dead.'

Catching the golden fish in the rehearsal room isn't hazardous or exotic; its as methodical, prolonged and uncertain as trawling for cod in the North Sea. A rehearsal is an exploration: the writer provides the territory, the director draws the map as the journey progresses. At the start of rehearsals the actors view the landscape with the innocent optimism of new settlers, sharing a common aim and bound by the same social rules. They are stridently individualistic, and yet have to bury their egos for the good of the whole; they have to work to a common rhythm, even if each chooses a different tempo; they are of uneven abilities and yet they have to subscribe to a democracy of talent, underwritten by a generosity of spirit. They must give credence to Marx's sampler: 'From each according to his abilities, to each according to his needs.' It's a sort of utopia, and, as Thomas More said, 'There are many things in the Commonwealth of Utopia that I rather wish, than hope, to see followed in our governments.'

I like the way this little model society mocks the real thing; it's come together not to change the world or feed the hungry, but for pleasure, to 'play', and this usually generates a special gentleness and magnanimity. It often survives the entire rehearsal period and then, like any self-regarding sect, is threatened by coming into contact with a world that owes no favours to its buoyant optimism. In the rehearsal room a spark has bred a flame, which may turn out to be as fragile as a candle in the wind.

The start of most rehearsals resembles others more than it differs from them. Rehearsals have to begin somewhere – usually it's a meeting of the cast, and a reading of the play. The director talks a little – or a lot, depending on temperament – and his words drift like incense over a group of actors who, regardless of their mutual familiarity, are united only in their nervous anticipation and social unease. The director stands like a heron, rigid with anxiety, and the pose is repeated several weeks later when the production is exposed to an audience for the first time.

A rehearsal has to be a time when actors can experiment, invent, explore, discuss, dispute, practise and become childlike, and it is the job of a director to create a world – private and secure – where this activity can go on without fear of failure. There is no method that guarantees a good rehearsal, and Eliot's advice on writing poetry, 'There is no method except to be very intelligent,' is rather far from being the whole story. It is as hard to know why some highly articulate, learned and intelligent directors seem unable to animate a cast of actors as it is to understand how the same orchestra can be inspired by some conductors, and seem commonplace in the hands of others – 'the masters of the brilliant wave', as James Galway calls them.

I once saw a masterclass in conducting led by Daniel Barenboim. He had six students, a pianist and a chamber orchestra. The exercise was to bring in the orchestra at the end of the soloist's cadenza. Easy, I thought, as I waved my hands in sync with Barenboim. Each of the students, all knowledgeable about the craft, took their turn; all but two of them failed to bring the orchestra in on the beat. I've come to think of directing like that. When I see a production, I think – as it were, after a few bars – ah, the director has brought the actors in on the beat, and even if I'm not altogether having a wonderful time, even if every moment of the production is not illuminated by the vital spark, I think: It's not drifting, it's being 'directed'. I was once at a seminar where Peter Brook was asked, 'What *is* directing?' to which he answered – only slightly disingenuously – 'It's getting people on and offstage,' which is a skill, a talent, and perhaps the only indispensable part of the craft of directing – like bringing the orchestra in on time.

The title of director is a comparatively recent creation; not as recent as social worker, family counsellor and sex therapist, but perhaps belonging to the same reductive urge of the twentieth century to label and professionalise all forms of human contact. It is often said that the function of directors is as recent as their title. This is not true; no one who has ever acted in a Shakespeare play, or suffered in the audience at amateur (or even some professional) productions could doubt that *someone* at least has to arbitrate, to sort out the flow of traffic across the stage, the exits and entrances, and the staging of the often bewilderingly confused codas to the comedies when the stage becomes crammed with couples all declaring that they are related to long-lost fathers, mothers, cousins or children.

Shakespeare and Molière were undoubtedly directors in all but name, just as much as composers were *de facto* conductors for many years before audiences started to applaud someone just for turning up on time and walking to the podium with a baton in their hand. Directing as a full-time occupation is an invention of our age, perhaps born more out of social and commercial imperatives than artistic ones.

There is much in the analogy of the director and conductor that seems compelling, but in practice they have little in common, even if both professions are thought to share the characteristics of tyranny, which our century has systematised and sophisticated beyond the dreams of the previous two millennia. The director works steadily over weeks or months, by accretion, layer after layer deposited to mature only in performance. However powerful he is (and more often than not it is *he*), however much he throws his weight around, however much he bullies and cajoles, however much the actors are subject to his conceit, directorial and personal, the moment the performance begins, he has less importance than the person who is showing latecomers to their seats. The conductor, on the other hand, is part of the performance, and, although possibly technically superfluous, is at its centre – the absolute autocrat, the sole lawgiver.

Music doesn't have to have a point; that is its point. Music *is*. With good music, as Auden says, you have only to listen to it, and be grateful. Theatre, on the other hand, prospers, or labours, under the despotism of logic. Most modern art is concerned with texture, with the surface of things; it's only the theatre that maintains a stubborn dependence on plot, and it can look merely quaint when set against such contemporary obsessions as graphic design, fashion photography and the design of the tail fins of Ford Cortinas. Theatre will always be unfashionable because of its form, its need for order in narrative and in structure, and it will always lag behind a society that is conspicuous for its formlessness. The theatre's concern with the frailty of being human will always look defenceless when set against *Mad Max III*, *The Exterminator*, or the confident certainties of politics or journalism.

What I like about the theatre is precisely what some people hate about it. I like being made to concentrate. I like the fallibility that goes hand in hand with its immediacy. I like the fact that it happens in the present tense, that it's vulnerable and it's changeable. I like its sense of occasion, the communal event: going in as an individual and emerging as part of a group. I like sharing *time* with strangers: a beginning and an end, a sense of birth and a sense of death. And I like the singular combination of magic and moral debate.

There are a lot of good reasons for *not* going to the theatre. For a start, you have to turn up on time and sit in the dark without talking for longish periods. I know many people who find this an insupportable restriction of their freedom. Judi Dench told me of a woman who had sat through a performance of *The Three Sisters* during which she contributed a seamless monologue. As the final moments approached and the three tear-stained heroines clung to each other, she achieved immortality as she muttered to her friend, 'You know, I think they're sisters.'

I once spoke to the financier James Goldsmith in the hope of luring him into sponsoring a play at the National Theatre. 'I never go to the theatre,' he said. 'My legs are too long.' And I have a friend, a film director, who hates going to the theatre because it's all in wide-shot. Many people prefer the cinema for its solitary, dreamlike disengagement. John Updike says:

> I've never much enjoyed going to plays. The unreality of painted people standing on a platform saying things they've said to each other for months is more than I can overlook.

For me this is missing the point; it's the re-creation that animates the art and makes it unique, and anyway all art forms are unreal in some sense. They have their formal rules, their conventions, their partiality, novels as much as paintings. A woman said to Matisse, 'Surely the arm of this woman is too long?' To which Matisse replied, 'It's not an arm, Madame, it's a picture.'

Each art form has its unique properties. There is no art that uses time, space, gesture, movement, speech, colour, costume, light and music in the way that the theatre does. It thrives on metaphor: things stand *for* things rather than being the thing itself, a room becomes a world, a group of characters a whole society. Theatre invokes the astonishment of the unreal, and the strange, magnified, proportions that occur naturally in childhood.

The British are supposed to have the finest theatre in the world. The same thing is said about our television, our judiciary, and our parliamentary system, so we can be forgiven for being a bit sceptical about this claim. If the British have an enthusiasm for theatre and an aptitude, perhaps it's because so many of the characteristics of the medium coincide with the characteristics of the nation. The theatre exploits ritual, processions, ceremonies, hieratic behaviour and dressing up; it depends on adversarial conflict, the stuff of our parliamentary and legal system, and it's concerned with role-playing, which is second nature to a nation obsessed with the signs and manners of class distinction, and inured to the necessity, as a nation and as individuals, of pretending to be what you aren't.

I learnt the credo of this national faith at school: Church, Queen, and Country. Like many seminarists, I responded poorly to the propaganda. When I was thirteen I sat formally with eighty other boys before our evening meal, and listened to Anthony Eden on the radio informing us that 'Colonel Nasser has naturalised, er, nationalised the Suez Canal. Britain must invade Egypt.' 'The honour of our country is at stake,' we were told by our housemaster. I was bemused. I was no less bemused twenty-six years later when I heard our Prime Minister say much the same thing about the Falkland Isles. As thirteen year olds we were not encouraged to ask questions, and it was left to a teenage wit to unearth Chesterton's *bon mot*: ' "My country right or wrong" is a thing that no patriot would think of saying except in a desperate case. It's like saying "My mother drunk or sober".'

I recoil still from appeals to 'country' and 'national culture', and in this I reveal my Englishness. We don't like to admit to nationhood or culture, or, especially, to ideology, although in some respects we are the most ideologically motivated nation in Europe. We used to be defined nationally by an Empire, and now we are condemned to live out Dean Acheson's truism that 'Britain has lost an Empire and has yet to find a role'. So we invent our roles on the domestic rather than the international stage. We put ourselves in inverted commas – 'Swinging London', 'The Rock Revolution', 'Punks', 'Fogeys', 'Sloanes', 'Beasties', 'Yuppies'. We put on funny accents; we make TV shows about TV shows; we make adverts based on old adverts; we have a whole culture that refers above all to itself. We have created a world fit for shop-fitting, in which presentation is paramount, and we excel in those media that put a premium on display: advertising and theatre.

For such a notoriously reticent and introspective nation we seem to have a great capacity for displaying ourselves in public. Maybe it's precisely because of this reticence that we like to express ourselves vicariously through the theatre, and that strain in our national character has given us what is unarguably the richest theatre tradition in the world. Whether it's the *best* must be left to those who keep statistics, write record books, and dream up a sport as daft as synchronised swimming.

Britain is gradually being converted into a theme park. Buildings, institutions, and ceremonies are appropriated, synthetically processed, and disgorged as 'national traditions'. If we really valued our heritage, then we would do everything we could to ensure the continuity of the most animated and longest-lived part of that cultural heritage – our national theatre (with a small *n*). We have a theatrical tradition that nurtures an astonishing number of actors who are not only gifted but resourceful, pragmatic, witty, humane, generous, irreverent and courageous. Shakespeare was an actor, spent his time in the company of actors, and in his work returned over and over again to the process by which people can *seem* to be one thing, and *be* another. It's become common to deride actors as sentimental, posturing, and self-absorbed – in a sneering word: 'luvvies'. It's true they can be as vain, difficult, petty and selfish as any group of journalists, or lawyers, or politicians, or chefs, but I'd rather spend my time with a group of actors than with any other professional body.

In life, acting breeds bitterness – pretending to feel what we don't feel, feigning interest when we're bored, being polite when we feel resentful, delighted when we're disappointed, but acting for a living breeds resilience and fortitude, a kind of stoicism. When you work with actors daily it's hard not to be infected by this philosophy. Stoicism may not be a path to virtue, but at least it gets you through the night. 'An actor,' said Macready, 'must affect an immoderate buoyancy of spirits while perhaps his heart is breaking.'

Once I saw a performance of Ralph Richardson, and afterwards I told a friend of mine who was in the production how remarkable I thought he'd been. 'Yes, it's amazing,' she said, 'I saw him looking very melancholy before the show, and I said, "Are you all right, Ralph? You look very sad." ' 'Oh, you know, I've had a bit of bad news,' he said. 'My brother's been killed. In a fire.' 'Oh Ralph,' she said, 'how awful.' 'Yes,' he said. 'Still, there's one consolation – it can't happen again.'

In some respects actors are like soldiers, veterans of many ill-conceived campaigns, and ever-sceptical of the leaders who have dragged them there. It can be unnerving to hear a group of actors discussing directors with all the affection of prisoners of war for their Camp Commandant, and actors don't discourage the widespread myth that directors seek their role model in Eric von Stroheim, complete with whip, boots, and jodhpurs. In reality directors resemble more closely the Woody Allen end of the personality spectrum. They are often surprisingly lacking in the gift and appetite for self-promotion, and, in spite of a high estimation of their own importance, are often reluctant to capitalise on it by making public pronouncements on their craft. It's all the odder therefore that directors occupy such an elevated status in contemporary mythology, often, like conductors, placed somewhere between the maestro and the magus, when they're more like teachers or doctors.

I've learned that it's better to be more like the pupil or the patient than the teacher or the doctor. The mistake is to pretend that you have all the answers, a lesson that it took me a longish time to learn. I directed *The Beggar's Opera* at the National Theatre in 1982. There was a scene in which Macheath flirts with several prostitutes, who then sit around talking about their work, while one of their number seduces him, and betrays him to the thief-catcher. It's a difficult scene to stage, and almost impossible to avoid slipping into those lazy, time-honoured, hand-me-down, cash-and-corset clichés.

It's all too easy to slip into received ideas about the behaviour of any profession. I was filming a scene for *Tumbledown* in a ward for patients recovering from brain surgery when I suggested to an actor playing a patient that he vomited; an extra masquerading as a doctor would stop to deal with him on his way through the ward. 'You must be joking,' said the medical advisor. 'The doctor would just leg it out of the ward as quickly as he could.'

Most of my knowledge of prostitutes since I was a teenager has been derived from watching earnest, or meretricious TV documentaries, but I did have a flat once above a prostitute, and she included acting as an essential component of her professional skills. She had one customer whose sole demand was that she stood naked in a transparent plastic mac by a portable bus-stop sign that he brought with him in his briefcase and assembled in her bedroom. She had to pretend to be irritated by his attentions while she waited for the bus and he silently masturbated at her side. He'd become exasperated if she showed less than total conviction in her performance.

This particular memory didn't help *The Beggar's Opera*. The cast had little to offer in the way of what one might tastelessly describe as first-hand experience, I could offer no immediate recipe to animate the scene, and for a long while we sat around paralysed and mute with indecision. Finally I said, 'I really don't know how to do this scene.' More silence, then a palpable sense of relief: the problem was shared, and patience and detailed examination would tell us how the scene should be played, not some specious staging notion offered up by an under-confident and over-anxious director. I learned the importance of having the courage to admit ignorance, and to welcome silence, not as a herald of despair, but as an ally.

Shortly after I had become a director, or at least called myself a director, and had found someone to support my calling, I wrote a play, an adaption of a novel about schizophrenia by Jennifer Dawson, *The Ha-Ha*. The novel was light, frightening, and witty. It had an epigraph by Blake, 'The Fly':

> Little fly,
> Thy summer's play
> My thoughtless hand
> Has brushed away.

> Am not I
> A fly like thee?
> Or art not thou
> A man like me?

Researching for the production of the play, I visited a mental hospital in Lincoln. I spoke at length to a doctor, who, unlike the other doctors, wore a white coat and had a stethoscope tumbling out of his pocket. There was little he didn't know about the pathology of schizophrenia, and little that I could do to stop him telling me. After twenty minutes I was anxious to leave to talk to some patients, and as I turned away he said, 'You know why I'm here, don't you?' 'Mmm, no, I don't think I do.' 'The Prime Minister is trying to kill me,' he said, and only then did I realise that the doctor was a patient. Am I not a fly like thee?

It's often said, sometimes by themselves, that directors are like gods, manipulating the destinies of lives. Occasionally, and only very occasionally, they are, but only if they are tyrants. Every director, at heart, wants to be God, or god-like, but however inventive, however imaginative, however inspiring, the creative pulse will always be derived from the people who are on show, whose souls are at stake: the writer and the actor. Directors are the negotiators, the diplomats the translators, the mediators, suspended between the writer's need to impel the play forward, and the actor's desire to stand still and create a character; directors are obliged to interpret the blueprint, not to re-draw it. They are the builders, not the architects.

It used to be said, properly if satirically, of Orson Welles, that there but for the grace of God goes God, but the only thing most good directors have in common with God is the need for their work to be invisible. 'The best directing,' said Billy Wilder, 'is the one you don't see.' This is not an invitation to indolence, for the director to step back and let the writing, like water, take its own course, but a demand that the production illuminate the play or the film rather than itself.

Many people can only see direction when it draws attention to itself, when it swishes and swaggers like a silk-lined opera cloak, shrouding its owner in awesome mystery, while ostentatiously advertising his presence. Then it's the opposite of good direction: it's covering up instead of illuminating. The craft of directing does not, or should not, depend on tricks of concealment or illusionism, and if it involves any device from the magician's repertoire, it's sleight of hand: making the audience look the other way at the same time as opening their eyes to what is in front of them. It's a paradox: you are exhorting the audience to forget they are in a theatre – to suspend their disbelief – while at the same time making them believe in the truth of what you are showing them. Conjurors have a name for this, in fact it's at the heart of their craft: they call it 'misdirection'.

Most of us have an indecent curiosity about what other people do in private. Sex and money, for instance: 'What do you do in bed?' and 'How much do you earn?' are the questions that underwrite all profile journalism and most biography. My own particular corner of prurience concerns the working habits of directors. I have no more than a moderately healthy interest in what directors do outside the rehearsal room, but I am inordinately fascinated by what they do within it. Directors are not very gregarious creatures, at least among their own kind, and if you were to search for a collective noun for them it would probably be a 'solitude'. When we do gather together, we are wary of discussing each other's work, and warier still of asking how it was achieved.

Rehearsals are a private province; no one likes to be observed, so it's hard to see enough to imitate, even if you have a model to follow. I started directing professionally – at least in the sense of getting paid – at the Phoenix Theatre in Leicester in 1965. While I was acting in *The Boyfriend* I had gathered a group of dissident actors together to do a Sunday-night production of *The Knack* by Ann Jellicoe. After the performance, Clive Perry, who was Director of the theatre, said this to me, 'If you want to be a director, you can become one. I'm not sure you'll ever be an actor. But you must choose.' And I did.

Clive asked me to do a production of the same play for a four-week run a few months later. I don't suppose doing what I do for a living will ever be as exciting, and I don't think I've ever felt quite so intensely the absurd privilege of getting paid for what you enjoy doing. I knew nothing about the process; all was intuitive – ignorance (or innocence) seemed a glorious asset. It couldn't last. Like a child's acting, it may be successful in short bursts, but to sustain it, to repeat it – to become a professional – takes application and technique.

You need to learn and you can only learn by doing it, by watching someone else do it, or by seeing other people's productions and learning by example. I thought I wanted to be an assistant, and the director I most admired was, and is, Peter Brook. I wrote to him (how I found his address I don't know) and he replied, said he didn't know how he could help me, but invited me to come and talk with him. I went to his house in Holland Park, to a large room with a pine floor, some lovely drawings and a grand piano.

We met; he talked; I listened. He spoke with great clarity, with unforced charm and without any sense of talking down to me, although I was thoroughly and obviously ignorant and awestruck. Like all exceptionally intelligent people, he offered me the gift of his intelligence and required me to give my best in return. He spoke of how plays were revealed during rehearsals, not mapped out beforehand by the director, of how rehearsals must be a journey, of how there was no such thing as a definitive production; of magic, of instinct, of showmanship. I asked if I might be his assistant. 'Why?' he said. 'You're a great teacher,' I said. 'You can only learn from yourself,' he said, 'from doing it yourself,' and I learnt the truth of what he was saying some time later.

I worked as an assistant on a production of *A Man for All Seasons* and I was useless. I was commuting, a journey of two hours, from a girlfriend who coupled a phenomenal sexual energy with a taste for prolonged argument, and almost daily during rehearsals I would sink from discontented lassitude into deep sleep. I'd wake to find the whole cast staring at me, indulgently amused, and the director less so, glowering unforgivingly. In my waking moments, I restlessly picked the scab of my unease about a play that seemed to reduce history to anecdote.

It would be hard to find a better model to follow than Peter Brook, but what marks him out is not so much his expertise as a teacher as his doggedness as a pupil; he keeps on asking questions. I have seen most of his work in the succeeding years. I have been occasionally exasperated, often overwhelmed, charmed frequently, repelled occasionally, awed now and again, bored never. His staging has consistently had the flair, brilliance and bravura that could be attention-seeking if it were not so obviously the consequence of trying to find the most expressive way of telling the story. In spite of his supreme command of stage machinery, he wearied early of the 'train set' side of theatre, what he describes as the '*quincaillerie*', the 'ironmongery', of stage production. He can make the terrible isolation of a mad king alone on a brightly lit stage as much of a *coup de théâtre* as a snake of flame on a bare earth floor, twisting out of the dark, pulling a dancer in its wake.

His search for a new theatrical language culminated, in its English phase, with his production of *A Midsummer Night's Dream*. It's magic was a true 'theatre magic', effected by the performer rather than the technician, and it's a paradox to many that Brook's work is always concerned with conferring authority on the performer rather than celebrating the director.

I admire in him what I'd call his spiritual quest. He has often, I think courageously, laid himself open to accusations of naivety at best, pretentiousness at worst. I remember a TV documentary in which a white-robed Brook was seen at the prow of a small boat, crossing an African lake. A gnarled old man advanced towards Brook as he disembarked, arms outstretched, crying, '*Kwabo, kwabo.*' Brook embraced him and replied, '*Kwabo, kwabo.*' Years later I was told that the meaning of the haunting salutation was : 'Buddy, can you spare me a dime?' Years later still I discovered that I'd been misinformed, and I cursed my own gullibility and the disingenuousness of my informant. '*Kwabo*' can indeed, I discovered, mean 'welcome' in certain parts of Nigeria.

I felt like the victims of a Czech translator I knew in Prague in 1969 – she had to teach English to Russian officers. Her Schweykian strategy was this: in every twenty words of vocabulary that she gave the officers to learn she would place one mistranslation. She would grin at the thought of the detonation of her infinitely patiently constructed time-bomb as a Russian officer signing a diplomatic concordat might refer to his fountain-pen as his penis.

Brook has cunningly resisted being perceived as an administrator or an entrepreneur, although he has performed these roles brilliantly. When I was about to be appointed Director of the National, he said to me, 'You don't want to do that. Can't you find someone to do it for you?' Perhaps he'd found the perfect partner in Peter Hall at the RSC. 'Peter was wonderful at the memos,' he said impishly.

Most of all I admire his refusal ever to be satisfied, ever to 'finish' a piece of work. For him theatre must always be alive and therefore always changing. I had lunch with him just after *The Mahabharata* opened in Paris, and he said he'd learned something really useful in putting on the Indian epic. I waited anxiously, fearing a gnomic riddle. 'What have you discovered?' I asked. 'Never to have a press night,' he replied. 'It stops you from going on working.'

The capacity to go on working is something for which all the directors I know envy Peter as much as they envy his talent. Something to do with his well-timed self-exile to Paris, they presume, which seems to have inoculated him against the plagues of self-doubt, the vagaries of fashion, the attrition of parochial sniping, against weariness and careerism. He seems to have managed to exempt himself from the mid-life crisis that affects theatre directors (not always in mid-life), which is something to do with a frustration at not being an '*auteur*', with repetition, constant barter and compromise, and something perhaps to do with an inability to re-invent the medium as he does. He inspires me to think that the theatre is not only important, it's indispensable.

If it was Peter Brook who opened my eyes to the possibilities of the theatre as an art, it was the actor John Neville who

121

made me see the attractions of a life in the theatre. When I was working in Leicester I went to see him play Richard II, and it still remains one of the best Shakespearian performances I've ever seen. John was tall, aquiline, a natural aristocrat with feline grace who disguised well the roaring boy underneath, who had for many years matched Richard Burton part for part and drink for drink at the Old Vic. I wasn't at the Nottingham matinée during which Judi Dench played one of the soldiers, dressed from top to toe in chain-mail, and the whole company, but for John Neville, shuddered hopelessly with contagious frenzy. If I'd been in the audience I'd have demanded my money back, but if I'd been onstage I'd have shamelessly joined in the caper. This was the anarchic side of John's company, the wild, larky, raffish side that, combined with their brio and skill, made for a heady atmosphere – onstage and off. I was drawn to the Playhouse as often as I could manage.

John unwittingly returned the compliment by coming to see my production of *The Knack*. To my surprise, within two days, he wrote to me and offered me a job directing a schools' production of Goldoni's play *La Locandiera*, which was to tour Nottinghamshire under the title *Mirandolina*. I remember little of the production, and it wasn't highly regarded by the schoolchildren of Ollerton, Mansfield, and Retford. The play ended with the (theoretically touching) reconciliation between the Mistress of the Inn, and her Manservant, which was invariably underscored by shouts of 'Go on, fuck 'er' from the youthful audience.

I saw the Berliner Ensemble with John. We spent some weeks casting for his new season in London before doing my schools' production, and I went with him to see *Coriolanus*, *Arturo Ui*, and *The Days of the Commune*. Everything about the productions confounded my expectations of Brecht's work. That it was lucid, robust and intelligent I'd expected, but I was unprepared for the visceral power of the productions, the bravura of Ekkehard Schall's performance as Coriolanus, the wit even, and the sheer beauty of Helene Weigel (Brecht's widow) as Volumnia. The single most expressive gesture I've ever seen on a stage came at the end of the scene where she says goodbye to her son, off to battle, certain that it is the last time she will see him. As Ekkehard Schall turned to go she raised her right arm in a military gesture, initially like a Nazi salute, then, as he left the stage, loosening with a faint, and infinitely touching, bending of the finger-tips; the iron woman became a mother, grieving for the loss of her child. After the performance John took me to meet Weigel and Schall. She was regal and detached, he was genial and, his hands covered in removing cream, he extended his elbow for me to shake. Ionesco used to say that Brecht's theatre was *un théâtre de* boy-scout'; I can't imagine anything refuting this more effectively than those productions that I saw in 1966.

If I had believed in portents and omens, my first sight of Nottingham Playhouse would have been depressing indeed. In the early sixties I visited Sheffield, as an improbable candidate for attachment to a steel company as a fledgling chemical engineer. I stayed with some friends of friends, and apart from seeing molten steel pour from the lip of a Bessemer converter, and a visit to an umbrella factory where the all-female workforce teased us with sexual banter that remains unrivalled in my experience, I remember nothing else apart from a mild flirtation with my hosts' daughter in the back of a cinema. It was the trip to Nottingham that sticks in my mind.

I had expressed a keen interest in theatre, albeit that at that time I had rarely attended a performance outside the realm of pantomime. So we visited Nottingham Playhouse. At the edge of Wellington Circus (a name that I still find exciting – redolent of clowns, elephants, sawdust and the military) there was a large crater, the kind of hole that looked as though it might have been created by the bomb that breached the Moehne Dam. Concrete was being poured into holes which sprouted rusty iron feelers. We watched the laying of the foundations for perhaps twenty minutes, and then, bored and dispirited, we drifted away.

When I returned to Nottingham Playhouse in 1965, the theatre had already opened, lost two of its trio of artistic directors – Peter Ustinov and Frank Dunlop – but retained John Neville, and established a national reputation. In those days we were mercifully free of those sanctimonious terms like 'regional' and 'community' which always succeed in making you feel diminished wherever you come from. The theatrical megaliths of today – the National Theatre and the Royal Shakespeare Company – weren't the size of a Third World Country, government hadn't been so remorselessly centralised, Mrs Thatcher hadn't become the High Priestess of Opportunism, and a theatre in Nottingham or Glasgow or Birmingham or Bristol had every chance of being (at least temporarily) the national focus of good theatre.

John was sufficiently encouraged by the schools' production to ask me to be Assistant Director on a tour of *As You Like It* and *A Man For All Seasons* which was destined for Sierra Leone, Ghana and Nigeria on behalf of the British Council. The Biafran War put paid to that plan, and we were transferred to South-East Asia, touring Malaysia, Borneo, Singapore, and the Philippines. I fell in love in Singapore with an Indian girl from Penang, deserted her; I fell in love with the East, with travelling, even with falling in love itself, and after the tour was over returned from Manila the slow way – via Hong Kong, Cambodia, Vietnam, Thailand, India, Egypt and Greece. It was, as they say, the time of my life, and for years acted as a kind of template against which all my other experiences were set. If I began to grow up after university, it was during the months that I spent travelling by myself. My father hadn't been so wrong after all.

I had a return ticket from Manila to London that could be routed more or less anywhere as long as I headed west. I used to decide my destination the day before I travelled, obtain a visa if necessary, and, like a nineteenth-century explorer, set off into what was, for me, uncharted territory marked by dawns and sunsets that have been inscribed on my memory like an illuminated text. Like the indelibly sentimental Anne Shelton song that became an anthem to all National Servicemen, I saw the pyramids along the Nile, the sunset on a desert isle, the jungle in the falling rain, and the ocean from a silver plane.

I saw Hong Kong first in fragments from the Kowloon Ferry; pampered by a thin grey dawn mist, it revealed itself flirtatiously, tall buildings prodding the clouds, little houses piled like silt on the hillsides. It struck me then that it was a monument to a single human activity: trade. Trade rules the city in all its aspects at all levels, and if an extraterrestrial were to take a look at this feverish anthill of activity, he would not be able to decide if man made money to live, or lived to make money.

I walked the streets, took trams, explored the island and marvelled at how – and why – so many people were packed into such a small space. The city clattered and shrieked, and the only way to escape the incessant din was to take the cable railway to the top of the Peak, where it was silent but for the rattle of crickets, and the steamy, sweat-ridden battle for survival receded to a picturesque panorama. The other side of the island, facing the Pacific Ocean, was barely populated; the ants were all drawn away by the jam of money-making spread along the harbour's edge.

Mainland China was at that time impenetrable: vast, mysterious, awesome and forbidding. I took a train through the New Territories to the border, and with a handful of other tourists, gazed with a kind of prurient curiosity at the 'enemy' beyond – small figures scratching at the ground with hoes, innocent of any intent greater than making a sparse living from the soil.

As if to remind us of the titanic and preposterous clash of ideologies, the American Pacific Fleet was in the harbour, a huge grey aircraft carrier, large as a small island, a cruiser basking at its side like a crocodile, and hordes of baby alligators – destroyers, corvettes, minesweepers and supply vessels. At night the US Navy went ashore and I watched the Snowdrops – naval police, named more for their white tin helmets than their charm – deal with some recalcitrant drunk sailors and an incipient riot by striking the heads of the participants with long truncheons as if they were brass gongs. The rest of South-East Asia, with the exception of Vietnam, had yet to be educated in the advantages of being protected by the United States – and nowhere more poignantly and painfully than Cambodia.

From Hong Kong I travelled to Angkor, the city of temples in the jungle in the North of Cambodia, and arrived there, by bus from Phnom Penh, near to sunset. I walked a short distance from the hotel, a dilapidated relic of French colonial rule, and watched the sun set behind the vast temple of Angkor Wat, the dark stone spire rising up against a great red gash bleeding between two thick clouds. The surrounding country was, on the one side, a solid mass of dark-green jungle, and on the other open plainland pocked with a sprinkling of shrubby trees. The huge stones of the temple still breathed the day's heat; the bats cut through the air with a wild swoosh, and the insects twanged like wires, a crescendo as the evening closed in. The gash of sun shrank to a small pink stain tinged with orange like a pomegranate. It became dark, the moon shone, I walked into the temple, and I met my ghost; in this country I felt at peace.

The writer Ian McEwan lives in Oxford; he came to see me with his small son when I was staying about thirty miles away in Gloucestershire, near Cirencester, which to his two-year-old son seemed a continental distance. They stayed until evening and as they left we stopped to look at the moon; it was full, a harvest moon. 'In my country,' said the little boy, 'the moon is small and white. Here it's big and yellow.'

In Vietnam I discovered that a far-away country of which I knew nothing had been invaded by the largest power on earth. The American presence sat like Goya's colossus of

Chaos on the beguiling and still graceful city of Saigon. When I returned to London – this was in 1966 – I could not persuade friends of mine of the scope of the outrage of the American occupation. I was a premature anti-war protester; within two years the same people were massed with thousands of others outside the American Embassy in Grosvenor Square.

During the months that I was away from London I never became able to conceal the face of the tourist behind the mask of the 'traveller', so carefully cultivated on journeys manufactured in quest of publishers' royalties. In India I saw poverty I could not have imagined, still less learned to be indifferent to: bodies dumped like refuse on the pavements, lucky if they had space to sleep, wealthy if they possessed a bed roll to sleep on, grubbing for fragments of food in piles of rubbish or mounds of shit, sustained perhaps only by the knowledge that there were others still worse off than them. I didn't learn how to harden my heart to beggars, particularly when they thrust a child towards me, crippled or blinded by their own hands. Oh brave old world that had such people in it.

I was no more prepared for the astonishing beauty of India in the landscapes of the Rajahstan, the delicacy of the Mogul architecture of Jaipur and Old Delhi and Agra, the black-and-white marble, filigree screens, gold-leaf inscriptions, cerulean blue tiles, and red sandstone that turned from deep terracotta to orange to water-melon pink as the nights came down like a hazy veil. In the Red Fort in Delhi there is a corridor of rooms clad in marble veined like a ripe white plum with a narrow channel of water running down the middle, and an inscription at the end:

If there be a paradise on the face of the earth,
It is here,
It is here,
It is here.

After India I was sated with travel, with history, and with my own company, and although I was grateful to visit the

Pyramids, the Valley of the Kings and the Cairo Museum, the only truly enjoyable thing that I did in Egypt was to hire a rowing boat and spend an afternoon idling past dhows sailing down the Nile as they had for several thousand years.

For most of the time I travelled with only three books: *The Idiot*, Angus Calder's *The People's War* and *The Virginian* by Owen Wister, a classic tale of the Old West. The three of them made a quaint mixture; in Dostoevsky I discovered the kind of spiritual solace that I suppose others might find in a Gideon Bible; in Angus Calder's book I discovered a way of looking at my own country that changed my thinking as much as any book I've read. In his introduction Calder said this:

> After 1945, it was for a long time fashionable to talk as if something like a revolution had occurred. But at this distance, we can see clearly enough that the effect of the war was not to sweep society on to a new course, but to hasten its progress along an old one.

I had discovered a book which could, to paraphrase Auden, teach the unhappy Present to recite the Past; I'm still unable to read it without feeling both nostalgia and pain for the unfulfilled promise of the world I was born into.

After Egypt I stopped in Greece where I would have remained if I hadn't felt the need to return home to get a job, and the compulsion to make something of my life. Owen Wister's Virginian supplied a laconic epitaph to my travels:

> 'You've done some moving.'
> 'I have had a look at the country.'

I worked sporadically for Nottingham Playhouse on my return, and it was than that I was offered an Arts Council Directors' bursary and was attached to the Phoenix Theatre, as assistant to Clive Perry. I returned to Leicester to live in digs with a Polish landlady who waged an incessant war of vituperation against the 'foreigners' in her street – Asian families who had lived there almost as long as she and had a far more complete grasp of the English language than she did. I lived a cosmopolitan life – arguing in pidgin English with the landlady, eating Indian food, taking my washing to the Chinese laundry, where a hatch opened, a hand emerged, took the clothes, tore a fragment of paper, scribbled an ideogram on it, thrust it back, and with an incomprehensible grunt, closed the hatch.

In Clive Perry I had found a patron; he was a short, shy man, who hid his feelings behind a closely preserved cladding of diffidence and sometimes spiky defensiveness which concealed an essentially kindly, if solitary, soul. His generosity to me was unstinting, and his support unfailing; without his faith in me I would never have become a director. I have often been asked how I became a director, to which I reply: nepotism, or bribery, or hard work, but the truth is this: I was lucky to have Clive as my patron.

If everybody needs a patron, they also need someone to model themselves on, a father if you're fortunate, or a father-figure. He may be a teacher, a prophet, a boss, a priest, perhaps, a political leader, or a friend. If you can't find a father you must invent him. No one could call Peter Brook a father-figure; he's too active, engaged, present, comradely, essentially too young. In some ways, not altogether trivial, my father-figure is a writer who I admire more than any twentieth-century English writer before the sixties – he's Chekhov with an English accent, he's the first modern British director, he's the real founder of the National Theatre, and, in his *Prefaces*, he's a man who, alone amongst Shakespearian commentators before Jan Kott, believed in the power of Shakespeare on stage: Harley Granville-Barker.

The history of the theatre in England in this century can be told largely through the life and work of Harley Granville-Barker and George Bernard Shaw, a triple-barrelled cadence of names that resonates like the ruffling of the pages of a large book in a silent public library. One was a brilliant polemicist who dealt with certainties and assertions and sometimes, but not often enough, breathed life into his sermons; the other a committed sceptic who started from the premise that the only thing certain about human behaviour was that nothing was certain. Both, however, possessed a passionate certainty about the importance of the theatre and the need to revise its form, its content, and the way that it was managed. Shaw was a playwright, critic and pamphleteer, Barker a playwright, director and actor.

The Voysey Inheritance is Granville-Barker's best play: a complex web of family relationships, a fervent, but never unambiguous indictment of a world dominated by the mutually dependent obsessions of greed, class, and self-deception. It's also a virtuoso display of stagecraft: the writer showing that as director he can handle twelve speaking characters on stage at one time, and that as actor he can deal with the most ambitious and unexpected modulations of thought and feeling. The 'inheritance' of the Voyseys is a legacy of debt, bad faith, and bitter family dissension. Edward's father has, shortly before his death, revealed that he has been cheating the family firm of solicitors for many years, as his father had for many years before that. Towards the end of the play Edward Voysey, the youngest son, confronts the woman he loves:

EDWARD: Why wouldn't he own the truth to me about himself?
BEATRICE: Perhaps he took care not to know it. Would you have understood?
EDWARD: Perhaps not. But I loved him.
BEATRICE: That would silence a bench of judges.

Shaw would have used the story not to moralise and polemicise. He might have had the son hate the father; he might have had him forgive him; he might have had him indict him as a paradigm of capitalism; he would never have said he loved him.

There was a myth that Granville-Barker was the natural

son of Shaw. He was certainly someone who Shaw could, in his awkward way, cherish and admire, educate and castigate. When Barker fell wildly in love ('in the Italian manner', as Shaw said) with Helen Huntington, an American millionairess, he married her, acquired a hyphen in his surname, moved first to Devon to play the part of a country squire, and then to France to a life of seclusion. Shaw thought that he had buried himself alive and could never reconcile himself to the loss. It was, as his biographer Hesketh Pearson said, 'the only important matter about which he asked me to be reticent'.

After directing many of Shaw's plays for many years, acting many of his best roles (created with him in mind), dreaming and planning together the birth of a National Theatre, not to mention writing, directing, and acting in his own plays while managing his own company at the Royal Court, Barker withdrew from the theatre, and for twenty years there was silence between the two men. Only on the occasion of the death of Shaw's wife did they communicate by letter. 'I did not know I could be so moved by anything,' wrote Shaw to him.

Out of this self-exile came one major work, slowly assembled over many years: *The Prefaces to Shakespeare*. With a few exceptions (Auden on *Othello*, Barbara Everett on *Hamlet*, Jan Kott on *The Tempest*) it's the only critical work about Shakespeare that's made any impact on me, apart, that is, from my father whose view of Shakespeare was brief and brutal: 'It's absolute balls.'

As much as we need a good father, we need a good teacher. Mine, improbably perhaps, was Kingsley Amis. The depth of my ignorance of English literature corresponded almost exactly to his dislike of the theatre. Nevertheless, he made me see Shakespeare with a mind uncontaminated by the views of academics, who he would never have described as his fellows and whose views he regarded as, well, academic. I would write essays marinated in the opinions of Spurgeon, Wilson Knight, Dover Wilson and a large cast of critical supernumeraries. He would gently, but courteously, cast aside my essay about, say, *Twelfth Night*: 'But what do *you* think of this play? Do you think it's any good?' 'Well . . . er . . . it's Shakespeare.' 'Yes, but is it any *good*? I mean as a *play*. It says it's a comedy. Fine. But does it have any decent jokes?'

I took this for irreverence, heresy even. Over the years, however, I've come to regard this as good teaching, or, closely allied, good direction. It's asking the right questions, unintimidated by reputation, by tradition, by received opinion, or by critical orthodoxy. This was shocking, but healthy, for a young and impressionable man ripe to become a fundamentalist in matters of literary taste. What you have is yourself and the text, only that. That's the lesson of Granville-Barker: 'We have the text to guide us, half a dozen stage directions, and that is all. I abide by the text and the demands of the text and beyond that I claim freedom.' I can't imagine a more useful and more enduring dictum.

The Prefaces have a practical aim: 'I want to see Shakespeare made fully effective on the English stage. That is the best sort of help I can lend.' What Granville-Barker wrote is a primer for directors and actors working on the plays of Shakespeare. There is lamentably little useful literature about the making of theatre, even though there is an indigestible glut of memoirs and biographies, largely concerned with events that have taken place *after* the curtain has fallen. If I was asked by a visiting Martian to recommend books that would help him, her or it to make theatre in the manner of the European I could only offer four books: Stanislavski's *The Art of the Stage*, John Willet's *Brecht on Brecht*, Peter Brook's *The Empty Space*, and *The Prefaces to Shakespeare*.

Stanislavski offers a pseudo-scientific dissection of the art of acting which is, in some respects, like reading Freud on the mechanism of the joke: earnest, well-meaning, but devoid of the indispensable ingredient of its subject matter: humour. Stanislavski's great contribution was to demand that actors hold the mirror up to nature, that they take their craft as seriously as the writers whom they serve, and provide some sort of formal discipline within which both aims can be realised.

Brecht provided a manifesto that was a political and aesthetic response to the baroque encrustations of the scenery-laden, star-dominated, archaic boulevard theatre of Germany in the twenties. Although much of what he wrote as theory is an unpalatable mix of political ideology and artistic instruction, it is his theatrical instinct that prevails. He asserts, he insists, he browbeats. He demands that the stage, like society, must be re-examined, reformed, that the audience's habits mustn't be satisfied, they must be changed, but just when he is about to nail his 13 Articles to the church door he drops the voice of the zealot: 'The stage is not a hothouse or a zoological museum full of stuffed animals. It must be peopled with live, three-dimensional, self-contradictory people with their passions, unconsidered utterances and actions.' In all art forms, he says, the guardians of orthodoxy will assert that there are eternal and immutable laws that you ignore at your peril, but in the theatre there is only one inflexible rule: 'The proof of the pudding is in the eating.' Brecht teaches us to ask the question: what goes on in a theatre?

Brook takes the question even further: what is theatre? It's a philosophical, but eminently practical, question that Brook has been asking for over thirty years and which has taken him to the African desert, a quarry in Iran, and an abandoned music hall in Paris.

> I take an empty space and call it a bare stage. A man walks across this empty space while someone else is watching him, and that is all that is needed for an act of theatre to be engaged.

For all his apparent concern with metaphysics, there is no more practical man of the theatre than Brook. Like Brecht, like Stanislavski, like Granville-Barker, Brook argues that for the theatre to be expressive it must be, above all, simple and unaffected: a distillation of language, of gesture, of action, of design, where meaning is the essence. The meaning must be felt as much as understood. 'They don't have to understand with their ears,' says Granville-Barker, 'just with their guts.'

Brecht didn't acknowledge a debt to Granville-Barker. Perhaps he wasn't aware of one, but it seems to me that Barker's Shakespeare productions were the direct antecedents of his work. Brecht certainly knew enough about English theatre to know that he was on to a good thing adapting *The Beggar's Opera*, *The Recruiting Officer* and *Coriolanus*. Brecht has been lauded for destroying illusionism, Granville-Barker has been unhymned. He aimed at re-establishing the relationship between actor and audience that had existed in Shakespeare's theatre – and this at a time when the prevailing style of Shakespearian production involved *not* stopping short of having live sheep in *As You Like It*. He abolished footlights and the proscenium arch, building out an apron over the orchestra pit which Shaw said 'apparently trebled the spaciousness of the stage . . . To the imagination it looks as if he had invented a new heaven and a new earth.'

His response to staging Shakespeare was not to look for a synthetic Elizabethanism. 'We shall not save our souls by being Elizabethan.' To recreate The Globe would, he knew, be aesthetic anaesthesia, involving the audience in an insincere conspiracy to pretend that they were willing collaborators in a vain effort to turn the clock back. His answers to staging Shakespeare were similar to Brecht's for *his* plays and, in some senses, to Chekhov's for his. He wanted scenery not to decorate and be literal, but to be expressive and metaphorical, and at the same time, in apparent contradiction, to be specific and real, while being minimal and iconographic: the cart in *Mother Courage*, the nursery in *The Cherry Orchard*, the dining table in *The Voysey Inheritance*.

> To create a new hieroglyphic language of scenery. That, in a phrase, is the problem. If the designer finds himself competing with the actors, the sole interpreters Shakespeare has licensed, then it is he that is the intruder and must retire.

In *The Prefaces* Granville-Barker argues for a fluency of

staging unbroken by scene changes. Likewise the verse should be spoken fast. 'Character in action, not sound like the voice beautiful from the lectern . . .' Be swift, be swift, be not poetical, he wrote on the dressing-room mirror of Cathleen Nesbit when she played Perdita. Within the speed, however, detailed reality: *meaning* above all.

It is the director's task, with the actors, to illuminate the meanings of a play; its vocabulary, its syntax, and its philosophy. The director has to ask what each scene is revealing about the characters and their actions: what story is each scene telling us? In *The Prefaces* Granville-Barker exhumes, examines and explains the lost stagecraft of Shakespeare line by line, scene by scene, play by play.

Directing Shakespeare is a matter of understanding the meaning of a scene and staging it in the light of that knowledge. Easier said than done, but it's at the heart of the business of directing *any* play, and directing Shakespeare is merely directing writ large. Beyond that, as David Mamet has observed, 'choice of actions and adverbs constitutes the craft of directing.' Get up from that chair and walk across the room. Slowly. Add to this the nouns 'detail' and 'patience', and the maxim, 'Always remember tomorrow is not the first night', and you have said more or less all that can be said of the craft of directing.

Of course all this has to be underwritten by a clear view of the territory that's being described in order to be able to fashion the map: *what* the play is trying to say, and *why*. It's impossible for a director to stage a play without revealing something of his politics. Even the most innocent of drawing-room comedies reflects a view of the world that a director can endorse or criticise in a number of subtle or indiscreet ways. By making choices about design, costume, and performances it is impossible not to be taking a view about how people live, how they behave, how they are influenced by what they earn, where they were born and what they believe in. To affect a lack of interest for these matters is no less a political position than that of the Queen, who claims to be 'above politics'. Alan Parker said of Ken

Loach, whose films, however artful, always have a sense of life being artlessly observed, 'I ask how he gets such reality, such honesty. Ken always says, "It's nothing to do with the *how*, it's to do with the *why*." '

With Shakespeare as with any other playwright the director's job is to make the play live, now, in the present tense. 'Spontaneous enjoyment is the life of the theatre,' says Granville-Barker in his Preface to *Love's Labour's Lost*. To receive a review, as Granville-Barker did, headed 'SHAKESPEARE ALIVE!' is the most, but should be the least, that a director must hope for.

I regard Granville-Barker as not only the first modern English director but as the most influential. Curiously, partly as a result of his early withdrawal from the theatre, partly because his *Prefaces* have been out of print for many years, and partly because of his own self-effacement, he has been unjustly ignored both in the theatre and in the academic world, where the codification of their 'systems' has resulted in the canonisation of Brecht and Stanislavski.

My sense of filial identification is not entirely a professional one. When I directed *The Voysey Inheritance* at the National Theatre I wanted a photograph of the author on the poster. A number of people protested that it was the height, or depth, of vanity and self-aggrandisement to put my own photograph on the poster. I was astonished, I was bewildered, but I wasn't unflattered. I still can't see the resemblance and it's not through lack of trying.

Three years ago the National Theatre was presented with a wonderful bronze bust of Granville-Barker by Katherine Scott (the wife, incidentally, of the Antarctic hero). For a while it sat on the windowsill of my office like a benign household god. Then it was installed on a bracket in the foyer opposite a bust of Olivier, the two men eyeing each other in wary regard. A few months later it was stolen; perhaps it was an act of homage.

I began to learn something of how to direct by going to the

theatre regularly but discriminately. I'd not had much of a head start, the only 'serious' theatre I'd seen until I was eighteen was the *Hamlet* of Peter O'Toole at the Bristol Old Vic, and *Much Ado About Nothing* at Stratford with a school party which sat listlessly unengaged by the production. O'Toole was in his unreconstructed state – dark-haired, wild, violent, mercurial and thrilling – before stardom and Lawrence of Arabia turned him blond, small-nosed and epicene.

Theatrical energy and invention seem to coincide with periods of economic expansion: the Elizabethan and Jacobean ages, the Restoration, the late-eighteenth century, the late-nineteenth century, the mid-fifties, sixties and seventies in this century. Between 1961, when I started going to the theatre in earnest, and 1965 when I became part of it, I was able to see the work of Joan Littlewood at Stratford East, the Royal Court in its most fertile years, the newly formed RSC under Peter Hall, and the newly formed National Theatre at the Old Vic under Laurence Olivier. *Oh What a Lovely War, The Wars of the Roses*, Brook's *Lear*, Olivier's *Othello*; the young Maggie Smith, the young Albert Finney, the young Vanessa Redgrave; the plays of Arnold Wesker, of Harold Pinter, John Osborne, Peter Shaffer, Peter Nichols, Edward Bond, David Storey, Charles Wood, Tom Stoppard; Scofield, Richardson, Gielgud, Guinness, Peggy Ashcroft, even Edith Evans, and Kenneth Tynan presiding over this activity as a mandarin and godfather. To a young man who had only ever been to the Alexandra Gardens or the Pavilion Theatre in Weymouth to see Morecambe and Wise or Jewel and Warriss, or to the Victoria Palace to see the Crazy Gang, this was heady stuff. It seemed to me that anything and everything was possible.

If you took the theatre seriously in the early-sixties you had a choice of four companies to which you might pledge your loyalty – The National Theatre at the Old Vic, the Royal Shakespeare Company at Stratford and the Aldwych, the Royal Court, and the Theatre Royal at Stratford East. My head was with the Royal Court, but my heart was unequivocally with Joan Littlewood's company at Stratford East, and remains there to this day. She managed, at least for a while, to run a company which combined high ideals, no pretensions, artistic integrity, political sincerity, and commercial success. Her troupe of actors brought together a chaotic patchwork of styles, making a seamless unity without diminishing their individual colours. Her work was witty, skilful, vulgar, populist but not patronising, and the most indelibly memorable production I saw there – *Oh What a Lovely War* – is still the only show I have ever seen that has successfully yoked together the traditions of popular entertainment – music hall – with the aims of propaganda. This was political theatre that, unlike most of the genre, neither patronised its audience, nor did it try to reprimand or reform them. It sought to inform and to entertain, and it broke your heart in the process. It's one of the very few things I've seen in the theatre that I'd call 'great'.

Joan Littlewood hasn't worked in Britain for twenty-five years, and it's been our loss; I don't know if she's missed it. Time hasn't diminished her resentment of the theatrical establishment in any form. When I asked for the rights to present *Oh What a Lovely War* at the National Theatre (a show which I've directed in Leicester, Edinburgh and Nottingham) her refusal was as firm as an ayatollah's fatwah. I sent her a card on her eightieth birthday. I got a postcard back. It read:

> Thank you for your card, Richard. I really don't know what you're up to. Whatever it is, you'd do better to bomb that building. I had to put up with an old slum in London. Yours need never have been. JL.

Toscanini said that when people spoke of 'great' performances they were talking of 'some fool's memory of the last bad performance.' What he meant, and expressed so biliously, is that it is hard to challenge the orthodoxy of 'great' performances. It's true that some critics have a gift for describing a performance, but however vivid their powers of description they are doomed to the status of obituarists:

we don't have the originals to test against our own experience and our own taste.

Those who work in the theatre, at least most actors, don't have much interest in memorabilia or in history. They are not particularly intrigued by how the great X or Y, or even Z, played a particular part. They glory in the fact that their performance exists only in the present tense and in the future, and denies the past. The past is for the critics and the archivists. No one works in the theatre for posterity; it's ephemeral: when it's there it's there, when it's gone it's gone. That is the joy of the medium. That is its allure, its mystery.

It's hard to subscribe to the authorised version of the 'great' performances. Either we haven't seen them or we choose to dissent. I have much admired Laurence Olivier in performances on film from *Wuthering Heights* to *Term of Trial*, and in the theatre from *Dance of Death* to *The Party*, but no critical catechism will make me accept that his Othello was anything more than mildly risible. And in spite of the overwhelming evidence of countless critics' polls I am unconvinced that *Citizen Kane* is the greatest film ever made. Like the 'great' performances beloved of critical orthodoxy it draws attention in every frame, however brilliant, precisely to its own brilliance. The machinery, as in a hi-tech building, is there to be marvelled at, and the heart is left unengaged.

The worlds of pop music, broadcasting, football, the cinema, politics, and love, all have lost domains occupied by the memories of great past performances, which are sought out for solace or to shame the shabbiness of the present – 'When Churchill was Prime Minister' . . . 'When we were in the World Cup Final' . . . 'When we were first married' . . . David Hare calls the curators of these golden worlds the 'whenwes.' They guard their territory with a dogged devotion. The theatre isn't immune from this virus – 'The National Theatre under Laurence Olivier' . . . 'The Royal Court under George Devine' and 'Joan Littlewood at Stratford East' are particularly robust strains. In the case of

Joan Littlewood there was a 'genius' (in the religious and secular sense), an innocent virtue, that can never, and will never, be replicated in any form. There has been as good work recently at the National Theatre and the Royal Court as in any preceding generation, but this doesn't diminish the power of the elegiac rhapsodies which celebrate the Royal Court arcadia – known by its most infected adherents simply, monarchically, and without irony, as the 'Court'. For all its espousal of working-class playwrights, its animosity to 'university' theatre, its alienation from the values of the West End, and my unreserved admiration of it, during the sixties it seemed to me as remote, as exclusive, and as inaccessible as – well, a royal court.

I saw most of the productions at the Royal Court during the sixties and I was drawn to the humanism, as much as the rigour and the asceticism of the work, even if it did sometimes dip into sanctimoniousness. The thing I learned above all was that what you left off the stage was as important as what you put on it, and that being 'theatrical' could have as much to do with austerity as excess. The productions of Bill Gaskill, Lindsay Anderson, and Peter Gill, and the designs of Jocelyn Herbert embodied this aesthetic. 'A theatre stage should have the maximum of verbal presence and the maximum of corporal presence,' said Samuel Beckett to Gaskill, and there seemed to me no better theatrical maxim than that. It was an approach that demanded that the text came first, and that the director and designer served it with clarity, lucidity, realism, and grace. Lindsay Anderson cited the Periclean ideal as the model for the Royal Court aesthetic: 'We pursue beauty without extravagance and knowledge without effeminacy,' which made it all sound to me rather too much like Sparta than Sloane Square, and it exacerbated the comic contrast of the meticulous observations of working-class life on stage with the furs of the audience and the chauffeur-driven cars parked, when the theatre had a real hit, two-abreast outside the foyer.

The golden age of the Royal Court invoked by today's

'whenwes' is the era of the early years of the English Stage Company, the company started in 1955 by George Devine and Tony Richardson, although the theatre enjoyed at least as luminous a period from 1904 to 1907 when Granville-Barker was its Artistic Director. The Royal Court is the ideal size for a playhouse; it seats about 400 people (200 less than in Granville-Barker's day), it has perfect acoustics (if one can ignore the occasional rumble of the Circle Line), its stage has humane proportions, and it's perfectly placed between the (now) ersatz Bohemianism of Chelsea, and the wealthy austerity of Belgravia. It had a long pedigree as a theatre which had played host to refugees from the West End, struggling to make a bridge between art and show-business. Granville-Barker had a policy of presenting exclus-ively new plays, amongst which where his own and Shaw's. Of the thirty-two plays that he presented over a period of three years – including premières of Galsworthy, Ibsen and Maeterlinck, eleven were new plays by Shaw. In addition to running the theatre and writing plays, Granville-Barker directed and acted in many, if not most, of them, and if I could say I shared anything with George Devine it would be that he, too, appeared to have found a spiritual father in Granville-Barker, whose determination to make the thea-tre an art to be respected, rather than a respectable art, mirrored the evangelical purpose that drove George Devine.

It was serendipity that brought Tony Richardson and George Devine together, just as it brought them eventually to rent the Royal Court Theatre. They met when Tony Richardson was directing at the BBC, an organisation that he regarded, characteristically enough, as an out-front-and-proud-of-it bastion of mediocrity. Devine was an actor/direc-tor who had run the Old Vic School with Michel Saint-Denis and Glen Byam Shaw. They trained actors along French and Russian models, serious above all about taking the theatre seriously. For a while they ran the Old Vic, and for a while seemed, plausibly enough, to be the triumvirate that would run the National Theatre when it was founded. They were fired by the capricious Tyrone Guthrie; Glen Byam Shaw went to Stratford and George Devine returned to acting.

When they talked about forming a theatre company neither the young Tony Richardson, nor the much older Devine, knew what they wanted: 'A new theatre – he didn't know what. I wanted a new theatre too, and I didn't know how.' If the ambitious young Oxford graduate didn't know how to go about it, then the older actor did, and together, for a few years, they made a happy marriage – the young adventurer with the (not-so-old) visionary, the impatient entrepreneur with the fastidious craftsman. George Devine came to be known by succeeding generations as a 'secular saint', not a bad description for a man who said, 'The theatre is really a religion or a way of life,' even if, as Richardson said, 'He always had the cement and truck dust on his hands – that's why the hod-carriers would follow him to the top of the scaffolding.'

All theatre has a tendency to decline to the condition of trivia – ephemeral, impermanent, frivolous. Every now and then someone comes along and shakes up that notion – Shakespeare, Jonson, and Molière in the seventeenth century; Goethe, Schiller and the Duke of Meiningen in the nineteenth century; Stanislavski, and Namivorich-Danchenko, Meyerhold, Brecht, Shaw and Granville-Barker in the early-twentieth; in the late-fifties and early-sixties, Joan Littlewood, George Devine, and, in recent years, Peter Brook in Stratford and in Paris. All of them demonstrated, implicitly or explicitly, the notion that the theatre is an art, a forum, a faith, something to be fought for. At the Royal Court George Devine engendered a system of values that gave the theatre of his time a goal: to be 'about something', to be ambitious for the work before the career, and to be unsanctimoniously unembarrassed about being serious – in short, he taught self-respect.

If it can plausibly be said that modern British theatre started with the production of *Look Back in Anger* in 1956, then it's an extraordinary comment on the state of the theatre (and of British society) at the time. The play that effected this seismic breakthrough, that defined the English State Company for ever, was a play that now seems, for all its abrasive, excoriating, maudlin, self-pitying, iconoclastic rhetoric, to belong more to the world of Noël Coward than to Edward Bond, and far from looking back in anger, looks back with a fierce, despairing, nostalgia. Is there a more solipsistic cry from the post-war years, when the world has become better informed than ever about mass starvation, tyranny, injustice, plague and poverty, than that of Jimmy Porter: 'There aren't any good, brave causes left'?

In the fifties, until the birth of the English Stage Company, the British theatre was, as Arthur Miller has said, 'hermetically sealed-off from life' – and from the American theatre. When *Look Back in Anger* was produced Miller had written *Death of a Salesman, The Crucible, A View From the Bridge* and *All My Sons*, Tennessee Williams *The Glass Menagerie, A Streetcar Named Desire, Camino Real* and *The Rose Tattoo*. On the London stages there were intermittently fine productions, 'revivals', of classics at the Old Vic, and under the not always benign supervision of 'Binkie' Beaumont, many glittering West End First Nights. While the newly formed Arts Council had started to make an impact outside London in building up a network of flourishing repertory theatres, some of which had begun to present work percolated by real life, in London the insulation from contemporary realities was almost complete.

The fatuous inhibiting presence of censorship in the shape of the Lord Chamberlain merely reinforced the notion to a generation now used to drama on television that the theatre was an archaic, redundant and class-bound form of entertainment. I directed one play, John McGrath's *Events While Guarding the Bofors Gun*, which had to be submitted to the Lord Chamberlain. I received a letter from him which read something like this:

The following words are to be eliminated from the text:

fuck

143

bugger
prick
bugger
bloody
go for a piss
bloody bastard
the late King George VI . . .

And so on. You knew where you were then.

Censorship now takes a rather more devious route. A few years ago I made a film for Channel 4 of Tony Harrison's poem 'v.' The film was heralded, sight unseen, by the *Daily Mail* with the headline 'TV FURY OVER FOUR-LETTER POEM'. This did not indicate an unprecedented interest in poetry from an upmarket *Sun*. It was rather an indication that, just as there are always those prepared to do the hangman's job, there are also contenders for the Lord Chamberlain's.

George Devine introduced two canonical sayings to the theatre in Britain on the cusp of the age of subsidy: 'Policy is Who You Work With', and 'The Right to Fail' – the first is endearingly pragmatic, a sort of embodiment of English empiricism, the second is a kind of arrogant, absurd, self-righteous, and necessary principle that must underlie any artistic endeavour. The demand for a 'Right To Fail' is more often a plea for the right not to *have* to succeed, but as a slogan it reveals much of the heart of Devine's character and ethos: ascetic, patrician, stubborn, cocky, and courageous.

The partnership between Richardson and Devine lasted for nearly eight years, which is perhaps as long as any partnership in the theatre can survive. I worked once with Leslie Sarony, a musical-hall performer who had an act with another Leslie, and for thirty years they worked as *The Two Leslies*. I was working with Leslie when his partner died. 'You must be very upset,' I said. 'Upset?' he said. 'Upset? I couldn't stand the cunt.'

The most famous partnership of directors was at the Moscow Art Theatre, that of Stanislavski and Namirovich-Danchenko. Their collaboration ostensibly lasted forty-one years, but only about seven of these years were unmarked by conflict, and for most of thirty or so years they didn't speak to each other. To anyone who has run a theatre much of their story has an eerie familiarity: discussions about 'accessibility', debates about an 'open' theatre, about the composition of the audience: balancing the repertoire, balancing the accounts; art versus the commercial, seriousness against trivia; coaxing plays from authors (in their case Chekhov, Gorky and Bulgakov amongst others) and performances from actors, struggles with sponsors and patrons, pleas to playwrights, the frustrations and exasperations of trying to retain a company, the vortex of egos. As Olga Knipper wrote to Chekhov, 'Dear God, this is a crazy life!'

There are those, Tony Richardson, for one, who felt the life went out of the Court after George Devine's death but I never felt that. The tradition of unmannered acting, devotion to the text, unostentatious direction, simple and expressive design has been maintained until recently. So also, until recently, has the Calvinistic fervour with which the Royal Court has always separated itself from the rest of the theatre. There was a time when it was frowned on to attend productions at the RSC if you worked at the Court, professional suicide not to be seen leaving before the interval, and actual suicide to profess enjoyment of the production. The Royal Court was Arcadia to the RSC's Utopia. I wasn't an active party to either side of the sectarian divide, but I leaned more to the Royal Court in spite of (or because of) its rigorous puritanism than to the collegiate fervour of the RSC. The one seemed to possess an aesthetic, the other a system. You can see why, I thought (as in Auden's 'Horae Canonicae') 'Between my Eden and his New Jerusalem, no treaty is negotiable.'

If I didn't go to the RSC as diligently as the Royal Court in the late-sixties it was not so much that my tastes didn't lead me in that direction, as that I was living four hundred miles away in Edinburgh.

When Clive Perry was asked to become Director of the Royal Lyceum Theatre in Edinburgh, and for six years, interrupted by intermittent productions in London, Edinburgh was where I worked and lived. One of the productions outside Scotland was at Hampstead Theatre Club – my own play *The Ha-Ha*, which was successful enough for me to be courted for a while by carpet-bagging American film producers, looking for cheap English writers.

Another venture outside Edinburgh was a wholly unsuccessful play which ran for ten days in the West End. It was a new play by Ann Jellicoe, called *The Giveaway*, a would-be comic satire on consumerism. Judging by the fact that its stars – Dandy Nichols, Roy Hudd and Rita Tushingham – had been cast before I arrived on the scene, I was one of a long line of directors to whom the play had been offered. When I read the play it became obvious why. Much as I liked Ann Jellicoe, and much as I loved *The Knack*, I did not warm to her new play. I went along to a meeting with the producer, the small, sparrow-like, cocky and patronising Oscar Lewenstein, to say to him, 'Thank you for your offer, but no thanks.' But he pre-empted me by telling me how pleased he was that I was going to do the play, and out of vanity and opportunism I found myself agreeing. At least I salvaged from this one indelible lesson: always work in good faith – if you don't, and it goes wrong, you will be left with nothing but a mouthful of bitterness.

I embarked on a *folie à deux* with Ann Jellicoe, heavily pregnant with her first child. Together we convinced ourselves (in my case with an increasingly self-deluding urgency) that the play and production were working, and armed by the confidence of denial I blundered my way towards the first night, when, certain of the play's failure, the boos of the gallery first-nighters still fresh in my ears, I left the Garrick Theatre stage door carrying a bottle of champagne which, with perfect aptness, slipped from my hands and broke on the pavement. I went to the cast party, drunk and gloomy as sin, and, once again with perfect aptness, was very nearly sick on the shoes of Oscar Lewenstein. 'No blame,' he said to me generously of the whole venture, 'no blame.' It was one of the very few occasions that I remember the critic Harold Hobson writing a review with which I concurred. He wrote, 'This was badly written, badly acted, and badly directed.'

The Royal Lyceum Theatre in Edinburgh was a large, amiable proscenium theatre, with an auditorium of endearingly faded cream-and-gold plaster, shiny dark oak banisters, bars and panels, doors embellished with brass fittings, and thick but threadbare red velvet seating; the stage was equipped with the original machinery – staid but workable, an antique lighting board, and a wonderful physical relationship between the actors and the audience. The proportions seemed right: the slope of the stalls, the rake of the stage, the elevation of the circle, the width and height of the proscenium. The Lyceum is one of many theatres designed in the late-nineteenth century that really work: the actors can be seen and heard, the audience feels comfortable with them, the attention is focused, and everyone shares more or less the same viewpoint of the action. I have never understood why architects, or at least those who design theatres, seem so reluctant to draw on the lessons of the past. A theatre, more than any other building save perhaps a public lavatory, must be defined by its function: it's there in order for a few hundred human beings to sit in the dark and watch and listen to a few other human beings on a lighted platform. Yet almost without exception theatres built in the last thirty or forty years provide bad sightlines, poor acoustics, stage proportions that don't relate to the human figure, and self-advertising architectural features that intrude on the audience's attention, they demonstrate an arrogance that in a theatre professional would be simply laughable.

Prior to Clive Perry's period as Director, the Lyceum Theatre had been the home for an ambitious, but ill-fated enterprise (one of many over the years) to create a Scottish National Theatre. It was led by Tom Fleming, had a large company of talented Scottish actors, and a European repertoire that fiercely avoided any taint of parochialism. The Edinburgh public didn't take to it, and the venture crumbled. Perhaps the theatre-goers weren't ready to accept the change of the Lyceum from a Howard and Wyndham number-one weekly touring date to a theatre whose manifesto determinedly set its sights on demonstrating that the city was indeed the Athens of the North.

We're ready enough to look for any excuse for why people don't come to the theatre – the rain, the cold, the heat, recession, their conservatism, their timidity – and Edinburgh has always been castigated (by Glasgow) for its demure taste. They were certainly slow enough to rally to Clive Perry's new regime, but after a year or two of a programme based on Shakespeare, the classics of the twentieth century, some new Scottish plays, and some judiciously placed squibs, a loyal core audience started to grow. I directed plays by Chekhov, Ibsen, O'Casey, Arthur Miller, Webster, Middleton, Shakespeare, Kleist, Brecht, new plays by Scottish writers, new plays by English writers, and I counted myself extraordinarily lucky.

The Lyceum was managed by a die-hard from the Howard and Wyndham days, a tenacious, anxious, warm-hearted worrier called Charlie Tripp. He could never reconcile himself to plays that could alienate even a small part of an audience; he defended the right of the artist to say anything, as long as it didn't have to be in his theatre. 'The most beautiful word in the English language is compromise, Richard. Why don't you try it?' I must have exasperated him with my arrogant certainties, but I never tired of sitting on his padded fire-surround with a huge gin in my hand ('Just a wee one, Richard') and listening to his tales of the Wilson Barrett company, the Fol de Rols, The Five Past Eight Shows, Flora Robson, Sybil Thorndike, Douglas Byng, Marlene Dietrich ('Marleeny, the most unpleasant woman I've ever met, Richard'), Currie's Magic Waterfalls, the iniquities of the City Council, the improprieties of the councillors, and the weekly returns for the last twenty odd years. Much of his morning was spent studying the racing form, and he was one of the very few gamblers I've known who has made a substantial living from his hobby or obsession.

Edinburgh was a small enough city to be in touch with a theatrical past that was disappearing in other parts of the country. There was still a variety theatre – the Palladium – where Archie Rice would have felt at home, and a healthy crossover between performers nurtured in that world. It was also small enough for the avant-garde – located in the Traverse Theatre which was then situated up a narrow close on the Royal Mile – to rub shoulders with the *ancien régime*. I was fond of Sadie Aitken who used to run the Gateway, an Edinburgh rep theatre, who was a sort of Scottish Lilian Baylis, forthright and outspoken, but ostensibly Morning-side genteel. An actor in her theatre once dried in the middle of a performance, said oh fuck I've dried, mumbled a bit, asked for a prompt, and continued when it came. The next morning he was summoned to Sadie's office and given the sack. 'I suppose it's because I said fuck on stage,' he said. 'No,' replied Sadie, 'It's because you're a fucking bad actor.'

The Traverse provided a meeting place – a bar and restaurant – as well as an opportunity to see a lot of theatre, partly home-grown, partly imported, that was the seed of what later became the 'Fringe' in London. The first show I saw there was a sort of college review called *The Case of the Walking Policeman*. It was memorable for the performance of the Judge by the Director, Max Stafford-Clark, and for my first meeting with the actor Tony Haygarth, who I've worked with many times since; he played a police sergeant and asked me to dance at the policemen's ball in the interval.

Much the same thing happened when I first saw a show of Lindsay Kemp's at the Traverse. It was *Salome*, an early version of a show that became increasingly sophisticated over the years. Lindsay was, onstage and off, outrageously, heroically, majestically camp, and the first time I saw him he was also heroically drunk. A member of the audience audibly objected. Lindsay rounded on him: 'I may be drunk, but I'm a bloody sight more interesting drunk than you'll ever be sober.' Several of us applauded him; I sat on the front row, and he curtsied low like a ballerina and offered me a flower. I worked with him a couple of times; he once performed the entire opening chorus of *Oklahoma* for me, solo, on the Lyceum stage, reliving his days as a dancer in the chorus. He worked and lived with an extraordinary ex-ballet dancer, Jack Birkett, who looked a little like Genet: big-featured like a boxer, and totally bald. He was also totally blind. I've seldom seen a more haunting sight than an almost leglessly drunk Lindsay being led home by Jack late at night down the Royal Mile: the blind literally leading the blind.

This was the era of 'Swinging London', but while London may have believed its own advertising copy, Edinburgh followed its own pace, and the life I led owed more to Fitzroy bohemia than King's Road psychedelia. Not that there was a shortage of sex, drugs, and rock and roll, but there were a lot of congenial pubs available that hadn't been Disneyfied (as in: 'It disnae know whether to be a pub or a wine bar'). I wasn't drinking to obliterate anything, it just became a social habit, perhaps an unconscious mimicry of my father. For a while it became chronic but I pulled back when, one night when I was saturated with whisky, I lurched to the lavatory to be sick and after I had wrung my body like a wet dishcloth, and decorated the lavatory floor with the sort of design chronicled in amply repellent detail by Billy Connolly – a mosaic of tomato skins and Russian salad – I staggered to the sink, washed my face and encountered a stranger in my mirror. The small veins in my face had broken, purpling my nose and cheeks like a birthmark. The doctor diagnosed scurvy.

I pursued sex with the same recklessness and self-destruction, chasing the shadow of my father. Absolute sexual licence seems enviable but, at least for me, in practice it meant being clamped with fear, on the one hand fear of being trapped, and on the other of being free. I can't claim that I was happy then.

I lived in a small flat at the top of a narrow close in a

mews street with eight pubs in a few hundred yards in the centre of the city. It was called Rose Street and is a narrow cleft between the well-padded flanks of George Street – an escarpment that borders the infinitely elegant New Town, and Prince's Street – the smart shopping street that looks out over the castle and the Old Town. I was within two minutes' walk of the subdued elegance of Charlotte Square in one direction, and in the other the National Gallery and a smart grocer's shop that placed passion fruit and pomegranates in its window like jewelled tiaras, and yet in my street, in my close, I could have been in a different city in a different century.

My flat consisted of a hallway the size of a wardrobe, a small but beautifully proportioned sitting room, a bedroom in which you could barely stand under the eaves, a kitchen in which I installed a bath with a cover that served as a work surface, and a lavatory on the landing outside my front door, in which I once discovered a sleeping drunk. I think the previous occupant of the flat had been a prostitute because I'd often be woken in the night by a tapping at the door and open it to find some half-drunk man standing there asking if Marie was in. Getting up the stairs on a Friday and Saturday night was hazardous, stepping round couples having a quick knee-trembler, or being sick, or worse, and on Sunday morning when I went out to get the papers my downstairs neighbour would be shaking her head in weary lamentation over the debris of condoms, fish suppers, bottles, and, occasionally, shit. 'Will you look at that midden,' she'd say. 'It's human, that is, it's nae dog do.' But for all that I liked living there, and walking out in the morning with the smell of Edinburgh which is all its own: of fresh dough, of malt from the brewery, of ozone from the sea, and I missed the Jekyll and Hydeness of Rose Street when I moved to a flat high in a terrace the other side of the city with a view of Arthur's Seat, the Firth of Forth, and on a clear day the Fife Hills. These days Rose Street is a seamless spread of gift shops, clothes boutiques and wine bars.

Edinburgh was also the Festival, which I always mildly resented for the way in which what I regarded as 'my' city would be rudely colonised by thousands of interlopers who clearly felt the same as I did. But it gave me the opportunity to hear a lot of music, and see a lot of foreign theatre that I would otherwise never have seen.

If you are more generous, and more forgiving, when you see a foreign production, it is partly on the principle that 'away' is always more attractive than 'home', partly that you want your guests to be impressed by the quality of their hosts, but also because, barred by your ignorance from the nuance of language, you are recognising character and plot solely by the tone of voice, and the language of the body. You sense by instinct more than reason the truth, the wit, and the talent of an actor. Your eye strays over a stage and rests, like an heat-detecting device, on the actor radiating the 'hot' emotion, and your heart seeks the echo of common humanity.

When you see a foreign company you are seeing a different culture in microcosm: to see Bergman's production of *Miss Julie* is to have an insight into the Swedish character, but then so is to see his production of *Hamlet*. Shakespeare productions in foreign languages are naturally diminished by the absence of the complex ambiguities and the musical cadences of the verse, but often enhanced by the lack of theatrical and historical baggage. In foreign productions the plays can seem like allegorical fables – a succession of images and incidents resonating like wind chimes. At their best – Sturua's *Richard III*, Bergman's *Hamlet*. Strehler's *The Tempest* – the productions seem to re-invent the original play and force you to consider it afresh.

It's no less true of familiar contemporary English texts. The most intense and effective production I've seen of *The Birthday Party* was at the Cinoherni Theatre in Prague in 1969, barely six months after the Russian invasion. In the context of the real tyranny of secret police, mutual fear and suspicion, and the cruel absurdity of life under a totalitarian government, Pinter's surrealistic play, set in an English boarding-house, seemed an enormously touching, funny, and closely observed account of daily life in Czechoslovakia; the surreal lost its prefix.

Our theatre reflects the strengths and weaknesses of our national character. It is almost wholly pragmatic, humane, often witty, often ironic, hardly ever didactic. The visual muscle is not well developed, but it is becoming more so, and it is the consistent exposure to productions from Europe, Japan and North and South America that has brought this about. We are beginning to see in British productions a willingness to exploit *all* the resources of the medium of theatre – words, movement, music, light and space – to animate and illuminate a text. In the eighteenth century the British theatre was castigated by critics for failing to match up to 'foreign' drama; in this respect nothing much has changed. What has changed – and I have heard it expressed in many European countries over the past three years – is Europe's view of what is valuable, and singular, about British theatre: its essential humanity, and its focus on the actor, rather than the director, as the principal agent of contact with an audience. I work frequently with one of the leading European lighting designers, who is French. 'I like to work here,' he says, 'because I can use warm colours. In Germany I can only use blue.'

Theatre has been a passport and a lingua franca for me, and I came to know Romania through a company that I encountered first in Edinburgh in 1971. The Bulandra Company from Bucharest were presenting two plays at the Lyceum Theatre: *Carnival Scenes* by the Romanian playwright I. L. Carigiale, and *Leonce and Lena* by Buchner. The two productions exemplified the best of Romanian theatre. Carigiale is a writer best described as a cross between Labiche and Gogol – witty, satirical, robust, farcical, energetic and humane. None of these characteristics is specifically Romanian, but the combination is distinctly so. The productions and the acting had an engaging, droll, and highly charged charm; and outstanding in a cast of richly talented and idiosyncratic actors was a young man described by Michael Billington as the most exciting young actor he'd seen since the debut of Ian McKellen.

In the following years I came to know Ion Caramitru and the work of the Bulandra Company well. The company was started in 1948 by Lucia Bulandra, who was like Olivier in combining a great acting talent with a formidable ability as a manager and talent spotter. She remained director until her death in 1965. Her funeral was a great public event. So many people turned out on the streets for the procession of the body from the theatre to the cemetery that the pall-bearers (who included the young Caramitru) were jostled, shaking the body. Her head nodded from side to side, indicating, as in life, that the answer to whatever they wanted was no.

She had, however, said yes to the appointment of her successor, Livie Culei. Culei presided over the company from 1965 until his dismissal in 1973. (He emigrated in 1979, becoming Director of the Guthrie Theatre in Minneapolis.) Under his direction the Bulandra went through a golden period, gaining a well-deserved international reputation. An uneasy relationship between the successful, but highly individualistic, company and the Cultural Ministry exploded in 1973.

A production of *The Government Inspector* was banned by the Ministry after three performances. The 'special ideological forces' of the Ministry, encouraged by their Russian colleagues, saw the production as unequivocally anti-government and anti-Russian. Gogol's stage direction at the end – 'a frozen tableau of consternation' – had been staged as an endlessly repeating whirl of robot-like bureaucrats stumbling about the stage in an ever-growing fog. The director, Lucian Pintilei, lost the right to work and emigrated. Culei was sacked; some leading actors lost their responsibilities within the administration, and an era of numbing censorship was ushered in. This was merely an echo of the repression happening on the larger, political, stage. The repertoire now had to be approved by the Councillor of Culture and Social

Education; individual plays unknown to the Councillor had to be submitted a year in advance, and a special committee of twenty-five bureaucrats attended special previews. The most effective form of censorship, and one that is not unknown in the West, was the gradual diminution of subsidy. In the last two years before the Revolution the company existed on a subsidy of less than one tenth of their subsidy at the beginning of the seventies. There was barely enough money to pay the actors, and none for the heating and electricity.

I visited Romania several times in the seventies, sponsored by the British Council as part of a Cultural Exchange programme. By the end of the decade Ion Caramitru had become a leading actor and the Deputy Director of the company. (The Director was a place man; a party member and a dull actor, to boot), and in the early-eighties on a visit to London he invited me to direct a play for the Bulandra. I suggested *Hamlet*, partly because it seemed an excellent part for Caramitru, partly because it seemed an all too appropriate play for Romania, and partly because I'd just directed it in London.

I'd been asked to direct a play for the Royal Court in 1980, I was producing 'Play For Today' at the BBC, and hadn't worked in the theatre for two years. I think Max Stafford-Clark hoped that I might suggest a new play, or a revival of a contemporary classic – in short, a 'play for today'. I thought I had, and so, I imagine, did he, for he accepted the notion of *Hamlet* with Jonathan Pryce with no visible ideological struggle.

If the production belonged in any way to a 'Royal Court tradition', it was in its casting (Jill Bennett as Gertrude, Michael Elphick as Claudius, Harriet Walter as Ophelia), and what I thought of as a strain of rational humanism. It was stubborn logic that led us to play Hamlet's soliloquy 'To be or not to be' to Ophelia rather than countenance the implausibility of having her present on the small stage (as Shakespeare indicates) without being noticed by Hamlet, and we dispensed with the Ghost in search of a plausible means of presenting the spirit of Hamlet's father to an audience (and actor and director) sceptical of paranormal phenomena. The spirit of Old Hamlet spoke through his son, and Jonathan made the phenomenon of 'belly speaking' terrifying and, at the same time, touching. His whole performance walked a knife edge between danger and an almost childlike vulnerability. Madness never seemed far away.

To do Shakespeare at the Court – at least in 1980, was to play to an audience who seemed largely unencumbered by the layers of myth that the great plays accumulate. A few critics were ecstatic, a few indifferent, and some patronising – 'Hamlet on a tram', said the *Evening Standard*, presumably mistaking the influence of Holbein in the design for the influence of Holborn – but the audiences were never less than enthusiastic. I became used to hearing excited speculation in the interval about the probable fate of the hero, and gasps during the last act when they realised that he would not survive the duel.

When I was preparing the production I was often drawn to Dürer's portrait of *Melancholia* – a drooping, long-haired androgynous figure slumped amidst the scientific artefacts of Renaissance science: compasses, a sextant, a globe, a telescope; a figure encircled by the tools of technology, immobile in the face of progress. I read an interview by Günter Grass. 'What will the eighties be like?' he was asked. 'If you want to know what the eighties will be like,' he said, 'look at Dürer's picture of *Melancholia* ... She knows so much that she gets sad about it. I think we are in this situation: we are victims of our own intelligence.'

I went to Bucharest in 1983 to cast the play and talk to the prospective designer. The city had changed since I was there a few years earlier. Armed with an image of *The Balkan Trilogy* of Olivia Manning, I had not been disappointed on my first visit; a city of wide boulevards, elegant and humanely proportioned *fin de siècle* houses often decorated with florid and flamboyant art nouveau features, and populated by a Latin people who bore their oppression with a beguiling mixture of diffidence and discreet subversion.

The Bucharest I encountered in 1983 was a drab parody if its former self. It had been harmed more by Ceauçescu than by the recent earthquake. Obdurate and systematic neglect and deprivation darkened the face of the city; at night literally so for all the street lamps and shop windows were extinguished in a misplaced scheme to save energy for industry. The downward spiral continued during the eighties. After ten o'clock a curfew was effectively introduced. Cinemas, restaurants, theatres, were obliged to close and 'night clubs', with a wonderfully absurd magnanimity, were allowed to open between eight and ten.

If I had any doubts about whether *Hamlet* was the appropriate play, I was given ample confirmation of its suitability. Bugged telephones and hotel rooms, the ever present Securitate, the smug, strutting arrogance of the Party's apparatchiks, the friends who lowered their voices and looked about them before speaking, the fear of prison and the familiarity with those who had experienced it, the swaggering display of the privileges of the nomeklatura; in short, it was Elsinor.

I was finally unable to do the production partly because, shamefully, I became increasingly reluctant to spend three months in Bucharest during a time of great privation, partly because I was becoming wary of doing the play in a language of which I spoke only a few words, and partly because I had got the go-ahead from Channel 4 and Goldcrest to make the film that I had been working on with Ian McEwan – *The Ploughman's Lunch*, a chronicle of the Thatcher Years. I was replaced by a gifted young Romanian, Alex Tocilescu. For about nine months he, a brace of poets, five actors, and a novelist worked to achieve a translation that they felt was true to Shakespeare and to the condition of Romania. The Ministry had accepted the idea of *Hamlet* until the ideological committee attended a preview. They found the translation too 'modern', too 'close', and the production too provocative. Caramitru came very near to an explosive confrontation with the Ministry: 'You can't stop Shakespeare, or at least you can't be seen to.' Surprisingly the appeal worked, the fear of becoming the laughing stock of the world outweighed the fear of inciting unhealthy thoughts.

The production opened triumphantly in 1985 and played 200 performances through the hardest years of the regime. Ceauçescu had graduated from being a malign clown to a psychotic ogre. His *folies de grandeur* consisted of razing villages to the ground in order to rehouse peasants in tower blocks, sweeping aside boulevards because the streets from his residence to his office were insufficiently straight, building miles of preposterously baroque apartment blocks which echoed in concrete the lines of Securitate men standing beneath them, and led the eye towards a gigantic palace which made Stalin's taste in architecture look restrained. They ran out of marble to clad the walls and the floors, and had to invent a process to make a synthetic substitute out of marble dust; and there was never enough gold for all the door handles of the hundreds of rooms, or the taps of the scores of bathrooms. It was a palace of Oz, built for a demented wizard, costing the lives of hundreds of building workers who, numbed by cold, fell from the flimsy scaffolding and were brushed away like rubble, to be laid out in a room reserved solely for the coffins of the expendable workforce. There was a photograph of Ceauçescu that showed only one ear, and there's a Romanian saying that to have one ear is to be mad. So another ear was painstakingly painted on the official photograph. Such are the ways of great men. I went to a conference in Bucharest after the Revolution. I was asked, 'What is the difference between Alexander the Great and the Buddha?' I had no answer.

The Bulandra Company had suffered, like the country as a whole, from a decimation of its resources, a crippling of morale, and a defection of talent (mostly directors). There was, however, one ironic gain. As the regime tightened its grip and the corrosive effect of tyranny leaked into every area of public and private life, the theatre gathered more and more power as the sole public medium of expression where thoughts could be spoken, ideas asserted, passions voiced, through allegory and metaphor.

The code was one that could be read by an audience but not challenged by the censors. When I saw *Hamlet* in Bucharest I was seeing a play whose resonances were, literally, painfully telling. Hamlet was seen unambiguously as a man fighting against Claudius/Ceauçescu, and if he vacillated, accused himself of cowardice, cursed himself for his inaction, it only reflected the audience's awareness of their own frailty. They sat enraptured in an unheated theatre for several hours on uncomfortable seats or crouched on the edge of the stage, swathed in scarves and overcoats. Line after line was greeted with the applause of recognition; this was their story.

Ion Caramitru was in London in December 1989 to give a poetry reading at the Barbican to celebrate the centenary of the celebrated Romanian poet, Eminescu. We spoke a lot about recent events in Eastern Europe. 'The Berlin Wall has moved to the Romanian border. There won't be any changes in Romania.' We're all prophets with hindsight. I ruefully said goodbye to him, promising to visit an unchanged Romania during the next year.

He returned to Bucharest on the 13th of December. There were reports of unrest in Timişoara on the 16th of December, but no one in Bucharest knew what had happened. Ion had to go to Cluj, in the north, to give a talk. While he was there he heard rumours of a massacre in Timişoara, flew back to Bucharest and found Ceauçescu on the TV at the airport speaking from a balcony to a huge crowd. Suddenly the TV broadcast stopped. Ion left the airport but could barely drive his car for the crush of coaches filled with riot police heading for the centre. He joined the crowd and the square was surrounded by soldiers and Securitate. Ion was recognised by students and teenagers, who asked him to help them persuade people to join the opposition. The Securitate were infiltrating the crowd as he enlisted support and gave encouragement. 'It was the beginning of a new world,' he said.

The next morning there were opposition slogans in office buildings, groups of people emerging all over the city. By ten o'clock it was known that the Commander of the Army had either committed suicide or had been executed. The soldiers embraced the people, and the Securitate started to fight. Hundreds of protesters were killed. Two months later you could still see where they died. In squares, on pavements, on street corners, in shop doorways, you could see small clusters of candles and bunches of flowers. Often they described the outline of a body and they haunt the memory like the shadows of the vaporized bodies in Hiroshima.

Nobody knew what to do. Nobody knew where to go. There was no order, no plan. They saw Ceauçescu's helicopter overhead; leaflets were scattered from it. They read: 'DON'T LISTEN TO FOREIGNERS'.

Finding himself with a group near the TV station, Ion suggested that they take it over. A General said to him, 'My army is at your disposal. Tell us where to go.' Heady stuff for an actor. And off they went. There was fierce fighting round the TV station but by the time Ion went in, the crowd parted for him and he found the TV station guarded by only one Securitate man, who was trembling too much even to raise his hand in a salute.

> Then a programme started, but it was the same announcer who had been broadcasting all these lies for *years*. So I said no. But the TV people said yes, let him speak. We are all guilty. I told him to apologise for his past. He did and then I went on and I said we're free, we've won. God is with us. Don't shoot anyone. Join us ... I was too full of emotion to speak properly.

After two or three hours Iliescu, Roman and Brucan arrived at the TV station. They decided to form a provisional government; a hundred or so dissidents, poets, artists, and teachers, joined the National Salvation Front. Ion became one of the twelve-man Executive Committee. He was the only one who had not been a member of the Party. The promise of the NSF was to administrate the country until elections could be held; it was never intended to become a political party itself. This was one of many broken promises. On the night of the 23rd of December, Ion tried to persuade Iliescu to go out on the balcony in front of the huge crowd, tear up his Party card and scatter the pieces in the wind; a simple theatrical gesture that could have changed the history of his government.

Ion fought his corner in the Provisional Government as Vice-President with responsibility for Culture and Education, and when the elections were announced he stood as an independent. Like all the other independents (with the exception of Andrez Plezu, who succeeded him as Minister of Culture), he failed to get elected. Many tried to persuade him to stand for President, and there is no doubt that he had a following that would flatter any politician. He refused, and decided to return to the theatre to become head of a newly formed Theatre Union, dedicated to getting revolution off the streets and into the revival of theatres. Perhaps Madame Bulandra was shaking her head at her protégé, fearful that a gain for politics would be a loss to the theatre, and I'm sure that no theatre could afford to lose the services of this wry, talented, intelligent and humane actor.

To be involved in a revolution is to take theatre to the streets. The difficulties that theatre faces in Romania are a microcosm of the difficulties faced by the Government: to rebuild a culture debilitated by years of deprivation and neglect. They used to call pig's trotters patriots in Bucharest butcher's shops; they were the only part of the animal that hadn't gone abroad in Ceauçescu's drive for foreign exchange. What the pigs left behind was a country close to famine, frozen in a Stalinist time warp like a mammoth in a glacier. If the British response to hardship is to maintain a stiff upper lip, the Romanian approach is 'haz de necaz' – to get fun out of tragedy. They've had ample opportunity to put this to the test in the last forty-five years.

It's been a depressing sight to see the Romanian government blundering into folly after folly, the Western governments withdrawing aid, and the public withdrawing their fickle affections when the sunburst of revolution gives way to the grey light of day. There used to be a giant statue of Lenin in front of the huge Stalinist wedding cake of the Ministry of Culture. It was torn down during the Revolution. A small placard was put in its place on the graffiti-covered granite plinth. It said: 'GOD HELP ROMANIA'.

The language of demagoguery in this century has a remarkable consistency: Stalin, Mao Tse-Tung, Ceauçescu and Bokassa shared a predilection for large banners, demonstrations, and military choreography, and the same architectural virus; totalitarianism consistently distorts proportion by eliminating human scale. Mass becomes the only consideration in architecture, armies, and death. The rise of a dictator and the accompanying political thuggery are the main topics of Shakespeare's *Richard III*, which could be said to be a handbook for tyrants – and for their victims. I directed the play with Ian McKellen as Richard in 1990 for the National Theatre and took it to its spiritual home in Bucharest early in 1991.

We have to keep rediscovering ways of doing Shakespeare's plays. They don't have absolute meanings. There is no fixed, frozen way of doing them. Nobody can mine a Shakespeare play and discover a 'solution', and to pretend that there are fixed canons of style, fashion and taste is to ignore history. When there is talk of 'classical acting', what is often meant is an acting style that instead of revealing the truth of a text for the present day reveals the bombast of yesterday.

How do we present the plays in a way that is true to their own terms, and at the same time bring them alive for a contemporary audience? It's very much easier to achieve this in a small space, and it's no coincidence that most successful Shakespeare productions of recent years have been done in theatres seating a couple of hundred people at most, where the potency of the language isn't dissipated by the exigencies of voice projection, and the problems of presentation – finding a physical world for the play –

become negligible. It's hard at one end of the spectrum to avoid latching on to a visual conceit that tidies up the landscape of a Shakespeare play, and, at the other end of the spectrum, to avoid imposing unity through a rigorously enforced discipline of verse-speaking. Verse-speaking should be like jazz: never *on* the beat, but before, after, or across it.

The life of the plays is in the language, not alongside it, or underneath it. Feelings and thoughts are released at the moment of speech. An Elizabethan audience would have responded to the pulse, the rhythms, the shapes, sounds, and above all meanings, within the consistent ten-syllable, five-stress, lines of blank verse. They were an audience who listened. To a large extent we've lost that priority; nowadays we see before we hear. Verse drama places demands on the audience, but a greater demand still on the actors, habituated to naturalistic speech, and to private, introspective emotional displays. 'You should be able to feel the language,' says Tony Harrison, 'to taste it, to conscript the whole body as well as the mind and the mouth to savour it.'

For a director, working with a designer can often be the most satisfying and enjoyable part of a production. You advance slowly, day by day, in a kind of amiable dialectic, helped by sketches, anecdotes, photographs, and reference books. The play starts as a tone – of voice, or colour – and a shape as formless as the shadow of a sheet on a washing line; through reading and discussion and illustration, it acquires a clear and palpable shape. There is no more gifted designer, and more generous collaborator, than Bob Crowley. When Ian McKellen and Bob and I started work on *Richard III* we had no plan for the setting; we never sought to establish literal equivalents between medieval and modern tyrants. We worked simply, day by day, reading the play aloud to each other, and refusing to jump to conclusions.

A story emerged: Richard's occupation's gone. He's a successful soldier who, in the face of great odds, has welded a life together in which he has a purpose, an identity as a military man. His opening speech describes his depression at the conclusion of war, his bitterness at the effeminacy of peace. He's a man raging with unconsummated energy, needing a world to 'bustle' in. This hunger to fill the vacuum left by battle is the driving force of the play. It has a deep resonance for me. When I made a film about the Falklands War, I saw this sense of unfulfilled appetite at first hand in people who had fought in the war and were unable to come to terms with peace. The experience of battle is a profound distillation of fear, danger, and exhilaration; nothing in peacetime will ever match it, and those who are affected by it are as traumatised as those who have been wounded, who at least have the visible signs of trauma to show for it. Soldiers are licensed to break the ultimate taboo against killing; some of them get the habit.

Richard has had to fight against many odds; he is the youngest son, coming after two very strong, dominant, assertive, brothers – and he is deformed, 'unfinished'. His eldest brother, Edward, is a profligate, and the spectacle of his brother's success with women is a sharp thorn in his flesh. The age, no less than today, worshipped physical prowess, and Richard is accustomed, though certainly not inured, to pejorative terms like 'bunch-back'd toad'; he has heard them all his life. We know that he is deformed, but the text repeatedly tells us he is a successful professional soldier. We have to reconcile the two demands of the text. Oliver's interpretation has become central to the mythology of the play, but the deformity that he depicts has never seemed to me plausibly compatible with what Shakespeare wrote. Ian McKellen played Richard with a small hump, he had chronic alopecia, and he was paralysed down one side of his body. These three handicaps taken together were sufficient to account for all the abuse he attracts and still allow him to serve as a professional soldier. Experience shows that even slight deformities are enough to inspire repulsion; modern reactions to disability haven't changed very much in this respect.

It is clear that Richard has been rejected from birth by his mother; she says so unequivocally to Clarence's children, and her words of contempt spoken to her son in front of his troops confirm this. It is impossible to escape the conclusion that Shakespeare is attempting to give some history, some causality, to Richard's evil.

The design of the production emerged empirically. We started with an empty model box, and put minimal elements into it – rows of overhead lamps to create a series of institutionalised public areas, a world of prisons and cabinet rooms and hospital corridors; palaces and areas of ceremonial display, set off against candle-lit areas of private pain. We drew some parallels with the rise of Hitler, but these were forced by Hitler himself; his rise shadows that of Richard astonishingly closely, as Brecht showed in *Arturo Ui*. Specific elements of Hitler's ascent to power, or Mosley's to notoriety, were echoes that bounced off a timeless sounding board. The play is set in a mythological landscape, even if it draws on an apparently historically precise period; I say apparently because Shakespeare treats historical incident with little reference to fact – incidents are conflated, characters meet whose paths never crossed. Tudor myths prevail.

Tyrants always invent their own ritual, synthetic ceremonies borrowed from previous generations in order to dignify the present and suggest an unbroken continuum with old traditions. Hitler played up all the themes of historical restitution. Napoleon, the little man from Corsica, designed the preposterous Byzantine ceremony that is represented in David's painting. Most of the English ritual, our so-called time-honoured ritual, is not very old either. The order of the last British Coronation, in 1953, had been almost wholly invented by Queen Victoria. Putting Richard in medieval costume in the Coronation, as we did, was a way of showing how tyrants – the authors of the Thousand-Year Reich – would have us believe that medievalism and modern time co-exist; the past is consistently made to serve the needs of the present.

Richard III is so much a one-man show in our acting tradition that the miseries visited on woman by the male appetite for power tend to be ignored or obscured. The female characters are as strong as in any of Shakespeare's plays. The legacy of men's cruelty is swept up by women who have been educated by the experience of grief. They have caused pain to Richard and they are taught by him to suffer: Elizabeth – proud, arrogant, and abusive of him, loses her brother and her sons; the Duchess of York – sealed in her own self-importance, openly contemptuous of her son, loses another son and grandchildren at his hands; Lady Anne – blinded by her grief and her hatred and seduced by him, loses her self-respect and, finally, her life. Only Queen Margaret needs no education at his hands: 'Teach me how to curse my enemies,' says Elizabeth to her. Their models in our times are only too obvious: the women who wait in Chile and in Argentina for news of their sons who have 'disappeared', and the mothers I saw in Romania shortly after the Revolution, putting candles and flowers in the streets on the spots where their sons had been killed. The play is called *The Tragedy of Richard III*, and it is the tragedy of the women that is being told.

The crude villain of melodrama has managed to overrule a play of considerable political subtlety. Richard does not appear in an untainted Eden; his England is the world of *realpolitik*. Clarence and Edward have both committed crimes in the Civil Wars, Clarence even admitting his guilt to the Keeper; Queen Elizabeth's family are greedy parvenus; Buckingham, Stanley and Ely are all morally ambiguous. At the beginning of the play Clarence has just been capriciously arrested; such behaviour may be exceptional and outrageous, but not unprecedented. What right have any of the characters to call Richard a villain?

Hastings, the Prime Minister, is a politician's politician, expedient, and amoral – when he is told of the impending execution of his political enemies, he can't fault this transparent abuse of justice; within minutes he is himself under sentence of execution. 'The rest that love me, rise and follow me,' says Richard, and at this point self-preservation takes over from courage, morality, or political expediency. We all hope that we will never have to face this choice; it takes formidable courage to say no when the consequence is imprisonment or worse, and where there is a crying need for reform, it's easy enough to agree that minor infringements of liberty are a small price to pay for the benefit of an able leader. We are comfortably insulated in our unchallenged, liberal, all-too English assumptions.

The play ends with the triumph of Richmond – a young man, almost a boy, in the hands of mature soldier-politicians who are promoting him. It is essential for their purposes that he succeed, and he is equally determined to show that he can succeed. I set his first entrance against a backdrop of a peaceful country village, in Devon in fact, near where I was born, the England of 'summer fields and fruitful vines'. If I was asked what I thought Richmond was fighting for, it would be this idealised picture of England. It was more than a metaphor for me; it was a heartland.

When I took my production of *Richard III* to Romania a year after their Revolution familiar landmarks in Bucharest were obscured entirely by the snow, and the people were unrecognisably changed from the years of oppression. Though some claimed that nothing had altered, the mere fact of being able to say this openly contradicted what they were saying. A stagehand said he wasn't at all frightened of being killed in the Revolution; after all, better to be dead than how it was. A small, pixie-like woman was helping at the theatre; she was slightly retarded but had some English. 'Are you happy? I am happy,' was her refrain. Like many others she was homeless, and lived in the theatre, where at least she could get hot water. Outside it was often one hour of hot water a day.

At the end of the last performance I went onstage with the actors and made a speech, starting through an interpreter. She was shouted off: 'English! English!' they chanted and I continued in English. I told them the production had come to its spiritual home, that this sort of cultural exchange was the only true diplomacy, and thanked them for their hospitality. They didn't want us to go, clapping rhythmically and incessantly, but we came offstage slowly, blinking back tears. As we left the stage a man walked up to us and handed a note and a bouquet to one of the actors. The note read: 'Nobody can play Sir William Shakespeare's plays better than his English people. I've seen with your remarkable help that somewhere in England Sir William Shakespeare is still alive. Thank you. Signed: a simple man.'

There's a prayer that people who run theatres often have hanging on their office walls, like a charm to ward off evil spirits. I think it was written by the American critic Walter Kerr who, perhaps as a punishment, has a theatre named after him on Broadway; it goes something like this:

> Give me success, but not too much of it; some failure to remind me what it's like; but for God's sake don't give me a building.

I didn't take his advice because after six years in Edinburgh I moved to run a theatre in Nottingham. I had met my wife in Edinburgh. In fact I'd bought the flat she was living in, and as a friend of mine predicted, the relationship between tenant and lodger deteriorated, or blossomed, into a somewhat unprofessional relationship. Then serendipity played a part: the two of us were sought out, independently, by Stuart Burge, who had succeeded John Neville – she to start a Theatre-in-Education company attached to the Playhouse, and me to be his successor. Unlike most fiction, this particular plot worked out rather well. We got married, had a daughter, and lived happily ever after. Mostly.

Nottingham was a thrilling place to be in the early-seventies. I was lucky enough to work with several of a new generation of playwrights who were young, ambitious, cocky and keen to repudiate the old avant-garde and establish a new one. Writers, not directors, have always been the motor of theatre. New styles of presentation have been found to embrace new meanings, not the other way round. I persuaded David Hare to become Resident Dramatist; he delivered, with Howard Brenton, a triumphantly successful epic comedy about corruption in local government, based on a current scandal in the North-East that was still *sub judice*. Together with a clutch of talented young(ish) writers (David Hare, Howard Brenton, Trevor Griffiths, Ken Campbell, Adrian Mitchell, Stephen Lowe), and actors (Jonathan Pryce, Tony Sher, Stephen Rea, Zoë Wanamaker, Alison Steadman, Tom Wilkinson, Mick Ford, Malcolm Storry) we embraced (or tried to) new forms of staging, vivid use of language, of music, of design. Of one thing we were certain, that the hub of the theatrical universe was Nottingham, not London. 'What we will do,' I would intone sanctimoniously, 'will be *our* work, not a watered-down version of what's happening in London.' And sometimes, perhaps, we succeeded.

Memory is often merciful, and never more so than in the theatre. Only the highlights remain, the rest – the unhappiness, the failures, the misjudgements – are washed away like silt, leaving the glinting ore behind. I remember many productions and many performances fondly in vivid detail but few with the intensity provoked by my collaborations with Ken Campbell and his performance as Professor Molereasons, the presiding genius of a German play for children called *School for Clowns*, adapted by Ken from the original by Friedrich Karl Waechter. Like many of Ken's most successful projects (or 'capers' as he'd refer to them) he'd taken someone else's idea, and turned it into something inimitably his own. Indeed, when it comes to expanding, developing, even appropriating other people's notions, Ken can be positively Shakespearian, if only in his resemblance to Autolycus, the 'snapper-up of unconsidered trifles'.

The play takes place in a (fairly) conventional old-fashioned schoolroom occupied by four pupils – clowns of largely irrelevant ages and sexes, and their teacher Professor Molereasons, a remorseless advocate of discipline. The play's structure is simple: the Professor opens his large book, finds a topic for the lesson (e.g., 'Help! Help! My aeroplane's on fire!'), and instructs the clowns on how to act it out. The clowns always start according to instructions, quietly and submissively. As their invention multiplies, and their enthusiasms grow, anarchy invariably brings on the intervention of the increasingly desperate Molereasons: 'SILENCE, CLOWNS!! I AM UNABLE TO CONTINUE IN THESE CIRCUMSTANCES!!' His final threat is to leave the room, aware even as he does so of the painful weakness of this sanction. There is no teacher alive, and no child, who would fail to recognise the dilemma.

The play is as good a metaphor as one can find for teaching, for learning, for the relationship of pupil and teacher, and for the connections between comedy, anarchy, and childhood. When Ken did the play, we had just opened Trevor Griffith's *Comedians*, which, as Ken observed, was *School for Clowns* for grown-ups.

I'd met Trevor Griffiths first when he was working for the BBC in Leeds, in charge of Adult Education. He looked stocky and fit, like a professional football player, perhaps not quite at the peak of his playing form, but quick, strong, and utterly confident of his own abilities. He was two people: the one a political thinker, loaded with gravitas; the other a demonic, mischievous, imaginative and sometimes wayward child, ready for anything. He was visiting Edinburgh, and brought me a play he'd written. I didn't put it on, but we became friends and when I took over Nottingham I asked him to write a play for us. He suggested the idea of *Comedians* to me in the bar of the Poetry Society in Earls Court, where I was auditioning for the opening season. A group of working-class men, he said, go to an evening class for club comedians. There's an old teacher, a liberal, a humanist, who believes in the idea of a 'good' joke, and there's a young skinhead, a hard man who won't compromise. It all takes place in real time. Do it, I said. He did, and wrote, in my view, the best play of the Seventies.

He delivered the first draft a few weeks after my daughter was born. My wife had gone back to work, and I rocked our tiny daughter in my arms while Trevor and I read the play together; she gurgled approvingly, immune to the firework display over her head. We announced the play, as we did many others, before a word had been written. It concentrated the mind wonderfully for writers, and irrevocably committed the theatre to doing the play. It was a sort of kamikaze policy: if the play didn't get written we were in bad trouble, if the play did get written and wasn't good enough we were in worse trouble, but I thought this reckless approach was preferable to what Ken described as 'brochure' theatre – deciding on the choice of play because the brochure has to go to print.

Unlike *Comedians*, which ends with a melancholic and equivocal debate, *School for Clowns* ends in total, glorious, unqualified anarchy as the clowns take over the classroom and, with the enthusiastic assistance of the audience, evict their teacher. In performance several hundred schoolchildren would bay for the expulsion of the Professor. He would straighten his wig, which was a plastic, carrot-coloured Mao-style hairpiece that looked as though it had been won in a raffle (in fact not unlike the hair of one of the teachers at my daughter's primary school), dust off the chalk from his academic gown, and step down into the auditorium. Not since Christians were thrown to the lions has so much public cruelty been enjoyed by so many.

With great dignity the Professor would process through the rioting schoolchildren, through the foyer, past the box office and into the street, shuffling, broken, but still proud, towards the stage door. I interrupted his journey one day, after a morning performance. 'How did it go, Ken?' I said. Professor Molereasons stared back at me with eyes misted by tears. 'I was unable to continue in the circumstances . . .'

Ken's work has always appealed to the child in me: anarchic, naughty, unreverential, silly even. When I started as Director at Nottingham it was more or less mandatory to pay homage to the local history of your 'community'. I had little taste for a dramatised documentary about laceworkers, and even less for a revisionist version of the Robin Hood story. I had heard about a little-known local hero called Bendigo, a prize fighter who was once champion of

England, and I asked Ken, who conscripted his friends Dave Hill and Andy Andrews, to dramatise the life of the boxer.

Ken was intrigued by his training methods. Bendigo used to go into pubs and spit in people's beer to annoy them, which would, unsurprisingly, provoke a fight. He once did it to a dancer who pranced about so much that Bendigo couldn't hit him, thus giving him the key to his distinctive, prancing style. In Ken's show *Bendigo: The Little-Known Facts* his inspiration to become a boxer came from his mother who, taunted beyond endurance by his indolence, flattened him with a rolling pin. He responded by thumping her with a powerful straight left. 'Ah son,' she said, ''tis a metaphor surely of your life to be.'

I thought this show certainly one of the most enjoyable things I had ever directed, and maybe that I had ever seen in a theatre. So did many of the audience, but not the man who Ken overheard in an interval say to his wife, 'I can't imagine the sort of person who would enjoy this stuff.'

This man would not have returned the following year when we staged another item of little-known local history based on the folk myth of the Nottinghamshire village of Gotham where the villagers discovered, round about the Middle Ages, that if they were declared insane they were exempt from the poll tax. Prescience indeed.

The show was called *Walking Like Geoffrey* and involved the villagers being taught to act silly by the village half-wit, Geoffrey, and a plot that went backwards in time, whose complexity would have done credit to Tolkien. The evening reached its climax in a mass demonstration of eccentric walking from the school of Max Wall for the benefit of the Tax Man, who was showered with a pyramid of bird droppings and an inflatable elephant, which was then bounced round the auditorium, as he fled from the village into insanity.

Shortly before he defected to an academic job in Canada the excellent Ronald Bryden, then critic of the *Observer*, wrote of *Walking Like Geoffrey*, 'If there's a future for British theatre it must lie here.' I wish I knew where it had all gone. More and more I find myself defending the theatre or proselytising for it as more and more people find excuses for not liking the medium or just not going out. We're made to feel like coracle-makers or morris dancers: participants in an archaic ritual performed only for the benefit of the devotees.

There was another review of the show that was less generous. The reviewer objected to almost everything about it, and in particular to the intrusive laughter of what he took to be friends of the authors. Ken was outraged. 'What does he mean friends, we *are* the bloody authors!'

There was a sketch from the show that Ken decided years later to perform at an Amnesty International concert at Drury Lane. Somewhat against my will I agreed to direct the piece again. It involved the death of an Elizabethan nobleman who was trying to cheat his destiny by breaking through the 'warp and weft of time': setting up a situation in which time passed quickly (pleasure) and time passed slowly (pain). Running between be-smocked wenches and nagging wife he failed to make the 'thread of marching time elastic' and 'pang' himself to 'other worlds', and died through a surfeit of blank verse. Or as Ken said, 'Death by RADA breathing.'

At Drury Lane Ken decided there had to be an extra ingredient to lard the nightmare of the dying time-traveller: live pigs. This was not a success. I don't mind working with children, and some animals can be perfectly docile, but take my advice: stay away from pigs. They aren't happy in theatres, and have the most disturbing ways of showing their unhappiness; they scream like scalded babies.

Most of Ken's capers look as if they are going to be follies and turn out to be inspired gestures of showmanship. *The Road Show*, like its subject matter – the dramatisation of pub myths and tall stories – eventually became a part of theatrical folklore. *Illuminatus*, a day-long play that I first saw in the Liverpool Theatre of Science Fiction, I would rank beside *The Wars of the Roses* and *The Hare Trilogy* as great days spent in the theatre. It's as ambitious, as long, and certainly as entertaining as *The Ring*. I was offered a job in *Illuminatus*. 'Peter Hall's turned it down,' said Ken. 'It's the part of the man who wants to run the world. It's not bad, you're only on for three minutes.' I regret not doing that as much as I regret declining the offer by a friend, a performance artist, to make love in public at the Round House in 1967, while wired to a microphone, an ECT machine, and a TV camera.

There are two sequels to *School for Clowns*: *Clowns on a School Outing* and *Peef*. They should be performed on the same day by the same actors, in a sort of clownfest. Ideally they would feature Ken as Professor Molereasons, but it would be wiser not to let him direct the plays. I once saw a rehearsal of his where an actor who had failed to provide the necessary energy and invention to satisfy Ken was hurled against the wall with Ken screaming in his all too imitable voice, like an exhaust pipe with a broken silencer, 'Act PROPER!'

Ken's evangelism, his enthusiasms of the moment, can sometimes be hard to endure, particularly on the phone at one o'clock in the morning: Gerry Webb of Space Consultancy and Interplanetary travel, EST, Max Wall, Spike Jones, Ian Drury, Charles Fort (the visionary not the hotelier), Robert McKee the script doctor, the Royal Dickens Theatre, the underwater show in the Liverpool swimming pool, the office on the Essex marshes, Werner the dog . . . There is no one who seizes the moment with quite so much enthusiasm and is quite so relentless in wanting to share it with others.

He once graphically displayed to me the two sides of his character, holding a hand in front of each half of his face in turn: the pirate and the char. The pirate is wild, sometimes savage, sometimes bullying, ambitious, brazen, loud. The char is mournful and melancholic, and sometimes, though not very often, quite tender.

In 1900, in Paris, there was a prize called The Guzmann Prize: 100,000 f. for anyone who could communicate with an extra-terrestrial being on another planet. The planet Mars was excluded on the grounds that it was too easy to communicate with Martians. I think Ken should, belatedly, be offered this prize. He told me of an encounter he'd once had with the Venusian Consul in London; I suspect he was talking about himself. He's been sent here to shake up our ideas about theatre.

The Board of Nottingham weren't too enthusiastic about Ken's work, but in spite of their reputation for strong government they forebore from openly criticising my decision to put the plays on. There had been a notorious episode which had resulted in John Neville shaking the dust of the city from his feet. The character of the Board was largely (but unfairly) fashioned in the shape of its Chairman, Cyril Forsyth, who was indeed a character. He looked like a cross between Khrushchev, a plump baby, and a member of the Crazy Gang, and he was capricious, bullying, wilful, loyal, and generous in equal measure. Even though I never got over the irritation of his pulling my hair and asking me when I was going to get it cut, I admired his passion for the theatre, and we developed an equable working relationship. He (and his Board) never transgressed the line between the responsibilities of the Board and those of the Artistic Director; the 'art' was my job, and if I messed that up, then it was all right with me if he handed me my cards. He didn't, and although we clashed on many occasions – a scene of Masonic induction in *Brassneck*, the bad language in *Comedians*, the politics of *The Churchill Play*, the nudity in *Touched* – we arrived at a point of mutual respect, and, if I'm not mistaken, mutual affection.

It's not putting a sentimental cast on it to say that I loved being in Nottingham: I loved the work, my family, our house, the theatre, our friends, and the wild, sweet, reckless innocence of it all. When I left the theatre, I took down all the posters and photographs in my office, and I stood for minutes, alone, looking at the sunlight through the slatted blinds falling on the bare walls, and listening to the sounds in my head. Mostly I heard the sound of laughter, and even though it may have felt like the end of *The Cherry Orchard*, there was more of Anya in me, welcoming the new life, than her mother lamenting the passing of the old one. To paraphrase William Shaw when he left *The New Yorker* after years as Editor: whatever our roles, we built something quite wonderful together. Love was the controlling emotion; we did our work with honesty and love.

I don't know any theatre director who hasn't wanted, at some time, to direct films. When you're in a rehearsal room for weeks on end fretting about the snail-like pace of improvement of the performances, the size of the auditorium you're moving to, how to get an actor offstage, how to get an actor onstage, how to move a piece of furniture, how to get rid of a piece of scenery, how to cope with the irreducibly unpoetic physical bulk of everything, the apparent fluency of the cinema seems irresistible. Every day spent making a film produces a finished piece of the puzzle, a complete element; rehearsals for the theatre stretch out for ever like a snake of DNA molecules. Film seems like a magic carpet that transports you across barriers of time and place without being bound by the unanswerable logic of real time and physical reality. It's a false allure, of course; there's a literalness about anything that appears on film. For all its apparent capacity to represent the landscape of dream (particularly in black-and-white), there's always an inescapable context of social reality that can't be dissolved even by the most expressionistic or surrealistic approach. In the theatre an actor can move from Ancient Rome to *Ultima Thule* by changing a hat, picking up a prop, uttering a few words.

But film has the wizard's gift of transforming scale: a face becomes as large as a house, an eye the size of a car; objects can threaten you, landscapes can engulf you. All is sensuous; everything conspires to draw you in, to make you feel, to defy thought. Television isn't like that; being smaller than life, it has problems handling subjects that are larger than life. It thrives on small subjects, small emotions; anyone who expresses extreme passion on television can look overheated; anyone in the cinema who doesn't looks tepid. The dominant medium of television – videotape – always looks undernourished compared to film; it's *too* present, too literal, unpoetic. But to be honest, after five and a half years running a theatre, it was not so much the lure of the different aesthetic of film, even in the muted and diminished form of television, as the promise of glamour and money.

There was precious little of either when I left Nottingham Playhouse to work for the BBC in 1978, even if my salary did double when I became a television producer, reminding me – as if I needed it – of the eternally low status of theatre in the hierarchy of our culture. I became responsible for *Play for Today*, a weekly slot devoted exclusively to contemporary drama.

Television drama used to influence the way we thought, and spoke, and felt; it helped to define the way we looked at the world. If that's rare nowadays it is not the fault of the TV institutions, or of the programme makers, but of a wholesale social revolution. Making good television used to be much easier. Expectations were low, and there was an amiable chaos, which made for a warm relationship between the programme-maker and the public. There's been a flight in recent years from the idea of a regimented culture where we sit down in front of the TV at a particular time, or turn up at a theatre, or put ourselves passively in the hands of any artist. While the writer, or film-maker, or composer, becomes increasingly concerned about controlling the conditions in which his work is displayed, the audience becomes increasingly reluctant to concede this control. If you make a film for television you are powerless to do anything but deliver the film to the best of your ability, and nothing in the world will prevent your audience from answering the phone, attending to the baby, kicking the cat or talking loudly during what you regard as the crucial and indispensable scene. After years of this attritional drizzle, the film-maker – consciously or not – becomes worn down, and withdraws, while the audience starts to rely more and more on watching bite-sized fragments on time-shift videos. It's a world away from watching a film on a large screen, sitting, dreaming, in the dark.

This goes some way to explaining why so many talented directors and producers have defected from television to work in the movies. That there is an aesthetic difference between television drama and the cinema is certain: the scale of the screen, the relationship with an audience, naturally make for a different species of experience to watching a film at home with the lights turned on. But often, I think, it's not as different as the propagandists would claim, and often the arguments made for the superiority of the cinema film over the television film are entirely specious. The truth is that all of us engaged in television drama are for a variety of reasons attracted to the 'movies', because the 'movies' represent an enchanted world: it's a bigger world, more glamorous, more sexy, it's not British – and above all it's richer. But it's not – at least in my opinion – invariably a better world. Many of my colleagues at the BBC fifteen years ago have gone to Hollywood, either literally or metaphorically, but only in the case of one director – out of perhaps a dozen – do I feel that they have made as good films there as under the aegis of the BBC. They have of course, sometimes, received critical acclaim, or at least critical acknowledgement – which is heaven enough for a director if you are used to your film being reviewed merely as a part of the day's viewing. They've received the status that they yearned for when they tramped the circular corridor of the Fifth Floor; they've visited many film festivals at somebody else's expense; they've wined, dined and pined for film stars; they've even made some films – and, of course, they have also made some money.

I'm not making a moral point – there is nothing wrong with any of this, even if there is an element of snobbery latent in the assumption that a film is inherently better if it's been made for the cinema. I'm simply observing that there has been a movement in television towards a system of values that mimics the movies, and this system of values has been underwritten by a generation of producers and directors new to television, who have been educated in 'film culture', paradoxically, not by going to the cinema but by watching old movies on TV. Channel 4 has offered the tempting hybrid, giving many films a tantalising half-life in the cinema. This has often amounted to the film equivalent of vanity publishing: the films have proved to be economically hazardous, and they have, largely, failed to find audiences in the cinema. The *Film on Four* phenomenon has served to illuminate brightly that uneasy cultural netherworld that exists between film and television, and continues to endorse the feeling that those whose films are destined only for television are somehow members of a culturally inadequate underclass.

There has at least been some visible change in television drama, which has been for the better – in the lighting, the camera operation, the design, and the graphics – but there's also been, in involuntary homage to present-day Hollywood, a deterioration in the writing and the acting. Television in Britain nowadays mimics Hollywood in its development deals, its view of the writer as a creature whose function is to create dialogue to fit storylines conjured by a director and producer from newspaper cuttings, and in the reliance on actors who are, vainly and wishfully, held to be 'bankable' in television terms – that's to say that they're best known for doing something other than being very good actors. I know that I'm parodying the truth, but television drama in this country used to be its own thing – quirky, idiosyncratic, and, for better or worse, reflecting the country that produced it – both in style and in content.

The position of the writer in television when I joined the BBC was a privileged one which owed much to its theatrical antecedents, even if these were far from an unmixed blessing – at best irritating, and at worst a millstone. For a newcomer to TV drama coming from the theatre it was infuriating to hear films referred to as plays, assistant directors as stage managers, and television drama as armchair theatre. I think it contributed to an attitude that discouraged visual expressiveness on the screen, and exaggerated the importance of linear story-telling; but it did have one strength – it gave an emphasis to content over style. In our concern with the look of things, the mood of things, the colour, the shape and the feel of things, we are in danger of forgetting the sound, the meaning and the story. The cult of *auteurism* married to the self-aggrandisement of directors has helped to confirm a view that writers are, at best, a necessary evil. It's rare that directors have a singular point of view of the world and those that do – Renoir, Ozu, Howard Hawks, for instance – are writers themselves. As they say, there are three things that make a good film – the script, the script, and the script.

I owed my job at the BBC to my predecessor, Margaret Matheson, who had suggested me to her boss as a likely replacement. Part of her legacy to me was the friendship of a writer called Tom Clarke who had yet to deliver a play she had commissioned a year or two before. I was soon to learn that she was not alone in this. 'Meet him,' she said. 'You may not get the play, but you'll get a jolly good laugh.' As it happens, to her surprise, and with hindsight, mine, I got both.

I met Tom in a restaurant specified by him, one that was seldom frequented by BBC producers for reasons that were later made clear to me. Our first meeting had many of the characteristics of our relationship over the years: it was fuelled by much food and drink; it was long, and loud, and full of argument and laughter; it solved most of the problems of the economy, of literary theory, and of the British film and television industry; it left few reputations intact; and the bill – to Tom's delight – got me in serious trouble with the keepers of the BBC's purse-strings. He was always keen to pass on his infectious disrespect for anyone who held authority.

The script that Tom delivered to me was about apartheid. Like all his work, it was idiosyncratic, irreverent, witty, and compassionate. There were no 'big issues' that could not be subverted by Tom; nothing was sacred – unless it was the principle that nothing was sacred.

If he gave the impression of a dilettante, it was a misleading one; he was a writer through and through, and this vocation, this will to write, informed his life as an article of faith, applied with an almost religious fortitude. If he often found writing painful, it was because he felt, with Graham Greene, who he admired unstintingly, that 'despair is the price one pays for setting oneself an impossible aim'.

He once wrote a television autobiography; it began something like this:

> A golden Roman chariot, drawn by two white horses, driven by a large, bald man with a high forehead, a nose that suits his vehicle, and a manner that is a mixture of self-aggrandisement and self-mockery, enters a television studio. 'The name's Tom Clarke,' he bellows to camera, 'and I'm a *writer*!'

Like much of Tom's work the project remained unfinished. In a sense the same was true of his life, and was part of his charm: he was always starting something new. He gave the impression of planning his life haphazardly, but actually he was impelled by a succession of enthusiasms, of crazes or passions, that accrued like the layers of clay on a maquette, each addition bringing him, at least in theory, nearer to the form he was seeking.

He was born, I think, in Essex, although it was never possible to be absolutely certain about the details of Tom's past. He had an American father, went to a prep school in Dorset, to public school at Tonbridge, left school early to be an electrical apprentice, became a call boy in a variety theatre, and, briefly, an actor in the West End. His anecdotes were alluring and inventive, but I don't think I'm imagining (or that he was) that he once had one line in a scene with Alec Guinness.

Tom's war was a 'good' war – a satisfying amalgam of high comedy and high adventure. He claimed to have spent much of it sitting in a deck chair in the desert reading a book and suffering from dysentery while shells fell all around him, but more of his time was spent in an aircraft spotting for bombers, and on one occasion being shot down.

He was not seriously injured and paradoxically, given his natural allergy to any form of authority, he became a Captain.

After the war he studied law, and was called to the Bar in 1951. He became impatient with the legal world, and left for Brazil, where he worked as a film editor, and documentary director. When he returned to London, he started to write for television after seeing a newspaper hoarding that read: 'RAB SLAMS SEX AND VIOLENCE ON TV'. That's for me, he thought.

Not even Tom's children could describe him as a father-figure, but he became a sort of mentor for me, a surrogate brother, older, perhaps, but for ever young. I relied on his spirited advice and ardent pessimism. There's a speech he wrote in one of his scripts for a rather faded good-time girl:

> I mean, say you go round thinking things are getting better, like people do. And say it *looks* as though things are getting better. Then, when you think they *have* got better you turn round and . . . well, it seems like they haven't after all.

Parodoxically Tom never lost his optimism that TV drama could recover its youthful buoyancy, and he never lost his belief in the obligation of the BBC to nurture utopian projects. In the last months of his life he was corresponding combatively with John Birt about the BBC's drama output. He met him for tea. 'What was that like, Tom?' 'Nice sandwiches,' he said. His lifelong view of the BBC's bureaucracy was triumphantly vindicated when, shortly after, he received a letter from an apparatchik that began: 'I am sorry that you feel our television drama is disappointing . . .' To which Tom replied, 'Let me say that "your" television drama is also mine, as a glance at my entry in *Who's Who* will confirm.' A glance at his CV would not have told you that his work was among the best that has ever been seen on television in this country, and that to anyone who cares about the future of television drama, his work, and his spirit, ought to be an inspiration; and it would not have told you that he could be the best company that anyone could hope for.

Tom resisted all attempts to make him clubbable, or 'suitable'. 'You can depend on me,' he said to me once, 'to be undependable.' But for all his gruffness, his scathing indictment of the bogus, the pretentious, the pompous, and the powerful, he was not a cynic; he was a realist – but a romantic one. Although no one could fail to describe Tom as an extrovert, in some ways his brashness was a carapace that concealed shyness and emotional reticence, and when I last saw him, he surprised me. 'It's good to see you. You see, I like you,' he said, and I was immeasurably touched.

I directed a film that he wrote, characteristically, about sex and old age. Its three stars – Denholm Elliott, Emlyn Williams, and Joan Greenwood – are now dead, and so is Tom. When he became ill, he said to me, unaware, I think, that he was quoting one of the characters from the film: 'People think you pop off just like that. But you don't. You drop off, bit by bit,' and I know what Tom, having popped off, would be saying about death, 'It's *awful! Awful!*'

I had agreed to become a producer on condition that I would be able to direct films for television, and on Tom's advice, I started to learn about directing films by employing good directors – in particular my friend, Stephen Frears. From watching and talking to them I acquired some basic film wisdom: that the director needs to hold the film in his head while shooting, that he needs to know what shot he is coming from and going to; that a film needs to move – if you can't move the camera, move the actor; that a film is not made in the cutting room; that photography captures everything it sees – what you see through the lens is what you get on the screen; that there is no alchemical transformation when the film is processed, and that light, as Fellini says, is 'the miracle worker, adding, blotting out, reducing, enriching, shading, emphasising, hinting, making the fantastic and the substance of dreams acceptable, or, on the contrary, adding quivering transparent effects and making an illusion out of the greyest everyday reality.'

When I say I learned these things, it was more that I observed them to be true without experiencing them. That came later, as I struggled to rid myself of the habits of years of working in the theatre, which is probably the worst preparation possible for directing films. Theatre is a linear medium, and the physical relationship between the actors and the audience is essentially static. Film is mobile; the audience's point of view is always being changed by the camera. When I started to direct films I learned, from cameramen – in particular Nat Crosby – how to tell a story with the camera, how to develop a shot, how to escape the conventional grammar of wide-shot, 2-shot, close-up, and how to avoid looking at a scene from a theatrical perspective. I'd stand watching a scene in rehearsal and Nat would beckon to me from the other side of the set, and I'd circle the scene, like an inquisitive bird, seeing the actors from fresh and unfamiliar angles.

The tendency of the theatre director coming to film is to duplicate sound and vision – to show the audience who is speaking, to be reluctant to assume the power of being able to change the audience's perspective by changing the size of the shot, by cutting, by music, by sound effects. It's all too easy, too, to assume that the visual image is paramount, and to ignore the capacity of film to exploit the dynamic of what you see and what you hear, sometimes complementary, sometimes in opposition. All the experience of a theatre director is to take the text as the unalterable given, and illuminate it, not shape it, carve it up, mould it, re-construct it as a director does in editing a film. Of course, if the material isn't there, if the performances don't exist, the editor can't conjure them from the ether; but if they do, the editor can minimise the flaws, disguise the follies, and, like a sculptor with a piece of marble, exploit the seams and shapes that exist in the stone. What film and theatre have in common is this: they both have to live from moment to moment, and to achieve this their essence – the matter that is worth preserving – has to be distilled from the raw material. That it's incomparably harder to achieve this in the theatre doesn't, of course, make either a superior medium.

I once went on a short course of film editing. The first afternoon we were given an editing machine and about a dozen shots of two men throwing a ball at each other watched by a woman who sat on a park bench. We were told to cut the shots together to make a sequence. I started off enthusiastically, assuming that the point of the exercise was a technical one, to decide when to make the cut from the man throwing the ball to the man receiving it, and when to cut to the face of the woman on the bench. After two hours I had a sequence; it lasted about a minute and although it had a coherent visual logic – people looking in the right direction, the action appearing natural – it was completely and irredeemably boring. It was then I realised the point of the exercise was to illustrate a necessary truth about editing: it doesn't have to be in the film just because it's been shot. The material we'd been given only had the potential of sustaining interest for a maximum of ten seconds; beyond that it had no life. It's always painful to realise you have to junk your favourite shot, but the audience has no curiosity about the hours that it took to achieve, you have to concede to the editor's unsentimental objectivity. I've done a number of films with an editor who comments drily if he doesn't like something, 'Doesn't get my rocks off,' and you can't argue with that.

I started working for the BBC at the end of what might be called a 'golden age' of TV drama, which can best be described, quite simply, as a period when the making of drama, and its quality, was the primary activity – more important than institutional politics, management initiatives, and making money. People in the BBC drama department were willing to work for less pay and lower conditions than 'outside' because they believed in a collective endeavour, that they were a part of an entire vision. It was a state of mind that could seem irritating to the outsider, and often seemed blinkered and insular. It was a sort of faith that was, on occasions, almost bewilderingly mystical. I was filming *Tumbledown* on a cold hill in Wales, at night, in the pouring rain, and talking to a prop man. 'I like working here,' he said. 'You get to make good programmes.' '*Here?*' I said. '*Here?* In Wales? In the Preseli Hills?' 'No, no,' he said, 'I mean at the BBC.' 'Here' was a territory of the mind – a heartland, if you like – and it's one that has been systematically eroded over the past few years.

Working for the BBC was described to me indelibly by Tom Clarke as like working for a cross between the Church and the Post Office; it seldom failed to live down to expectations. It could be infuriating and attritional to contend with official sanctimoniousness coupled with institutional inertia, but at the same time it was exhilarating to work with talented people who managed the system with guerrilla cunning and efficiency. It was possible to make a film for no other reason than the shared belief that it was worth making for itself alone rather than as a commodity or as a token in the ratings game.

There has been a crisis of faith in broadcasting, and it is hard to find a clearer example of working in good faith and working in bad than comparing the difference between the history of two BBC soap operas: *Eastenders* and *Eldorado*. The first was made in a spirit of innocence, enthusiasm and energetic commitment; the second was mired in cynicism, and the torpor of disaffection. We've all heard people say, after reading a Jackie Collins novel or seeing a West End musical, 'Oh, I think I could turn my hand to that and make a lot of money.' This misses a crucial point about popular culture: however it may appear, popular novels, films, musicals, and TV shows are not cynically constructed. Their makers – the writers, directors and producers – *believe* in them. If you try to manufacture popular culture synthetically, it won't work; you can't fake it, your bad faith will always betray you.

The necessary marriage of good faith and self-belief, even

if deluded, was illustrated for me by a story that a publisher told me about Jeffrey Archer. Archer said to the publisher, 'I'm thinking of writing a novel.' 'Ah,' said the publisher expectantly. 'Do you think,' said Archer, 'do you think that after writing several novels that I might – ' Here he paused; there was an awkward silence as the publisher waited for the inevitable request not only to read the novel but to publish it. 'Do you think,' said Archer, 'that I might ever win the Nobel Prize for Literature?'

Tumbledown was a film I made for the BBC in the autumn of 1986, and it was shown to an audience of over sixteen million the year after, almost five years to the day after the battle which the film's title celebrates. It was a film about war, or to be more specific, the Falklands War. That this was an incendiary subject was brought home to me sharply at a party just before I shot the film. I was talking to a woman who asked what I was doing. A film about the Falklands War, I said. Without troubling to hear more, she damned me for softness, liberalism, and woolly thinking. At the same party I encountered an ex-Labour peer, who said, 'I saw your *Guys and Dolls* three times. Wonderful. But last time you had a black man in the cast. Quite unacceptable.'

The film was written by Charles Wood and based on the experiences of a young Scots Guards officer, Robert Lawrence, who was shot during the war. It wasn't about the causes of the war, or the public aspects before, during, or after; it wasn't 'political' – or at least, polemical. It was concerned with the politics of the heart – the attraction of war to young men, the cost of it when it ends in triumph, and the inevitable cycle of tragedy that begins as soon as arms are taken up. There were strenuous attempts to prevent the film being made by the Scots Guards, the Ministry of Defence, and the Home Office, and it was soundly condemned in parliament before a single frame had been exposed. When the film was finished a friend of mine was invited to Chelsea Barracks for lunch by an officer of the Scots Guards. She was standing with a glass of sherry talking to her friend when the Colonel joined them. He discovered that she was working for the director of the notorious *Tumbledown*. Without hesitation he said, 'Your guest won't be staying for lunch,' and turned his back on her. He probably shared the view of the *Daily Telegraph* defence correspondent (who reviewed the film on the same principle as sending the crime correspondent to review *Macbeth*). 'I'm all for knocking the Establishment,' he said. 'but I'm choosy about who does it.'

The decision to make the film was spuriously confused with the decision *not* to make the bio-play of the Falklands conflict which featured Margaret Thatcher as its heroine. I was heartened by the encounter with the then Controller of BBC 1, Bill Cotton, who said he'd been contacted by 'someone who ought to have known better' who had suggested that both scripts were made 'so that the public could judge'. 'The public judge? The public *judge*?' said Bill. 'It's not a bloody panel game!'

The film wasn't a documentary, a quasi-documentary, or even a 'drama-documentary', the heart-sinking label that's attached to any piece of dramatic entertainment inspired by real events. It was a film drama whose characters were, like the best of fiction, drawn from life. Many of them could, if they chose, identify themselves in the story. The lawyers were therefore concerned that we were free from the stain of defamation. During long discussions it was often difficult to understand what constituted a defamatory statement. A character in the script, a young girl, was described in the stage directions as a punk. The lawyer said this was potentially defamatory. I was bemused. It could equally be seen as a satisfyingly flattering factual statement. To judge from reading newspapers it often seems that the unwritten law of libel is that it is defamatory to tell the truth about someone who has money, influence and a strong will. The lawyer argued that it could be defamatory to show a Scots Guardsman, who is a Londoner, speaking in a bad Scottish accent. Alan Bennett told me that when he was doing *An Englishman Abroad* he was advised that it could be libellous to say, 'Laertes looks as though he's got a couple of King Edwards down his tights.' It seems much more likely to have been received as a handsome compliment.

Preparing the film, I was constantly reminded of the vicariousness of my profession. I spent a large part of my days culling information from a young man who had been trained as a soldier, fought a war, killed several young men, and been horribly wounded. A Chilean actor came in to be interviewed for the part of an Argentinian. He had spent several months in Chilean jails being tortured. A Cypriot actor came in; he was in Cyprus during the Turkish invasion. 'Why,' he said, 'could the British go 12,000 miles to fight the Argentinians and not lift a finger to stop the Turks although there were RAF bases on the island and the British Army trained there?' I didn't know the answer. A black actress came in to meet me, whose brother was in the Navy during the Falklands War. He was now irrevocably brain-damaged from an explosion. We live constantly at second-hand, filching and borrowing and consuming the experience of others in order to write or act or direct.

It's a strange and depressing paradox that whenever films or plays turn their attention to their own world, the world of 'showbiz', the results are always, entertaining or not, fatuously poorly observed. Maybe we've come to believe in our own fictions and, like Warner Baxter in *42nd Street*, we believe that you can go out there a youngster and come back a star. This, according to Robert Lawrence, is how his contemporaries saw going to war – they were the stars of the movies in their own heads.

The BBC that I was working for needed reform. It was overextended and underfunded. It was overstaffed, it was inefficient, it was often lamed by inert bureaucracy, and for all the virtues of loyalty, continuity, and working together to get the job done, you could also find passive disobedience, stagnation, and working together to fuck the job up. But these characteristics effect any organisation at any time, particularly those like the BBC, the Arts Council, the

National Health and the National Theatre, that were founded in the post-war years in the zealous hope that all society would work together for the collective good. The fact that this has proved to be an inaccurate vision doesn't make it an inadequate one. I believe it is possible to change these organisations pragmatically, to make them more efficient, more cost-effective – 'efficiently managed', if you like – without altering the aims of their charters.

A few years ago I used to see Fred Zinnemann quite often. I remember him talking about the BBC. 'A wonderful organisation,' he said. 'It's like MGM used to be before movie-makers became businessmen – you have continuity, your work is allowed to develop.' Today this seems as remote as – well, as Hollywood in the thirties. I don't know how this can be recovered at the BBC, but without giving a sense of vision, common purpose, and continuity to the work of producers, directors, writers, actors, cameramen, designers, technicians and production teams, I know that BBC drama will always be less than the sum of its parts, and it will never achieve the collective confidence that transforms the ordinary into the distinctive, and the good into the excellent.

I dislike it when someone in my world speaks of their 'career', as if the life of an actor or a director or a writer were capable of being planned with the strategic caution of a business consultant. Apart from the (almost unique) privilege of getting paid for what you enjoy, the only goal that really matters is whether you do good work. I'm sure there are those who would argue that, divine vocation or not, every Catholic priest aspires to be a bishop, every bishop a cardinal, every cardinal a pope, but I don't think there are many theatre directors who embark on their professional lives with the aim of becoming Director of the National Theatre. If there are, I was not among their number, at least not until I walked into my office at the National Theatre after a lengthy, frustrating and inconclusive meeting with

Peter Hall and fellow Associate Directors. The office was occupied by Howard Brenton and David Hare, who were writing *Pravda*, their wonderfully prescient satire on the rise and rise of Rupert Murdoch. Howard paused for a moment in his two-fisted assaults on the typewriter. 'How was your meeting?' said Howard. 'Mmmm,' I grunted, for once sympathetic to Peter Hall's problems. 'I wonder if *I* could ever run the National Theatre?' 'But you must,' said Howard. 'It's your destiny.' And so it became.

It's a profound irony – at least to me – that I only became eligible to become the Director of the most prestigious theatre company in the English-speaking world by directing an American musical comedy. Prior to that, apart from running regional theatres, such reputation as I had derived from directing rigorous productions of acerbic new plays and TV films, and a highly successful production of *Hamlet* that dispensed with the Ghost. Still, as they say, everyone needs a hit.

The musical comedy that changed my life was *Guys and Dolls*, which I'd first become aware of through my father's overcoat, a loudish, belted, tweed coat with giant shoulders called Big Nig. 'Why is your coat called Big Nig?' I asked my father at the age of twelve. 'Read more than somewhat and you'll find out.' I already read more than somewhat, in fact my eyes ached from reading in torchlight under the bed-covers. '*More Than Somewhat*!' he growled. 'By Damon Runyon.' So I read Damon Runyon and I understood: Big Nig was a crapshooter and Damon Runyon was a magical writer.

About the same time the film of *Guys and Dolls* was released, a film based, according to the feed-box noise, on a story by Damon Runyon. I worshipped Brando, I was in love with Jean Simmons, I was cool towards Sinatra, and I was entranced by the songs and the dialogue – some of which I could even recognise from the original.

In the subsequent years I came to know the Broadway cast recording well, and had a nodding acquaintance with the script. While I was at Nottingham Playhouse I'd occasionally think about doing the show and then, daunted by the demands of the score and the book, think again. I never saw a stage production until my own – not even the 1979 Half Moon Theatre production, whose director told me that *Guys and Dolls* was so good, not even a director could mess it up.

In the middle of 1981 I agreed to join the National Theatre as an Associate Director. I had no clear programme of plays, and my first production was to be in the Olivier Theatre. Peter Hall was clearly apprehensive that I would be passionate to direct *Woyzek*, or a minor Ostrovsky, when what he needed at the time was a full-blooded crowd-pleaser. 'Could you think,' he asked plaintively, 'of doing a major popular classic?'

Composing the content of the repertoire will always be a balancing act between adventure and caution, between known classics and the unknown, recent plays and new ones, but the spine of the work will always be the classics. They are our genetic link with the past and our means of decoding the present. Every age sees its own reflection in these plays. We find in them not the past throwing a shadow on the present, but a distorted image of ourselves – our questions, our doubts and confusions. The classics survive not because they are relics venerated for their age but because of what they mean to us *now*. But the problem that anyone running a theatre faces is that there are a finite number of classics, and many of them rotate in the repertoires of our large theatres with the mechanical regularity of a prayer wheel. Voltaire was familiar with the problem:

> 'How many plays have been written in French?' asked Candide.
>
> 'About five or six thousand,' replied the Abbé.
>
> 'That's a lot,' Candide remarked. 'How many are any good?'
>
> 'Fifteen or sixteen,' replied the other.
>
> 'That's a lot.'

I racked my brains, but came up with nothing until I stood

in a record shop in Dean Street, which specialised in Broadway show albums and Ennio Morricone film scores. I saw the title *Guys and Dolls*, and knew that I was being given a nudge. I told Peter Hall, who was cautious but enthusiastic. I was, he said, the latest in a long line of claimants who had wanted to direct it at the National – including Olivier, who had planned to do the show at the Old Vic in 1970. He had cast it – himself as Nathan, Geraldine McEwan as Adelaide, Edward Woodward as Sky, Louise Purnell as Sarah, and dance rehearsals had begun; his coronary thrombosis nipped the production in the bud. Olivier always credited Ken Tynan with initiating the idea of doing *Guys and Dolls*, and my own adult enthusiasm owes a lot to Tynan's advocacy. He described it as the 'second-best American play' – the best being *Death of a Salesman*.

It seems anomalous to me now, when I feel so much more drawn to Europe than America, that America is such an ingrained habit of mind. I grew up in a landscape that seems to me now to define Englishness almost to the point of parody, the sort of landscape that could, and probably did, sustain colonial exiles in a comfortable fiction of an unchanged and unchangeable homeland. Physically, in spite of some small-scale speculative building of stuccoed breeze-block bungalows, it evoked the nineteenth century, socially an even earlier era: forelock-pulling country. I took the loveliness of the surrounding countryside for granted, and only fairly recently have I come to regret my indifference to the extraordinary privilege of growing up in a quite literally enchanted landscape – it was Arthurian as well as Hardy country. It's a landscape that, a friend of mine says, makes you see the point of England.

But isolated in the epicentre of Englishness, my brain was willingly, indeed eagerly, colonised by American culture – Marvel comics, rock and roll, jazz, fiction, movies, TV, even the theatre. Like many of my generation in the late-fifties, I was a cultural Fifth Columnist for most of my formative years. It wasn't just that American culture was something *other*, something not British, it was simply better than anything we had. The theatre of Arthur Miller and Tennessee Williams seemed to be the opposite of everything the British theatre stood for; it was ambitious, dense, political, poetic and heroic, where even the brightest talents of the British theatre seemed etiolated and petulant. We had nothing on TV to match the wit of *The Burns and Allen Show*, or *I Love Lucy*, or (unrivalled to this day) *Bilko*, which were the fruits of a comic tradition more robust, more adult, and not to put too fine a point on it, funnier than our own. And in music and the movies I celebrated the litany of my secular saints – Elvis, Buddy Holly, Jerry Lee Lewis, Little Richard, Fats Domino, Big Bill Broonzy, John Lee Hooker, Charlie Parker, Miles Davis, John Coltrane, Billie Holiday, James Stewart, Kirk Douglas, Cary Grant, Marlon Brando, James Dean, Grace Kelly, Ava Gardner, Rita Hayworth, Marilyn Monroe. The dazzle of their epiphany doesn't seemed much dimmed today.

Peter Hall gave the go-ahead to *Guys and Dolls* in early October – we had three months to cast and design the show before rehearsals started in January. I had directed musicals before but never on the scale that we anticipated in the Olivier; it seemed like moving from a back-garden paddling pool to the Pacific Ocean. I started work with John Gunter, the designer, in mid-October. We had worked together intermittently for about as long as Nathan Detroit and Adelaide had been engaged, and we operated by then a sort of shorthand. John quickly began to develop a scheme for the show. We realised our choices were simple – to opt for a standing set that would embrace all locations, with a production that laid little emphasis on the traditional values of the Broadway musical; or to go for broke – epic, flamboyant, extrovert and spectacular; Broadway in its heyday.

We talked a lot about movies – the fluency with which Gene Kelly's films blended the conventions of studio naturalism with extreme fantasy; the affectation, parody and bravura of Scorsese's *New York, New York*; the visual hallmarks of gangster movies. We discussed each scene in terms of staging it in a film version, and then translated those ideas into the appropriate gesture for the giant jaws of the Olivier stage. We failed to persuade Peter Hall to allow us a 'research' trip to New York, but we drew very heavily on Andreas Feininger's wonderful photographs of Manhattan in the forties. John began to create a structure that suggested Times Square by day. For night, we thought idly of neon – impractical, we thought, too bright.

I went for a weekend in Paris, and in the bookshop in the Beaubourg Centre I saw an American book: *Let There be Neon* by Rudi Stera. I lost no time in telling John that divine intervention had occurred. The book is a loving account of the birth, history, manufacture and current use of neon. We became entranced with it. 'Neon is writing with light,' said Rudi Stera, and John began to write with it. The set he designed was a joyous and ingenious invention, that fully exploited the most thrilling aspect of stage design – the ability to transform space; it moved effortlessly from the intimate to the epic, from the realistic to the fantastic, while making each location specific and detailed and full of character.

Sue Blane, the costume designer, matched John's invention and joined us, along with David Toguri, the choreographer, in long, discursive planning meetings. Sometimes we sat in silence; sometimes we chattered like parrots, and sometimes speculated ruminatively: 'What if we were to do . . .?' followed by a pregnant silence. We were much preoccupied by the low dive in Havana. At one stage we decided to have a café entirely populated by *émigrés* from film sets in Cuba – Humphrey Bogart, Lauren Bacall, Carmen Miranda, Sydney Greenstreet, Spencer Tracy – even the young Fidel Castro. We settled for a drag queen and eccentric local clientele.

To have the talents of John Gunter, David Toguri, Sue Blane, and David Hersey (the lighting designer) was luck of a rare degree, but when it came to casting it was clear the production had a charmed life. Casting is a lottery; it's an almost invariable rule of casting that the actor and actress you want has just signed for a film, two years with the RSC, or is planning to have a baby. In this case it seemed as if destiny had marked the actors' cards, and within a short time we had Julia McKenzie, Bob Hoskins, Ian Charleson, Julie Covington and a company of great individual and collective strength. 'We want people with bumps,' said Cy Feuer, the producer of the original *Guys and Dolls* production. Our cast was richly corrugated.

In the US there was a period of about thirty years from around 1930 when that 'marvellous invalid', the theatre, seemed to be in a state of constant ecstasy: O'Neill, Wilder, Odets, Hart and Kaufman, Hecht and McArthur, Williams and Miller – in addition to which it was the Golden Age of the Broadway musical. This was a dramatic form – drama, song and dance blended with energy, optimism and astringent wit – that for a few years reached a perfect equilibrium and then began to ossify, to decay, and failed to re-invent itself. There are not many great Broadway musicals but I believe that as examples of the dramatic art in a singular state of grace they have as much right to inclusion in a theatre dedicated to 'excellence' as any other. If I have to name them I would cite: *Guys and Dolls, Pal Joey, West Side Story, My Fair Lady, Gypsy* (possibly), *Oklahoma, South Pacific* and *Carousel*.

All these musicals address the emotional experience of an audience directly, and without inhibition. In this they are peculiarly American – devoid of irony, cynicism, and pessimism. No English writer could have ended the story that *Carousel* tells with the determination to purge darkness with hope; it's an assertion of a national faith: wilful optimism – 'You'll never walk alone.'

All musicals are love stories – *Guys and Dolls* is endowed with two of them. It's a 'fairy-tale of New York', peopled by many of Damon Runyon's characters but without the savage undertow of most of his stories – more Runyonesque than Runyonese. His world is a wholly successful fictional creation, as hermetic, consistent and original as Wodehouse's or Flann O'Brien's. It's always tempting to allow different criteria to apply to acting in musicals, to allow the artificiality of the medium to inform the performance. I wanted the actors to play truthfully, without sentimentality, to present a world larger than life without parody or facetiousness; to be true, in effect, to the 'fairy-tale'. Accents were studiously honed, the characters – even those on the periphery – were invested with offstage biographies. Runyon's stories were always on hand, and a professional croupier came in to teach us how to shoot craps.

We started rehearsals in early January – a seven-week stint, during which many of the cast had to learn from scratch to dance and sing harmonies, and all of them had to learn a tap routine. I was possessed by the idea that the show had to end with the entire cast tap-dancing down Broadway, and it was just as well that David Toguri was on hand to teach them. No choreographer I know has his skill and tact with actors, his invention and his indomitable good humour. And looking at the dancing of some of the cast at the early rehearsals, you'd have to say that he was an alchemist.

Guys and Dolls is essentially a play with music. The songs are always a logical extension of the dramatic situation and they always push the action forward, rather than allowing it to slow down or stand still. It's an irony that almost all the songs were written by Frank Loesser before the dialogue, which merely serves to highlight Loesser's genius as a dramatic lyricist. Abe Burrows wrote the book after an abortive script by Joe Swerling had been abandoned. 'Make it funny,' said George Kaufman, the director. 'But not *too* funny,' added Loesser. Abe Burrows certainly made it funny, but if I were looking for the catalytic talent that made *Guys and Dolls* so successful, I would lay 6 to 5 on Kaufman. He was a marvellous playwright (with Moss Hart and others he was known as 'The Great Collaborator') and, as director, a *play-maker*, and he was an exacting and utterly professional craftsman. He insisted on regarding *Guys and Dolls* as a play interrupted by musical numbers. He felt this so strongly that he regarded most of the songs as 'lobby' numbers – every time a song started he sprinted for the lobby for a cigarette. Abe Burrows once overheard him, mid-sprint, mutter, 'Good God, do we have to do *every* number this son-of-a-bitch ever wrote?'

'This beats working,' said Bob Hoskins on more than one occasion. There were times when it didn't seem fair to be paid for having so much fun; in fact there were times when I would have happily paid to do what I was doing. We worked hard, but it wasn't hard work; the show is so well crafted that there is an almost mathematical precision to it that demands that you get it right. 'Musicals are not written, they're fixed,' runs the adage. If you're doing a show that has been fixed to perfection, run for countless performances in countless productions, you know that if something isn't working, it's not the show's fault – it's yours. Ironically, this is comforting. For all this, there's nothing mechanical about the show; it has a life of its own and a heart as big as a skyscraper.

As the first night approached, everybody I met seemed to have seen the original Broadway production, or loved the film, knew every word of the lyrics, had played the parts or had married one of the chorus. If you do a major Shakespeare play you inherit the baggage of previous productions, and you are haunted by theatrical tradition. With *Guys and Dolls* I felt we were toying with something altogether more personal, and more passionate; a world of sentimental memories. The stakes were high, and gambling metaphors gushed in the press, like a burst water main. What they said was true: we had to win this hand or crap out in ignominy. In the end, the joy that we took in the show was shared by the audience; we had a success. Critics, immobile as Lazarus, spoke of dancing down the South Bank; one of them, correctly, described the show as a 'love letter to Broadway'; and, thanks to David Toguri, I even learned to tap.

The success of *Guys and Dolls* in 1982 made me a fancied runner for the National Theatre leadership stakes. Not that there seemed at the time any sign that Peter Hall would move on; he looked as enduring as Castro. I imagined that he was happy with his lot: the uxoriousness of his life at the National Theatre dovetailed with flings directing operas in Bayreuth, Glyndebourne, New York and Los Angeles, but three years later, in 1985, he told me he had decided to leave and, pointing out that it was not in his gift, asked if I might be interested in his job. Restlessness is Peter's natural condition; he has a protean energy, and an apparently insatiable appetite for work that, were he not so apparently self-assured, would denote a deep-set insecurity. No one that could twice contemplate suicide (as he confesses in his autobiography) could claim to be without self-doubt, but it is an enviable mark of his strength that he invariably radiates confidence, and when beaten to the ground by a particularly thorough drubbing from the critics, he emerges a day or two later like a large shaggy dog coming out of the river, shakes the hurtful abuse from him, and pounds enthusiastically towards his next production. I found him a consistently generous and acute producer who taught me that no advice is worth giving to a director when he is working for you. 'If the Board offer you the job,' he said, 'stick out for your own terms.'

The Chairman of the Board of the National was Max Rayne, a dapper, wise, affectionate, curiously indecisive man who had made his fortune out of property in the sixties, became a generous philanthropist, a shrewd and enthusiastic art collector, and had been Chairman of the theatre since the early-seventies. Over several months I was sniffed at, sounded out, dined at the Savoy to see if I knew (half metaphorically) which knife and fork to use, and politely interrogated in a series of meetings with members of the Board's inner caucus. Max, from a radical Lithuanian Jewish background, tested the severity of my political convictions. He told me that his grandmother used to say, 'If he says he's a communist and has holes in his shoes, he's a communist.' I stared at a hole the size of a shilling and shiftily hid my feet under a chair.

When I became Director I wasn't sure whether I expected people to commiserate or congratulate. I held a press conference, wearing suit and tie for the first time (professionally) for many years. 'Beware of any enterprise that requires new clothes,' said Emerson. I returned from the press conference and was violently sick, so much so that my ribs ached for days. Was this a metaphor for my life to come? I sat on a train the next day, cutting through a frosted amber landscape in the early morning sun, and read of a character called 'Richard Eyre', who seemed only vaguely familiar, who had woken up one morning transformed like Kafka's beetle into a creature alien even to himself.

In the Polish epic *The Knights of the Teutonic Order*, set in the early Middle Ages, a knight is tortured, his tongue is cut out, and he is imprisoned in an iron box for several years. He is eventually liberated from his confinement and he shambles out, grey-haired, sightless and tongueless, to rediscover a world whose features he can now only guess at. This is not light years aware from my nightmares about the Château d'If on the South Bank.

However much I might self-dramatisingly exaggerate, the reality is different enough to be comforting. The National Theatre is not an immutable bureaucracy, nor is it a cultural colossus riddled with institutional inertia. It is, to state what ought to be obvious, a theatre, or to be more obvious still, three theatres within one building. It exists to do work that, either by content or by execution or both, could not be performed or would not be initiated by the commercial sector. It provides continuity of 'investment', of employment, and of theatrical tradition, and this requires a subsidy to supplement the income from the box office. Recently an attempt has been made to blur the distinction between the commercial and the subsidised theatre in order to argue that there is no longer any real need for subsidy: if market forces can prevail for large nationalised businesses, so they should for large theatre companies. This conveniently ignores the fact that six nights a week, fifty-two weeks a year, the NT places 2,300 seats for sale in the 'market place', and depends for its survival on the sale of at least 1,750 of them.

No doubt the subsidised theatres have conspired in undermining their status by presenting shows that appear to be governed by a commercial imperative indistinguishable from the West End, and the relentless emphasis on productivity, cost-effectiveness, mixed economies, and profit margins has obscured the real issue which is not about money but art. The case for the existence of subsidised theatres is made on their stages and the only questions worth asking are, 'Is what I see on the stage any good?' and, 'What does it mean to me?' The commercial theatre is defined by its need to make a profit; the subsidised theatre is defined by its need to be good.

Any organisation that has the word 'National' attached to it must be expected to fulfil some sort of exemplary function, and a theatre's activities are rather more conspicuous than a hospital or sports centre. When I worked for many years in theatres outside London I looked, with a mixture of envy, irony, and longing, at the large metropolitan 'centres of excellence'. When I became the National Theatre's Director I was acutely conscious of the obligation for the theatre to live up to its name: the title of the National Theatre of Great Britain and Northern Ireland can be viewed with some cynicism if its work is constantly confined to its concrete bunker on the South Bank. I thought it was imperative that the National Theatre toured extensively on a small and large scale, nationally and internationally, and that we formed significant links with regional theatres through co-productions. We had to replace the upper case of 'National' with the lower case of 'national', an aim that was somewhat at odds with plans for the addition of 'Royal' to the theatre's title. My arrival coincided with this re-christening and provided me with my first, and to this date only, confrontation with the Board; it was as serious as it was comic.

The addition of 'Royal' made the theatre into another British oxymoron. The nation, the people of Britain, are subjects, possessing nothing in their name – it is Her Majesty's parliament, her armed forces, her postal services, her opera, her animal protection league, her life-boat service, and now her national theatre. The 'ploughman's lunch' was an adman's fiction in the sixties, an attempt to conjure up a glorious bucolic past, unbroken eating traditions carried on in every ale-house in the kingdom. The 'Royal' appellation was a similar piece of synthetic memorialising. The job of the theatre should be to raise two fingers to the establishment; I know it's irritating for the patrons of the arts – politicians or monarchs – to endure the often noisy dissent of an apparently arrogant and self-interested clique, but it has always been difficult for rulers to license the jester as well as the judge.

The problem for the Board, in the shape of Lords Rayne and Mishcon, was that there was a 'matter of protocol and precedent' involved in the representation of the Queen in Alan Bennett's play *A Question of Attribution*. I would have gone a long way to have avoided the agony of embarrassment that I caused the two Labour peers by forcing them to state the indelible matters of principle on which their objections were based. I would not, however, have missed the opportunity of hearing Lord Mishcon read the part of the Queen in his finest court-room baritone. The unexpressed implication of my possible resignation was intended to be pre-empted by the hint that 'Larry didn't resign over *Soldiers*', but when, by conviction rather than gamesmanship, it became obvious that I wouldn't do the decent thing and concede, the meeting was closed, cordiality resumed, and my induction as Director of the Royal National Theatre was complete.

There were other trials. Directors are not naturally public people, and are, mercifully, seldom obliged to endure the thumbscrew, rack, and strappado of publicity that's an occupational liability for an actor. I was working with Maggie Smith when a biography of her came out. I asked her if she'd read it; she made a vinegary face. 'Good God, no,' she said. 'I couldn't. I'm an ostrich, I can't bear publicity.' I have more of the mole in me than the ostrich – emerging briefly into the light and then with relief scuttling back below the surface, but my job at the National Theatre has obliged me often to disguise myself as a politician, and strut around in the company of less retiring species.

Politicians live in a sort of hell, condemned to wear a public mask of optimism and decisiveness, and to mouth fictions as if they were objective truths. Doubt is banished; ambiguity prohibited. To concede fallibility is to admit weakness, and to agree with the opposition is to embrace folly. A politician will tell you, as you stand on the deck of a sinking ship, with the water lapping your chin, that the vessel is still on course. Politicians do not talk; they assert – 'The fact of the matter is' – and since their faces are unmarked by the confusions and uncertainties that the rest of us endure, it is small wonder that they enjoy so little public esteem. When people are asked what professions they admire, politicians always limp home last – well behind the journalists and the tax inspectors. John Updike says that 'celebrity eats the face' – and maybe the soul in the case of politicians.

I've had to become a politician of a sort, lobbying politicians, sponsors, even audiences. The rite of passage which, for me, marked my accession to this new role was the eightieth birthday of Olivier, which was the last time he came to the National Theatre. A gala evening had been arranged, one of those elephantine occasions that stand in danger of being suffocated under a blanket of earnest and well-meant litanies of adulation. I'd only just been made Director, and so I was standing rather diffidently by the stage door waiting for Olivier in the ample shadow of Peter Hall. There was an enormous crowd and hordes of paparazzi in the street. The atmosphere was somewhere between that of St Peter's Square when the crowd are waiting for the appearance of the Pope on the balcony, and that on the pavement outside one of the large hotels before an awards ceremony to which Joan Collins has been invited.

As the car pulled up there was a wail from the crowd, almost Iranian in its tone and intensity, and out of the car stepped Olivier, smaller, almost unrecognisably so, a very,

very frail man supported by Joan Plowright. There was a cascade of flash bulbs and screams and hoots. For a moment he was completely dazed. Then he moved slightly towards the crowd, hesitating between terror and intense joy.

At the same moment Peter Hall started to move to welcome him, his arms outstretched in greeting. There was a moment when Larry looked at Peter as if he was unsure why he was being approached by this large genial man with a beard and benign smile. They shook hands, Larry now certain of who he was meeting. Then he turned and, politely bemused, stared at me as if I was the wrong suspect in a police identity parade.

The three of us were then prodded into an awkward line for the designated, and dreaded, 'photo opportunity'. We all had reasons to feel uncomfortable, and the three of us stared mirthlessly at the cameras in almost total embarrassment: the Past, the Present, and the Future of the National Theatre. Never did I feel history sit quite so heavily on my shoulders.

The evening proceeded as those evenings do; very emotional, very effusive, very long. The climax, and indeed the point of the evening, came at the end. Larry sat in one of the 'ashtrays' at the side of the theatre that had been named after him. The whole audience stood up, turned to him, and applauded him. He smiled, an enchanting, childlike smile of pure pleasure. He was a man for whom applause was almost better than life itself. He acknowledged the applause in a beautiful gesture, raising his right hand and turning it as if he were cupping butterflies. Joan made several attempts to lead him out but he was not going to be led. The applause went on and on. And on. The audience would happily have stayed for an hour. He was asked once what his policy was for the National Theatre. 'To make the audience applaud,' he said.

On his way to the stage door, he was lured, without much protest, at least from him, through the Green Room on to a balcony above the street, still packed with a mass of fans and photographers. They shouted, whistled, applauded, and when he left he seemed to be crying, certain that this was the last time he'd hear such a sound, his life's music.

It's not necessarily that he was *the* actor of our time; he wasn't necessarily the best or the wisest or any particular superlative, even if those critical categories have any meaning at all. He simply satisfied a desire for actors to be larger than life, and to be able to be *seen* to be acting at the same time as they are moving you to tears or to laughter. It's the desire to be knowingly seduced.

He satisfied so many of people's needs and longings both within the theatre and without. People want greatness, glory, extremes. That's why they want to go to the theatre; they want it to be bigger, more daring, more physical than their own lives. Kafka said, perhaps unexpectedly, 'If theatre is to affect life, it must be stronger, more intense than ordinary life. That is the law of gravity.' It could be Olivier's epitaph.

It's always said of Churchill that he was a man who exactly matched the moment of history, and it's a leaden truism that we shall never see his like again; the same can be said of Olivier. It's completely impossible, for a catalogue of reasons to do with finance, the structure of the film industry and the theatre, the spirit of the age and the taste of the times, that we will ever again see a great buccaneering actor-manager who is also a Hollywood film star, who is equally celebrated in the theatre, and who is capable of remaking his life and his art so often and so judiciously as he did. It's said, 'Happy the land that needs no heroes.' Happier, perhaps, but duller certainly.

To have three theatres in one building is, to say the least, a noble project. It was Olivier's will, his wilfulness, his ambition, that realised Granville-Barker, William Archer and Shaw's vision. When the National Theatre was built, a 'dream made concrete' (a metaphor made literal), Olivier, was asked what he thought of it. He smiled wryly. 'It's an experiment.' Witty, I think.

Like a youth sitting round the campfire listening to the tales of the village elders, I've heard countless stories of the genesis of the National Theatre building. I've often sat late at night after a technical rehearsal with a designer puzzling over the idiosyncracies of the design of the Olivier Theatre. There was a building committee which comprised many directors (Peter Brook, Bill Gaskill, John Dexter, Michael Eliott), and designers (Jocelyn Herbert, John Bury). All of them, in recollection, are unanimous about one thing: it was Larry's baby. It's not only for that reason that it's appropriate that it's named after him. It embodies him as he was – grand, grandiose, bold, ambitious, difficult, exasperating even, but often thrilling and occasionally unique. When it works there's no auditorium in the world that is as intoxicating as the Olivier; that was as true of the actor as it is of the theatre.

I was lucky with my first outing in the Olivier Theatre with *Guys and Dolls* and I've still never encountered anything as addictive as standing at the back towards the end of the show, night after night, as the audience, banked on the slopes of the auditorium like eager pilgrims, erupted like the roll of an avalanche, swamping the stage with warmth and approbation. When Olivier (who had wanted to play Nathan Detroit at the Old Vic) came to see the show he was generous. He loved it. 'But the accents,' he said. 'A bit of a mélange.'

Over the last few years I have tried to address some of the inherent problems of the National's building, not least the capriciousness of the acoustics of the Olivier auditorium. For my pains I have been described as a barbarian by the architect Denys Lasdun, who, much as he reveres the art of architecture, shows less respect or understanding of the art of the actor and the needs of an audience. Like a French farmer dumping trailerloads of manure on the steps of the Ministry of Agriculture, I am sometimes tempted to send him the mountain of letters of complaint about the acoustics accumulated over many years. But he has no intention of allowing any changes to his 'room', the Olivier auditorium, even if they are manifestly to the benefit of those who use it: the actors, directors, designers – and, of course, the audience. 'Pure form nakedly displayed/ And all things absolutely made,' he says, citing the poet Arthur Clough. Albert Finney is an actor who knows the Olivier stage as well as any actor. I quoted Peter Brook to him once: 'A theatre should be a musical instrument.' 'Yes,' said Albert, 'and who'd make a violin out of fucking concrete.'

For a while I felt dogged by the shadow of my predecessors. Interviewers would ask me how it felt to be following in the footsteps of such 'big men'. I would oblige them by telling the truth: I was daunted. I sat with Peter Hall for a photograph in front of a large photographic blow-up of Olivier. We were both, unwittingly, identically dressed – black shirts (mandatory directorial costume), grey-and-white flecked jackets – and we looked, and I felt, like a Country and Western duo in front of the icon of Hank Williams. In the early days I found it extraordinarily difficult to sustain the public act of self-confidence while crippled by private insecurity. Fear of cowardice sustained me: the certain indignity of resignation and the public admission of failure were outweighed by the uncertain perils of continuing.

Deciding to direct *Hamlet* for the second time reflected this insecurity. Olivier had opened his regime with Peter O'Toole as Hamlet, Peter Hall with Albert Finney, and I followed their precedent with a production that was no more successful than theirs.

I have rehearsed productions which, within the rehearsal room, have generated a febrile excitement, the air charged with urgent meaning, and yet they have failed to translate this sensation to the stage. When I rehearsed *Hamlet* with Daniel Day-Lewis there was universal consensus in the rehearsal room that we were watching a performance of great delicacy and great danger, and yet I was unable – or my production was unable – to do justice to this performance in the Olivier Theatre. Somehow the size of the theatre and the context of the production diminished rather than amplified the performance, and I felt as if the precious liquid that I'd been carrying in the palms of my hands had drained away, and only a clammy dampness remained. It's a mark of Dan's generosity that he never blamed me for it.

I had worked twice before with Dan; he was a definitive Kafka in a film I directed of Alan Bennett's *The Insurance Man*, and equally memorable as the Russian poet Mayakovski in *The Futurists* – a play about the years just after the Revolution. He is a remorselessly honest, mercurial, technically skilful, physically expressive, chameleon-like actor, with the beauty of an El Greco Christ; highly intelligent, and extremely well read, he seems happiest free of intellectual baggage, testing his body against the elements – a short run of ten miles, a bicycle ride of forty.

He is a good friend and it was his loyalty, coupled with his determined fastidiousness, that compelled him to drive himself to a pitch of pain to improve his performance. He had been terribly injured by the notices, which showed the critics in their least attractive light, saturated with snobbery about a 'film actor' who deigned to grace the classical stage, and riddled with perplexed anger and confusion: his performance, they said, was well spoken, badly spoken, adventurous, dull, highly intelligent, devoid of ideas, lucid, opaque, Byronic, Jewish – whatever that might have meant. There was a disturbing vein of *schadenfreude* in many of the reviews, and there was certainly enough despair between Dan and myself to take joy in, if you were so inclined. At least I had the solace, or the distraction, of the work of running the theatre, but Dan had to battle on night after night. When he left the stage in the middle of the scene with the Ghost, it was because, with his remorselessly punishing honesty, there was nothing else he could do. His problem was not so much his relationship with the Ghost of his father, as his relationship with the play. He wrestled nightly with its subjects – fathers, mothers, sons, grief, suicide, sex, love, revenge, intellect, violence, pacifism, discipline, and death and if they floored him he was guilty not of neurosis or incompetence, but of an excess of ambition.

I'm fairly sanguine about critics, even if I sometimes feel

after a bad notice that the appropriate fate for the critic is what they did to the dead Pharaohs before embalming them – having their brains drawn out with a long hook. I'm consoled by Christopher Hampton's observation that we are bound to feel about critics as lampposts do about dogs, but I'm temperamentally unable to affect the detachment of Picasso, who recommended that artists regard critics as ornithologists do birds. Critics are anomalous creatures in the theatre's ecology: the only people in our world who pay no penalty for failure. Steven Berkoff describes them as worn-out tarts. Alan Bennett is nearer the mark when he points out that if only they were, criticism would be in a better state. 'In fact,' he says, 'they're like dizzy girls taken out for the evening, just longing to be fucked and happy to be taken in by any plausible rogue who'll flatter their silly heads while knowing roughly the whereabouts of their private parts. A cheap thrill is all they want; at least tarts have got past that stage.'

I know of no practitioner in the theatre who does not suffer, painfully and unphilosophically, from bad reviews. At the moment when you are most tired, vulnerable, optimistic and subjective, and your work is the centre of a Ptolemaic universe, who can deal with a bargain-basement Galileo telling you that the sun doesn't go round the earth?

Having bad reviews is like being in mourning; you wake up each morning hoping that they've gone away, but there they are, immutable and corrosive as radioactivity. It didn't seem inconsistent in the wake of the sadness when Dan left the production to ask Ian Charleson to take over the part. When I asked him to play Hamlet I knew he'd been ill, had even had pneumonia, and that he still had a chronic sinus complaint which give him large, swollen bags under his eyes. On bad days it was barely possible to glimpse the face beneath the swelling, a malicious parody of his beauty. He was without vanity, but not without hope. He told me that he was HIV Positive and that he thought that the eyes would respond to treatment. When we embarked on rehearsals he was having regular, and immensely painful, acupuncture treatment, and later on, chemotherapy which exhausted and debilitated him. Later in his illness he defiantly rejected all treatment; he wanted to be himself, however painful that was.

I didn't know Ian well until I worked with him on *Guys and Dolls* in 1982. I knew him then as an actor of charm, of wit, of skill, with a kind of engaging melancholy of the Mastroianni variety, which he could dispel with a sardonic and self-mocking wit. He often looked truly beautiful, even angelic; then a mischievous smile would appear and all thought of angels would fly away like frightened starlings.

I'd offered him the part in *Guys and Dolls* on the basis of his acting and hearing him sing at parties. It was typical of him that he insisted on singing the score for me before he accepted the part, and equally typical that when he'd finished singing he said to me, 'You enjoyed that, didn't you, Richard?' He knew he could make an audience (and a director) cry with a romantic ballad, and he loved to do just that as much as he loved to torment me with his relentless mockery of my attempts to learn to tap-dance alongside the cast.

He was a fine, light, unfailingly truthful romantic actor, something that the French value more than we do. Like Cary Grant, he had the gift of making the difficult look effortlessly simple. But with Brick in *Cat on a Hot Tin Roof* and with his Hamlet, he discovered a new gravity in his work. He became, in my view, a real heavyweight.

We had talked some time ago about the parts that he desperately wanted to play – Richard II, Angelo, Benedick, and Hamlet and, as he said to me shortly before his death, 'Lear – God willing.' He had a real passion for Shakespeare, rather rare in his generation. He really loved the density of thought, the great Shakespearian paradoxes, the lyricism, the energy of the verse. He didn't want to paraphrase it; the meaning was for him in the poetry and the poetry in the meaning.

About halfway through the rehearsal period we discussed the future – an unspecified projection. 'Do you think I can go on as Hamlet looking like this?' he said. 'You'll get better,' I said. 'We have to be positive,' he said. And we were. Our text was, of course, from *Hamlet*: 'There's nothing either good or bad but thinking makes it so.'

Hamlet is a poem of death. It charts one of the great human rites of passage – from immaturity to accommodation with death. Hamlet grows up, in effect, to grow dead. Until he leaves for England ('From this time forth/ My thoughts be bloody or be nothing worth') he is on a reckless helter-skelter swerving between reason and chaos. When he returns from England he is changed, aged, matured, reconciled somehow to his end. We see Hamlet in a graveyard obsessed with the physical consequences of death, and then in a scene with Horatio prior to the duel he talks to him about his premonition of death:

> Thou wouldst not think how ill all's here about my heart.
> But it is no matter ... it is but foolery ... We defy augury.
> There is a special providence in the fall of a sparrow. If it
> be now, it is not to come; if it be not to come, it will be
> now; if it be not now, yet it will come. The readiness is all.
> Since no man of aught he leaves knows aught, what is't to
> leave betimes? Let be.

We talked a great deal about Hamlet's accommodation with death, always as a philosophical proposition, his own state lurking just below the surface, hidden subtext. Ian was very fastidious about the 'Let be'. It wasn't, for him, a chiding of Horatio, or a shrug of stoic indifference, it was an assertion, a proposed epitaph, perhaps: don't fuss, don't panic, don't be afraid.

I've no idea if it was Kennedy's coinage, more likely one of his speechwriter's, but the definition of courage as 'grace under pressure' was perfectly suited to Ian. It was something more than stoicism. He defied his illness with a spirit that was dazzling, quite without self-pity, self-dramatisation, and at least openly, without despair. During rehearsals he was utterly without reserve. Where there had been a kind of detachment or caution, a 'Scottishness', perhaps, there was a deep well of generosity, of affection – a largeness of heart, and the only 'Scottish' characteristics that he showed were his doggedness and his persistence.

In his last performance of *Hamlet* he acted as if he knew that it was the last time he'd be on stage. He'd had flu and hadn't played the previous two nights; he was feeling guilt about what he saw as his lack of professionalism. 'If they pay you, you should turn up,' he said. His performance on that Monday night was like that of a man who had been rehearsing for Hamlet all his life. He wasn't playing the part, he became it. By the end of the performance he was visibly exhausted, each line of his final scene painfully wrung from him, his farewell and the character's agonisingly merged. He stood at the curtain call like a tired boxer, battered by applause.

When he became unable to perform, it was a real deprivation to him. Without that there was nothing to hang on to. 'You know me, Richard, if there are two people out there who I can impress, I'd be there if I could.' And he would, if he'd had the strength. We're often accused of sentimentality in the theatre, but it can't be sentimental to miss terribly someone whose company gave so much joy, whose talent really *did* add to the sum of human happiness, and whose courage was beyond admiration.

I had a letter from him a few weeks before he died, just before Christmas. He said:

> One day when I'm better I'd love to attempt Hamlet again, and all the rest; and together we can revitalise Shakespeare. Anyway I hope this is not a dream and I can't tell you how much of a kick I got out of doing the part, if only for the short time I could . . .

He was buried in Edinburgh on a cold, clear, sunlit day in a graveyard tilted on the side of a hill by a railway line. I will never forget the sight of his father teetering on the side of the grave, sobbing helplessly, as the Minister intoned, 'God so loved the world that he gave his only begotten son.'

Let be.

The best day I've spent at the National Theatre is the first day we performed David Hare's trilogy of plays about British institutions: *Racing Demon* on the Church of England, *Murmuring Judges* on the Bar, the Prisons, and the Police, and *The Absence of War* on the Labour Party. The performance began at ten-thirty in the morning and ended twelve hours later. I wish I had been able to enjoy it more but I felt overwhelmed: ludicrously tired and even more ludicrously tense, coiled like a clenched fist, willing everything to go right. It did, but before I was able to relax and enjoy the day, it was over, and I was standing at the back of the auditorium having to jump aside to avoid the buffalo charge of self-advertising critics running for the exits as if their trousers were on fire. Then I went backstage and Robin Bailey told me his wife had just died, and I never quite got to the moment of ecstatic exhilaration that I'd been promising myself for four months.

The idea of a trilogy of plays developed from the success of the first play, *Racing Demon*, in 1990. This play started as nothing more than a shiver of curiosity. David visited the Church of England Synod in York in 1987, with a vague idea that the spectacle of vicars playing politics might make good theatre. He encouraged me to visit the Synod in London and until I read the first draft I had no higher expectations than an astringently satirical look at a largely irrelevant expiring British institution. The play he wrote examined a spiritual landscape with as much detail and wit and compassion as it did the political: is it possible to love God and love man? How does a good person change people's lives for the better? Can an institution established for the common good avoid being devoured by its own internal struggles and contradictions? Is man a social animal interested in justice, in equality, in love?

The two subsequent plays, *Murmuring Judges*, and *The Absence of War*, looked at the worlds of legal and social justice, and begged many of the same questions. I acted as a midwife for David over the three years during which the plays were written, cajoling, encouraging, and occasionally bullying, and I was spoilt by the experience. After their opening I dreaded the return to the business of having to whip up enthusiasm for plays by dead playwrights, and face the habitual crisis of the director – what is the *point* of it? It can often seem an occupation that has much in common with the life of an opposition politician – you're not quite sure what you're for, but for the four months of working on the trilogy I had no doubts, and I mourn for the passing of those days of high excitement and complete fulfilment.

It was not so much the quality of the writing that moved me, nor the excellence of the ensemble of actors, the seamlessness of the presentation, even the evident enjoyment of the audience. What touched me was the paradox at the heart of the occasion: a day dedicated to three plays about the crisis of public institutions demonstrated that one British institution at least does work for reasons that can loftily be dismissed as sentimental: a sense of community, a sense of 'family', a desire to share a common purpose. The whole is greater than the sum of the parts: that's the point of institutions – we do together what we cannot do alone. If we don't try to make our institutions work, what have we got? They're the only formal evidence of man as social animal; they're all imperfect but they're the only instruments of society that represent the belief, the hope – the faith, if you like – that mankind is capable of working together.

I always took Thatcher's dictim, 'There's no such thing as society,' as a figure of speech. I didn't realise that she was so literal, so serious, and so determined to prove her proposition. Her legacy is a sort of political epidemic, a determination to subject every organisation, every institution, to ideological reform at best, abolition at worst, all driven by the Three Horsemen of the contemporary Apocalypse: Money, Management and Marketing.

Are we really so helpless, so apathetic, that we need to deconstruct or destroy all the institutions that we've created in order to improve them? And why do many of the urgent demands for their destruction come from within the institution most conspicuously in need of radical reform – the House of Commons? Even such an inexhaustibly voluble and self-righteous reformer as Tony Benn becomes mute in the face of this question. The hours, the procedures, the electoral system, the adversarial head-banging, the complacency, the inefficiency, the deceit, the clubbiness, the blokiness, all persist without serious demand for change, and the House of Lords – inequitable, indefensible, ineffably absurd – continues with scarcely a murmur for its reform or abolition. Meanwhile, the National Health Service is dissipated, the BBC is diluted, British Rail is parcelled out, the GLC is abolished, and the network of regional theatres is diminished by the very body that is constitutionally charged with protecting them.

Perhaps it's overdoing it to say that it was bliss to be alive and run a theatre in the seventies, but at least we were helped by an Arts Council that was willing, financially and philosophically, to play the role of the unappreciated protector of the ungrateful young, and a society that believed that the value of certain things – like education and the arts – couldn't be quantified and was important precisely for that reason. But the ecology, and the economy, of the theatre has started to resemble the country as a whole; it has become infected by the virus of opportunism. A kind of impatience has grown: actors and directors who might previously have been content to do a year or two in a repertory theatre have begun to look anxiously for jobs in TV, in films, or the national companies, and the previous *de facto* form of apprenticeship for actors in smaller repertory theatres has started to disappear – as has the unspoken sense of shared experience between theatres in Newcastle, Nottingham, Exeter, Birmingham and London. A feeling has grown like a debilitating fungus that maybe these theatres aren't worth saving, and maybe this park serves no useful purpose, and maybe this hospital should be closed down, and maybe we can't justify these courses for adults, and maybe we don't need all these people who don't have jobs and take up all this space and all this money.

I don't believe that it's possible to retrace the steps of the last few years, to perform a sort of social surgery that would change our hearts and minds. We are what we are, and it is we who have made our world as it is. The gift of the post-war era was the promise of freedom: political, and economic, and sexual. It was an illusion: we are prisoners of our own social and economic structures. But because we know it was an illusion that shouldn't stop us from wanting a better world with our limited resources. We are not a poor country. Ion Caramitru told me in shocked tones, expecting my sympathetic support, that he had only 0.2 per cent of the Public Spending Budget of Romania to spend on culture. Ah, I said, if only we had that much.

It's impossible to make any recommendation about arts funding without straying into politics but it's an affectation to pretend that the arts and politics *aren't* connected. I wish that instead of having 'YOU DON'T HAVE TO BE CRAZY TO WORK HERE BUT IT HELPS' on their office walls, ministers would tack up this observation of Auden's:

> In our age the mere making of a work of art is political. So long as artists exist, making what they please and think they ought to make, even if it's not terribly good, even if it only appeals to a handful of people, they remind the management of something managers need to be reminded of, namely, that the managed are people with faces, not anonymous numbers, that *homo laborens* is also *homo ludens*.

The historian, the late E. P. Thompson, said, 'It is in the archipelago of dissenting islands that the only forces are mustered which may at some time liberate the mainland.' I felt this when I saw the miners marching down Kensington High Street to protest against the closure of their pits – hardly a hotbed of dissent. They were being joined by shoppers, applauded by office staff, and cheered by waiters from restaurants who had changed their menus to placards: 'WE SUPPORT THE MINERS'. All of these people were trying to express the same feeling: we are more than the sum of market forces, we are not mere 'economic units', we share a common humanity and a common society and we'd better make the best of it because it's the only one we have.

We've all got a limited capacity for compassion. Show us an injured Bosnian child or a starving Somalian and our hearts bleed, we dip in our pockets, we demand something must be done, and then time and our own self-regard wash away our concern as surely as the tide does a sandcastle. There's a peculiarly obnoxious euphemism used to describe this phenomenon: its called 'compassion fatigue'. Compared to the hell of the victims of civil war or starvation, to talk of the crisis in education and the arts seems like bathos of a high degree, but an equivalent weariness and encroaching deafness are engendered when we speak of *our* hardship.

I'm not playing naive if I say that I really don't understand why the government doesn't support the arts more fully, but then I'm no more able to understand why the government can't see that education is the key to our future, and that those who work in education might know as much about it as the politicians. In the eighties, in London, we were so diffident that we stood by and warmed our hands on the pyre of our city government and uttered barely a murmur of protest. We mustn't let scepticism, cynicism, or apathy lead us to be mute in the face of any attempts to dismantle those organisations and institutions which were set up in the spirit of optimism, and belief that there is such a thing as society.

In the latter years of the Age of Thatcher, I was once invited to a dinner party with several Cabinet members. It was at the house of that now celebrated exile, Alistair McAlpine. We dined well – he'd ordered a take-away from La Gavroche, at that time incontrovertibly the best res-taurant in London. The point of the dinner was to bring together the few government ministers sympathetic to the cause of culture with, as they say, 'leading figures in the arts'.

They'd rounded up many of the usual suspects, and we dutifully made the obvious points about the government getting so much money back from the arts in VAT, tax, employment, tourism, and national self-esteem. Yes, yes, of course, they said, and how can *we* help you? Well, er – we were tongue-tied now in the face of the obvious – give the arts more money, we said. It's not as simple as that, said Geoffrey Howe, there's a problem. Oh, you mean convincing the Treasury, said one of our lot. No, said Geoffrey, convincing the Cabinet. And that's when I felt a euphemism coming on: 'conviction fatigue'.

Tennessee Williams was once asked by a journalist, 'Mr Williams, would you please give us your definition of happiness?' He leant back, rolled his eyes, and said, 'Insensitivity, I guess.' If I were asked for a word to describe running the National Theatre, the word would be 'grief'. Not that it makes me sad, or ill, or wasted; sometimes it does all these things, but just as often I am elated and exhilarated by being responsible for something that is licensed, even obliged, to give pleasure, and that really is more than the sum of its parts. Running the theatre is like grief in that it sneaks into every corner of one's consciousness like a chill east wind, and the only protection is a thin cladding of anxious optimism. I've never been able to develop the carapace adopted by Lord Goodman, who, as Chairman of the Arts Council, was confronted by an indignant friend of mine protesting at the withdrawal of his grant. 'Doesn't it worry you when you leave this office – ' 'Let me stop you,' said Lord Goodman. 'When I leave this office I never worry.' And I've never acquired the sleight of hand of George Kaufman who, desperate to avoid the inevitable conclusion of a rehearsal – 'Could I have a word with you?' from an anxious actor – would start running a scene and slip out of the back of the auditorium, unnoticed until the rehearsal ended.

There is always a problem in a theatre: an actor is ill, a director is no longer available, a writer has withdrawn his play, a lavatory is blocked in the foyer, the box office is showing a haemorrhage, a new season of plays has to be decided, planned, cast, rehearsed, advertised, and once again you're giving a party and wondering if anyone will turn up. In his autobiography Bergman describes what it was like to run the Royal Dramaten Theatre in Stockholm, Sweden's National Theatre:

> Fun in an insane way, both awful and fun. I remember often feeling ill with anxiety, but at the same time I felt a burning curiosity for each new day. I remember climbing up the narrow wooden stairs up to the secretary's and director's room, with a mixed sense of panic and cheerfulness. I learnt that everything was a matter of life and death, but not particularly important, that reason and misunderstanding went hand in hand like Siamese twins, that the ordinary fixed proportion of failure predominates and lack of self-confidence is the most dangerous thing in the world, that the desire to give up affects even the strongest, and that the daily grumbling which runs like a humming note through ceilings and walls represents a kind of security. We scream and complain and moan, but we often laugh.

If you run a theatre it is hard to find time to think about your own productions. You are always tempted, as Bergman says, to 'reach backwards for already proven solutions'. All theatre directors dream of being able to develop their own work, but the reality is that when you run a theatre it consumes you; you become its creature. Jérome Savary, the French director, gave me some excellent advice for self-preservation, marinated in Gallic cynicism, that I've never quite succeeded in following:

> Don't go and see the plays – get someone to do it for you who you trust. And make sure you have a good restaurant: people care more about eating than theatre.

It's the sort of advice that my mother might have given me, with a well-intended innocence. She would have understood that a theatre director needs to be somehow assertive and yet self-effacing, dogged and yet pliable, demanding yet supportive, because it sounds like a prescription for a perfect marriage partner. Directors are ever hopeful of making a successful marriage of actor and character, text and design, play and audience, and if they are hesitant, doubtful, and diffident, it is because they know just how difficult it is, as in real life, to make a marriage work. My mother might also have given me the advice she gave to my father when he slipped off a sofa, limp with drink, after an over-indulgent dinner, 'Bloody fool, I told him not to do that.' But, in spite of her advice, she would have been glad that I'd tried.